Butterworths Compliance Series
Risk-Based Compliance

Stuart Bazley LLB, LLM
Barrister, Head of Compliance and Legal Counsel, Edward Jones Ltd

Dr Andrew Haynes BA (Hons) Law, PhD, CertEd, FSALS
Head, Institute of Finance Law, University of Wolverhampton

Tony Blunden FCIS
Director, Risk Management and Regulatory Services, Ernst & Young

Butterworths
London
2001

United Kingdom	Butterworths Tolley, a Division of Reed Elsevier (UK) Ltd, Halsbury House, 35 Chancery Lane, LONDON, WC2A 1EL, and 4 Hill Street, EDINBURGH EH2 3JZ
Argentina	Abeledo Perrot, Jurisprudencia Argentina and Depalma, BUENOS AIRES
Australia	Butterworths, a Division of Reed International Books Australia Pty Ltd, CHATSWOOD, New South Wales
Austria	ARD Betriebsdienst and Verlag Orac, VIENNA
Canada	Butterworths Canada Ltd, MARKHAM, Ontario
Chile	Publitecsa and Conosur Ltda, SANTIAGO DE CHILE
Czech Republic	Orac sro, PRAGUE
France	Editions du Juris-Classeur SA, PARIS
Hong Kong	Butterworths Asia (Hong Kong), HONG KONG
Hungary	Hvg Orac, BUDAPEST
India	Butterworths India, NEW DELHI
Ireland	Butterworths (Ireland) Ltd, DUBLIN
Italy	Giuffré, MILAN
Malaysia	Malayan Law Journal Sdn Bhd, KUALA LUMPUR
New Zealand	Butterworths of New Zealand, WELLINGTON
Poland	Wydawnictwa Prawnicze PWN, WARSAW
Singapore	Butterworths Asia, SINGAPORE
South Africa	Butterworths Publishers (Pty) Ltd, DURBAN
Switzerland	Stämpfli Verlag AG, BERNE
USA	LexisNexis, DAYTON, Ohio

© Reed Elsevier (UK) Ltd 2001

A CIP Catalogue record for this book is available from the British Library.

ISBN 0 406 932 506

Typeset by Columns Design Ltd, Reading, England
Printed and bound in Great Britain by Thomson Litho Ltd, East Kilbride, Scotland

Visit Butterworths LexisNexis *direct* at www.butterworths.com

Butterworths Compliance Series
Risk-Based Compliance

Butterworths Compliance Series

General Editor: Professor Barry AK Rider, LLB (Lond), MA (Cantab), PhD (Lond), PhD (Cantab), LLD (HC) (Penn State), LLD (HC) (UFS), Barrister

Series Editor: Graham Ritchie MA (Cantab), Solicitor

Other titles available in this series include:

Market Abuse and Insider Dealing Barry Rider, Lisa Linklater, Kern Alexander

Money Laundering Toby Graham, Evan Bell, Nick Elliott QC, Sue Thornhill

Investigations and Enforcement Dr Peter Johnstone, Richard Jones QC

Conflicts of Interest and Chinese Walls Dr Chizu Nakajima, Elizabeth Sheffield

Managed Funds Daniel Tunkel

Preface

On 20 May 1997 the UK government announced the reform of financial services regulation in the UK. The focal attention of that reform was the creation of a single financial services regulatory organisation. The Securities and Investments Board ('SIB'), formally changed its name to the Financial Services Authority ('FSA') in October 1997.

The first stage of the reform was completed in June 1998, when responsibility for banking supervision was transferred to the FSA from the Bank of England.

The Financial Services and Market Act 2000, which received Royal Assent in June 2000, recognises the FSA as the UK's single regulatory authority. On 12 July 2001 the UK Treasury announced that the new law would be brought into force no later than midnight on 30 November 2001. From that date the FSA will take responsibility for the regulatory functions of the Building Societies Commission, the Friendly Societies Commission, the Investment Management Regulatory Organisation, the Personal Investment Authority, the Register of Friendly Societies, and the Securities and Futures Authority.

The parliamentary debate and drafting of this new legislation, however, is not the limit of the preparation for the new regulatory regime. The practical application of much of the new law will be embodied in the rules of the FSA.

All of the FSA's proposed new rules have been extensively consulted on, and since October 1997 the FSA have issued 113 consultation papers. This consultation process has been a massive undertaking for both the FSA and the financial services industry.

In January 2000 the FSA set out its proposed approach to future regulation in its the publication 'A new regulator for the new millennium'. The FSA summarised its goal as being 'to maintain efficient, orderly and clean financial markets and help retail consumers achieve a fair deal'. This new approach is referred to as 'risk based supervision'; it is based on the FSA's realistic aims, and recognises both the proper responsibilities of consumers and of firms' own management. The FSA has also stated that it recognises the impossibility and undesirability of removing all risk and failure from the financial system.

The FSA has gone on to state that its approach to risk-based supervision is driven by the basic questions: what developments, events or issues pose significant risk to its objectives? And how should they use resources to focus on the risks that matter most?

We consider that risk-based compliance provides benefits to firms that operate in a regulated environment. Firms that adopt a successful risk-based approach to their own compliance management can focus their attention in a more structured and cost-effective manner.

In preparing this book we have considered both the legal and practical framework within which a compliance function must operate. The work is primarily intended as an overview and explanation of the issues faced by those engaged in managing the risks associated with financial services compliance. We have chosen not to analyse and comment on every aspect of regulation in the UK, but merely to concentrate on those areas which will be of particular interest to all firms. We then go on to provide practical comment on how such compliance responsibilities may be discharged effectively.

The approaches addressed in this book will be of particular interest to both compliance officers and money laundering reporting officers. They will be relevant when planning a compliance regime in an organisation for the very first time, or when re-engineering a firm's compliance procedures to meet the new UK legislation or the growing demands of an organisation. In addition, anyone holding a senior position in a financial services business should find this work valuable with regard to its explanation of the role of risk-based compliance and how a regulated firm should balance the firm's business with its compliance obligations. The book should also be of interest to professional advisers such as accountants, management consultants, lawyers and academics who may be required to understand the approach their clients should take in managing regulatory risk.

In preparing the book, we have focused largely on the new Financial Services and Markets Act 2000. We did, however, take the view that the discipline of compliance and areas of good practice required under this legislation would also be applicable to firms operating in regulatory environments outside of the UK. We consider, therefore, that this book will be of universal interest to compliance officers and regulated firms around the world.

We would like to thank everyone who assisted us in the preparation of this book and helped us to understand the new legislation. We would especially like to thank: Claire Davies and Jayne Owen of Ernst and Young for their assistance with Chapter 2; Katie Stone for giving up her spare time to prepare the manuscript; and Mary Dowd and Anna-Marie Heritier de la Roche for their support and encouragement. We would also like to thank the Committee of European Securities Regulators for their kind permission to reproduce the FESCO memorandum of understanding in Chapter 9.

The views expressed in this book are ours personally and are not attributable to our employers.

The law is stated as at 30 October 2001.

Stuart Bazley
Tony Blunden
Andrew Haynes

November 2001

Contents

Preface   v
Acronyms   xiii
Table of statutes   xv
Table of statutory instruments   xvii
Table of cases   xix

Chapter 1   The role of compliance   1
Introduction   1
The need for risk-based compliance   1
Relationships with others   2
Requirements and risks   6

Chapter 2   Risk analysis and surveying   13
Summary   13
Introduction   13
Building a systematic approach to compliance risk
analysis and surveying   14
Tools to use in compliance risk analysis and surveying   16
Risk identification   20
Control identification   22
Risk and control and monitoring   23
Risk and control framework   23
Measurement   27
Line management of compliance risk   28
Special areas of compliance risk   28
Training and competence   29
Change   30

Chapter 3   Fashioning compliance systems   31
Summary   31
Policy   32
Understanding   38

Rule review   39
Consolidated procedures   39
Monitoring procedures   39
Cross-reference documents   39
Procedures manual   40
The compliance department   41
Training and experience of compliance staff   43

Chapter 4   The complaints process and internal complaints investigations   45
Introduction   45
What the legislation states   46
Internal complaints procedures   49
Complaints disclosure   50
Complaints investigations: acknowledgements and time limits   53
Offers of redress   54
Compliance officer and complaints management   55
Scope of investigation   56
Interviews   56
Analysis of documents   57
Obtaining expertise   58
Balancing the evidence obtained   58
Complaints conclusion   59
Post-investigation matters   59
Complaint trends   59
Notification to professional indemnity insurers   61
Conclusion   62

Chapter 5   Relevant provisions in the Financial Services and Markets Act 2000   63
The new regulatory structure   63
The Financial Services Authority   63
Regulation   65
FSA Principles for Business   65
Approved persons   66
Statements of principle for approved persons   66
Relevant bodies other than the FSA   67
Wholesale market activities   71
Investment business in the UK   73
Gaming   86

Chapter 6   Special compliance obligations: money laundering   89
Introduction   89
The criminal offences – laundering drug proceeds and the profits of crime   91
Terrorism   93
Relevant parties   94
Checking identity   96

What is 'suspicion'?   97
Civil law issues   99
The role of the FSA   105
The Wolfsberg Principles   112

Chapter 7   Special compliance obligations: insider dealing, market abuse and other criminal offences   123
Introduction   123
Insider dealing   124
Market abuse   132
Other criminal offences   138

Chapter 8   Enforcing compliance obligations in multi-level and multi-business enterprises   141
Introduction   141
FSA Principles for Business   142
Senior management and compliance responsibility   143
Employment issues   153

Chapter 9   Ensuring international and national co-ordination   157
Introduction   157
Organisations   158
Key standards   159
Monitoring regulatory observance   164
Facilitating regulatory observance   165
Key issues other than regulatory observance   165
Consequences of regulatory failure   166
Memoranda of understanding   167
Appendix: Multilateral memorandum of understanding on the exchange of information and surveillance of securities activities   170

Chapter 10   Dealing with regulators and law enforcement   179
Managing the relationship with your regulator   179
Managing enforcement proceedings   186
Conclusion   196

Chapter 11   Authorisation, permissions and approved persons   197
The requirement for authorisation   197
Investments   198
Threshold conditions   198
The granting of permission   204
Procedure for making an application   205
Granting of permissions with conditions   208
Approved persons   208
Contravention of the requirement to be authorised   211
Authorised person acting without permission   211
Enforceability of agreements   211

Fitness of approved persons   212
Appointed representatives   213
Undertaking a review of business structure   213
Fit and proper status   214
Access to criminal records   216
Matters of concern to the FSA   218
Applications for approval by the FSA   218
Whistleblowing and employment law   218

Index   225

Acronyms

APACS	Association of Payment Clearing Services
AUTH	Authorisation Manual
CEO	Chief Executive Officer
CGO	Central Gilts Office
COB	Conduct of Business Handbook
CRB	Criminal Records Bureau
EEA	European Economic Area
ENF	Enforcement Manual
FESCO	Forum of European Securities Commissions
FSA	Financial Services Authority
FSMA 2000	Financial Services and Markets Act 2000
ICCH	International Commodities Clearing House
IMRO	Investment Management Regulatory Organisation
ISD	Investment Services Directive
JMLSG	Joint Money Laundering Steering Group
KRI	Key Risk Indicator
LIFFE	London International Financial Futures Exchange
LOCH	London Options Clearing House
NCIS	National Criminal Intelligence Service
OPRA	Occupational Pensions Regulatory Authority
OTC	Over the Counter
PIA	Personal Investment Authority
PRIN	Principles of Business Handbook
ROA	1974 Rehabilitation of Offenders Act 1974
SEC	Securities and Exchange Commission (US)
SFA	Securities and Futures Authority
SIB	Securities and Investments Board
SUP	Supervisory Manual
SYSC	Senior Management Systems and Controls Manual

Table of statutes

References in this table are to paragraph numbers

PARA

1845 Gaming Act
s 18 .... 5.97, 5.98
1892 Gaming Act
s 1 .... 5.97, 5.98
1968 National Loans Act 5.51, 5.64, 6.21
1969 Industrial and Provident Societies Act (Northern Ireland)
s 6 .... 6.22
1972 National Debt Act
s 11(3) 5.51, 5.64
1974 Rehabilitation of Offenders Act 11.11,
                                        11.64, 11.67
1979 Credit Union Act 6.21
1985 Companies Act
s 323(1)(a)–(c) 7.23
                                        744, 5.47
1986 Building Societies Act ....
s 119 .... 5.46
Sch 1 .... 5.49
1986 Financial Services Act 5.99
s 43 .... 5.33, 5.38
46 .... 6.22
63 .... 5.98
Sch 1 .... 5.78
para 8 .... 5.61
Pt II (ss129–139) 5.78
1986 Industrial and Provident Societies Act
s 6 .... 6.22
7(3) 6.22
1987 Banking Act 6.21
1988 Criminal Justice Act
s 51 .... 6.10
93A 6.9
93c 6.10
93d 6.16
1993 Criminal Justice Act ... 7.1, 7.12, 10.38
s 53(1)(b),(c) 7.16
(2)(b),(c) 7.16
(3)(a),(b) 7.17

PARA

1993 Criminal Justice Act—*contd*
s 53 (6) 7.16
55 .... 7.13
56 .... 7.10
57 .... 7.5
58 .... 7.6, 7.9
61(1)(a),(b) 7.20
62(2) 7.30
Sch 1
para 1 .... 7.18
2,3, ... 7.18
5 .... 7.18
Sch 2 .... 7.12
1994 Drug Trafficking Act 6.15
s 49 .... 6.9
50 .... 6.10
3(b)(ii) 6.11
51 .... 6.13
52 .... 6.14
53 .... 6.16
1995 Proceeds of Crime Act 7.22
s 1 .... 7.79
1996 Employment Rights Act 11.75
s 47b 11.75
1998 Bank of England Act 5.1, 5.2, 5.3,
                                        5.16
1998 Human Rights Act 8.46, 11.84
1998 Public Interest Disclosure Act ... 11.75
s 43c 11.79
ss 43g-43h 11.76
1999 Welfare Reform and Pensions Act
s 1(2)–(9) 5.57
2000 Financial Services and Markets Act 1.1,
                  2.65, 4.8, 4.12, 5.18, 5.24,
                  5.41, 5.90, 5.98, 6.59, 6.60, 6.61,
                  7.47, 7.74, 7.77, 8.2, 8.31, 10.30,
                  10.39, 11.2, 11.11, 11.39
Pt I (ss 1–18) 11.10
s 3–5 .... 5.7

PARA

2000 Financial Services and Markets Act—
contd
s 6 ....3.34, 5.7, 6.59
      (2)..6.60
      (3)..6.59
Pt II (ss 19–30)...
    19.................................... 8.55, 11.4, 11.48
      (1)..11.4
    20(2)...11.40
    21...7.78
    22...11.5
    23...11.39
    26...11.41
    27...11.43
    28...11.42
    29(1)...11.44
Pt III (ss 31–39).............................. 4.41
    31...11.7
      (1)(a) 11.7
    38...11.8
    39.................................... 8.56, 11.8, 11.49
      (4) 8.57, 11.50
      (6) 8.57, 11.50
Pt IV (ss 40–55)........... 10.59, 11.10, 11.19,
                              11.20, 11.40
    s 40 ....8.58, 11.51
    42(6), (7) 11.13
    45 .... 5.24
    49................................... 11.10, 11.25
    51(6)...11.24
    52...11.26
Pt V (ss 56–71)............................. 5.90
    s 59 ....11.38
    60 ....11.38
    62(4)...11.73
Pt VI (ss 72–103)
    s 95 .... 5.3
Pt VIII (ss 118–131)
    s 118 ....7.38
      (2)................................... 7.38, 7.43
      (5)..7.68
      (8)..7.52
    119..7.49
    120..7.61
    122..7.52
    123..7.47
Pt X (ss 138–164)..................... 4.12, 5.90
    s 138 ....4.12
    146 ....6.59
    150 ....4.53
      (1)..5.10
Pt XI (ss 165–177)......................... 5.90
Pt XII (ss 178–192)........................ 5.90
Pt XIV (ss 205–211) 5.90
Pt XV (ss 212–224).......................... 5.90
Pt XVI (ss 225–234) 5.90
    s 225 .... 4.8
      (1)... 4.8

PARA

2000 Financial Services and Markets Act—
contd
    ss 226–234 .... 4.8
Pt XVII (ss 235–284)
    s 235 .... 5.55
    236 ....5.56
    237 ....5.56
Pt XIX (ss 314–324)
    s 314 .... 5.24, 5.66
                              315, 5.24
      (1)... 5.89
      (2)... 5.89
    316
      (1) 5.24, 5.90
      (3)... 5.90
    317.. 5.24
    318.. 5.24
      (1)... 5.90
    320 (1) 5.91
      (3)... 5.91
Pt XXII (ss 340–346)......................... 5.90
Pt XXIV (ss 355–379)........................ 5.90
Pt XXV (ss 380–386)
    s 384–386.. 5.90
Pt XXVI (ss 387–396)........................ 5.90
Pt XXVII (ss 397–403)
    s 397 .... 7.71
      (1)... 7.71
      (2)... 7.72
      (3) 7.73, 7.74
      (9)... 7.72
    400 .... 7.77
    402(1)(b)... 6.61
Pt XXVIII (ss 404–416)
    s 412 .... 5.98, 5.101
Sch 1 .... 5.73, 10.37
    para 6(3) 10.37
Sch 2 .... 11.5
Sch 3 .... 5.32, 5.41
    para 5... 5.32
      (d)... 5.79
Sch 6
    para 3 (2)................................... 1.11
      41(1)... 11.9
Sch   17... 4.41
    para 3, 4 .... 11.10
      13... 4.12
      (4) 4.12
    16... 4.41
2000 Terrorism Act 6.18, 6.19
    s 15(2)... 6.18
    18 .... 6.18
    19(2)... 6.18
      (5)... 6.18
    22 .... 6.20
Sch 2 .... 6.19

Table of statutory instruments

References in this table are to paragraph numbers

PARA

1985/1204 Betting, Gaming, Lotteries and Amusements (Northern Ireland) Order ....
art 170 ....5.98
1985/1205 .Credit Unions (Northern Ireland) Order 6.21
1992/3218 Banking Co-ordination (Second Council Directive) Regulations
Sch 1..6.21
Sch 2
para...6.21
1993/1933 Money Laundering Regulations
6.25, 6.74, 6.84, 10.38
reg 4 (1) 6.21
(2)...6.22
1998/3132 Civil Procedure Rules
Sch 1

PARA

Rules of the Supreme Court
Ord 85..6.58
2001/1335 Financial Services and Markets Act 2000
(Financial Promotion) Order 7.78
2001/544 Financial Services and Markets Act 2000
(Regulated Activities) Order 5.41, 5.70
Pt II (arts 4–72) 5.41
Pt III (arts 73–89) 5.41, 5.75
art 84 (3)...5.61
(7)...5.61
Sch 1 ....5.44
2001/1261 Terrorism Act (Proscribed Organisations) (Amendment) Order 6.19

Table of cases

References in this table are to paragraph numbers

PARA

A

Agip (Africa) Ltd v Jackson [1990] Ch 265, [1992] 4 All ER 385, [1989] 3 WLR 1367, [1990] BCC 899, 134 Sol Jo 198, [1990] 2 LS Gaz R 34; affd [1991] Ch 547, [1992] 4 All ER 451, [1991] 3 WLR 116, 135 Sol Jo 117, CA 6.51, 6.109

Albert and Le Compte v Belgium (1982) 5 EHRR 533 .... 11.84

A-G for Hong Kong v Reid [1994] 1 AC 324, [1994] 1 All ER 1, [1993] 3 WLR 1143, [1993] NLJR 1569, 137 Sol Jo LB 251, PC 7.31

A-G's Reference (No 1 of 1975) [1975] QB 773, [1975] 2 All ER 684, [1975] 3 WLR 11, [1975] RTR 473, 61 Cr App Rep 118, 139 JP 569, 119 Sol Jo 373, CA 7.14

B

Barnes v Addy (1874) 9 Ch App 244, 43 LJ Ch 513, 22 WR 505, 30 LT 4 .... 6.43

Boardman v Phipps [1967] 2 AC 46, [1966] 3 All ER 721, [1966] 3 WLR 1009, 110 Sol Jo 853, HL 7.31

Borland's Trustee v Steel Bros & Co Ltd [1901] 1 Ch 279, 70 LJ Ch 51, 49 WR 120, 17 TLR 45 .... 5.47

C

City Index Ltd v Leslie [1992] QB 98, [1991] 3 All ER 180, [1991] 3 WLR 207, [1991] BCLC 643, CA 5.100

Coleman v Myers [1977] 2 NZLR 225, NZCA 7.34

Cowan de Groot Properties Ltd v Eagle Trust plc [1992] 4 All ER 700, [1991] BCLC 1045 .... 6.56

E

Eaves v Hickson (1861) 30 Beav 136, 7 Jur NS 1297, 132 RR 213, 10 WR 29, 5 LT 598. 6.46

El Ajou v Dollar Land Holdings plc (No 2) [1995] 2 All ER 213 .... 6.55

F

Fyler v Fyler (1841) 3 Beav 550, 5 Jur 187 .... 6.46

G

Ginikanwa v United Kingdom 55 DR 251 (1988) 11.88

Grey v Pearson (1857) 6 HL Cas 61, 26 LJ Ch 473, 3 Jur NS 823, 5 WR 454, 29 LTOS 67 .... 7.6

Guchez v Belgium 40 DR 100 (1984) 11.88

PARA

H
H v Belgium (1987) 10 EHRR 339, ECtHR 8.72
   Halford v United Kingdom (1997) 24 EHRR 523, [1997] IRLR 471, [1998] Crim
   LR 753, 94 LS Gaz R 24, ECtHR 11.86
Hazell v Hammersmith and Fulham London Borough Council [1992] 2 AC 1, [1991] 1
   All ER 545, [1991] 2 WLR 372, 89 LGR 271, [1991] RVR 28, HL 5.97
Heydon's Case (1584) 3 Co Rep 7a 7.6
Holland v Russell (1861) 1 B & S 424; affd (1863) 4 B & S 14, 32 LJQB 297, 2 New
   Rep 188, 11 WR 757, 8 LT 468 .... 6.53
Hussien v Chong Fook Kam [1970] AC 942, [1969] 3 All ER 1626, [1970] 2 WLR....441, 114
   Sol Jo 55, PC 6.31

L
Langborger v Sweden (1989) 12 EHRR 416, ECtHR 11.88
Levy v Abercorris Slate and Slab Co (1887) 37 Ch D 260, 57 LJ Ch 202, 36 WR 411,
   [1886–90] All ER Rep 509, 58 LT 218, 4 TLR 34 ....5.50
Lipkin Gorman v Karpnale Ltd [1992] 4 All ER 409, [1989] 1 WLR 1340, [1989] FLR
   137, [1989] BCLC 756n, 134 Sol Jo 234, [1990] 4 LS Gaz R 40, [1989] NLJR 76,
   CA; varied sub nom Lipkin Gorman (a firm) v Karpnale Ltd [1991] 2 AC 548,
   [1992] 4 All ER 512, [1991] 3 WLR 10, [1991] NLJR 815, 135 Sol Jo LB 36,
   HL 6.50
Lombardo v Italy (1992) 21 EHRR 188, ECtHR 11.84

M
Mackender v Feldia AG [1967] 2 QB 590, [1966] 3 All ER 847, [1967] 2 WLR 119,
   [1966] 2 Lloyd's Rep 449, 110 Sol Jo 811, CA 7.30
Morgan Grenfell & Co Ltd v Welwyn Hatfield District Council, Islington London
   Borough Council (third party) [1995] 1 All ER 1 .... 5.99

N
Nanus Asia Inc v Standard Chartered Bank [1990] HKLR 396 .... 7.31

O
Obermeier v Austria (1990) 13 EHRR 290 .... 11.84

P
Polly Peck International plc v Nadir (No 2) [1992] 4 All ER 769, [1992] 2 Lloyd's Rep
   238, [1992] NLJR 671, CA 6.52
Prince v United Kingdom (1984) 6 EHRR 583 .... 11.84

R
R v Goodman [1993] 2 All ER 789, 97 Cr App Rep 210, 14 Cr App Rep (S) 147, [1994]
   1 BCLC 349, [1992] BCC 625, CA 7.21
Regal (Hastings) Ltd v Gulliver (1942) [1967] 2 AC 134n, [1942] 1 All ER 378, HL 7.34
Ringeisen v Austria (1971) 1 EHRR 455, ECtHR 11.88
Royal Brunei Airlines Sdn Bhd v Tan [1995] 2 AC 378, [1995] 3 All ER 97, [1995] 3
   WLR 64, [1995] BCC 899, [1995] 27 LS Gaz R 33, [1995] NLJR 888, PC 6.44

S
Springfield Acres (in liquidation) v Abacus (Hong Kong) Ltd [1994] 3 NZLR 502 .... 6.54

T
Tournier v National Provincial and Union Bank of England [1924] 1 KB 461, 93
   LJKB 449, 29
Com Cas 129, [1923] All ER Rep 550, 68 Sol Jo 441, 130 LT 682, 40 TLR 214, CA 11.80

CHAPTER 1

The role of compliance

Introduction

1.1 The bringing into force of the Financial Services and Markets Act 2000 represents more than a restructuring of the financial regulatory regime. The new FSA regulatory approach is based on the premise that a financial services business poses risks to the FSA's objectives. The regulations passed by the FSA are a means to making sure that this is being done. Thus, the days of 'compliance', where maintaining a satisfactory set of systems was determined by whether a set of rules were being complied with, are gone. What it has been replaced with is a system of risk-based compliance which involves satisfying a series of principles and rules in the course of managing the necessary risks. In some areas, such as mainstream conduct of business, the consequences of this should not be too great. In others, such as market abuse, it will be fundamental.

1.2 The culture of risk management is one that is being widely adopted through the financial world. It can be seen in the conclusions of the Basel Committee and a range of other bodies (see **Chapter 10**). Thus, a major national regulator such as the FSA, whose work has international ramifications, needs to adopt an approach that is consistent with this. In any event, it is an approach that they regard as desirable.

The need for risk-based compliance

1.3 There are a number of reasons for the need for such a system. It forces the investment business firms to adopt practices that in a perfect world they would choose to adopt. Given the pressures that inevitably exist in a business between compliance personnel on the one hand and sales and marketing on the other, there will tend to be pressures operating to stop this happening. Thus the regulatory system must require the adoption of techniques by firms to minimise the regulator's exposure to risks. The consequences of this occurring provide the remaining reason: namely that it operates as risk reduction for the firm. Thus, a firm operating a system of best practice in risk reduction will face a much lower risk of litigation from those it has dealt with and a major reduction in being made to suffer loss through financial crime. Perhaps most importantly from the regulated firm's point of view is the evidence that it leads to a reduction in the risk of major failure.

1.4 In large, complex, multi-national financial services conglomerates the management of risk becomes highly complicated. Of particular importance is the risk of systemic failure where the failure of part of the business causes knock-on effects throughout the group. In extreme cases this could result in the failure of the entire group. As a result there has been a trend by such organisations to draft risk-avoidance strategies which form the basis of their multinational and multi-activity business. Regulators will usually negotiate with such organisations to satisfy themselves as to whether or not risk is being managed on a satisfactory basis. If so they will, on occasion, agree to exemptions from specific regulatory rules. This is much less likely to arise in the case of smaller firms, though were such a firm to have a specialist business that did not fit easily within the rules, negotiating a derogation can be explored. Whilst regulators wish to see the regulations compiled with it is the satisfactory management of risk rather than the existence of the rules that will be the overriding factor.

Relationships with others

General

1.5 Relationships that a compliance department manages both within the firm and externally are complex and often conflicting. The expectation of many managements that the compliance department is the conscience of the firm is an almost direct contradiction to the need for all employees to comply with minimum ethical standards. If a single department is perceived to carry out a function, it is much easier for others in the firm to abrogate their responsibility. Furthermore, the due diligence that compliance is required to carry out in order to ensure that the firm adheres to the rules and regulations imposed on it is often seen as conflicting with the need to make a profit.

The control departments: internal audit

1.6 The conceptual conflicts generated by these two points are added to by the relationship of the compliance department with the other control departments of the firm. There is possible considerable overlap with the internal audit, legal and risk management departments. Although internal audit should operate as an independent review and verification arm of the highest levels of management (ie the Board of Directors), there is a possibility that internal audit is viewed by management as an additional oversight and review function. When this mistake occurs there is a real likelihood of significant conflict with the compliance department, one of whose main functions is to review and oversee the compliance of the firm with the regulations imposed on it. The relationship of internal audit to the compliance department should be one where internal audit independently reviews the processes undertaken and the risks controlled by compliance.

Legal department

1.7 The relationship with the legal department is also one which is potentially fraught with difficulty. Although much of compliance can ultimately be traced back to legislation, the spirit of implementing regulatory rules and guidelines is often far removed from the enabling legislation. A legal interpretation of the precise meaning of words in a law crafted by parliamentarians can often be tangential at best with the spirit of regulatory guidelines and the regulator's day-to-day interpretations of the guidelines and rules.

Risk management department

1.8 It is also possible for there to be friction with the risk management department of the firm. This may become increasingly so as regulators move towards risk-based compliance. The risk management function can provide the compliance department with a source of subject matter expertise in terms of assisting the management of the firm in identifying risks and controls for managing and mitigating those risks. The general risk management expertise of the risk management department can be utilised by the compliance department in validating the compliance department's use of the compliance risks facing the firm and the appropriateness and effectiveness of the controls over those risks.

Credit department

1.9 The processes undertaken by the credit department are often very similar to (and complementary to) those undertaken by the compliance department. The due diligence performed by credit on a client will frequently be more than that which is required for client identification purposes. Although the ultimate outcomes are different (ie credit will grant a credit line and compliance will approve a client from a regulatory perspective), the two departments have much to gain by working together as the data required to make the decisions are similar. Whilst it is possible that the departments may have to perform small additional pieces of work in order to fully complete their separate needs, there is a potential cost-saving as well as the general raising of awareness of another department's processes by working together on the 'know your customer' needs of the firm.

Front office departments: trading and sales

1.10   The relationships with the trading and sales departments can range from proactive and positive to close to destructive. In a firm where the compliance department is seen as a profit prevention department the compliance officer will have a very significant uphill struggle. However, with significant training and the backing of senior management it is possible for the compliance function to be viewed positively and as part of the business qualification process. A wise compliance officer will build on this perception and ultimately achieve proactive feedback from the trading and sales departments. In such happy circumstances, the main compliance risks facing the firm are accidental breaches of the rules, deliberate fraud and external events beyond the control of compliance.

Research department

1.11   One of the more complex interactions of the compliance department is with the research department. A major objective of the research department is to produce commentary on a firm, sector or country that has not previously been considered by the investment community. Such commentary may therefore be capable of moving prices in the market and requires care in the handling and release of the information. However, such commentary is often time sensitive and a rapid response is necessary by the compliance department to a request for a compliance review of such material. Additionally, the acquisition by the research department of inside information during the writing of and preparation for the publication also needs careful handling.

Corporate finance department

1.12   The relationship between the compliance department and the corporate finance function is traditionally viewed as one of the most complex relationships for compliance. The inevitable acquisition of inside information by the corporate finance department on many, if not all, of its clients poses potentially significant problems for the firm. An innocent off-guard remark by a corporate financier runs the risk of being overheard or misinterpreted by others and action being taken that jeopardises the firm. There is, of course, no direct compliance action that can guard against such circumstances. However, good effective periodic training reinforced by frequent communications from the compliance department will ensure that there is a real and ongoing awareness of the compliance risks run by corporate finance.

Clients of the firm

1.13 The relationship of the compliance department with fellow financial institutions often revolves around complaints. These may be, for example, disputes between the trading and sales departments of the two institutions and are often resolved through a review of the tapes of the telephone conversations or of the documentation passed between the two firms. Institutional clients, however, may genuinely misunderstand the terms of a contract, particularly if it is a complex derivative. In a firm where the compliance department is viewed positively the compliance officer can often act as an honest broker in the dispute. Retail clients are, of course, an area where compliance spends a considerable amount of time. The greatest compliance risk to a firm often lies in this area through the misunderstanding, ignorance or sheer greed of either the client or the firm or both.

External auditors

1.14 External auditors can provide an additional check to the compliance department that compliance policies and procedures are being followed. The compliance officer can also provide further confirmation for external audit as a compliance officer is routinely interviewed during the due diligence process conducted by the external auditors. Additionally, the external auditors can give useful further weight to the compliance officer whose arguments and imperatives may not be fully understood (or may not wish to be fully understood) by senior management.

Regulators

1.15 Similarly, a regulatory review will provide a firm with confirmation that compliance monitoring of its procedures is sufficient. However, any regulatory review will almost inevitably find at least small technical breaches by the firm. It is important that the regulator ensures that the severity of such matters is put into context or the regulator will risk reducing communication with the firm. Equally, of course, if significant regulatory breaches are uncovered the compliance department will be key in developing policies, procedures and monitoring to ensure that such a breach will not happen again.

Rating agencies

1.16   Given the importance of compliance regulations, the rating agencies often have a relationship with a member of the compliance department. This helps to ensure that the agency fully understands the control exercised by management of the firm and the level of compliance awareness within the firm.

CEO's office

1.17   Finally, it is vital for the compliance department to build a good relationship with the CEO's office. Whilst this relationship should not be abused by compliance, easy and immediate access to the CEO is a necessary requirement for the good functioning of a compliance department.

Requirements and risks

Independence

1.18   A compliance department should be independent of any other function given the complex relationships that exist between it and the rest of the firm. Conflicts of interest for a compliance department should be eliminated wherever possible so that an independent and reasoned view, free of any encumbrance, can be developed by the compliance department on any matter of interest to the firm. The head of the compliance department must be perceived as a senior figure within the firm.

Access to senior management

1.19   There must be easy access to the highest levels of the management structure, eg the CEO or the Audit Committee Chairman (who will very likely be a member of the Board of Directors). The wide perception of unfettered access to senior management is as important as actual access.

Natural conflicts of interest

1.20   The paradox of the requirement for independence with the need to ensure compliance with the rules and regulations through comprehensive risk-based monitoring of the firm leads to a difficult balancing act. This is made still more difficult by the compliance staff being paid by the firm but being required to report breaches to the regulator. Although in concept such conflicts have been managed for decades, if not hundreds of years, by other control functions such as accounting, the problem is compounded by the penalties imposed by regulatory bodies.

Restrictions on compliance staff

1.21   Compliance department staff today are subject to a number of strictures that have not been deemed necessary in earlier eras. For example, personal accounts dealing by any member of a compliance department is subject to significant review if it is allowed at all by the firm. Some organisations have considered preventing members of compliance departments from undertaking any personal account dealings. All compliance staff are expected to have the highest ethics and morals (which requirement should, of course, apply to all members of staff).

Compliance policy drift

1.22   A further general risk to the firm with regard to compliance is the problem of ethical creep. Given the innovation of many sales and marketing staff, the spirit of regulation is continually being pushed at its edges. Unless compliance staff are very careful at clearly explaining the boundaries of acceptable products within a regulatory context, it is likely that those boundaries will move over time within the firm. Such movement may be difficult to detect on a day-to-day basis as it can be very gradual. It is most easily detected during periodic reviews of compliance policy against recent compliance decisions. Such reviews provide a valuable benchmark and mechanism for ensuring that compliance policy does not drift. Although the review can be performed by compliance management, an independent review is more likely to provide the check and balance necessary. Such independence can be found in the internal audit department or externally either through the external auditors or external legal advisers.

Regulatory ability

1.23   A regulatory lack of understanding of the business is also a potential compliance risk. Although the home regulator may be able to develop a full understanding of the firm, it is more likely that a host regulator of a subsidiary or branch will have difficulty comprehending the more complex parts of the business. This is particularly so when hybrid products are involved which span a number of businesses or geographic areas. Political or religious considerations in certain parts of the world may also lead to regulators not wishing to understand the firm's business.

Size of a regulated entity

1.24 The size of a regulated entity can be a disadvantage whether it is large or small. Small firms are unlikely to have sufficient resources, skills or knowledge to ensure full compliance. In a small firm it can be a never-ending battle balancing the business needs of generating money with the compliance needs for monitoring and record keeping. Many small firms use firms of compliance specialists who provide part-time periodic compliance reviews. However, a large firm can suffer from the view that a regulatory admonishment of a large firm is likely to be far more effective in disseminating an awareness of the regulator and a perception that the regulator's enforcement team is effective.

Staff turnover

1.25 Staff turnover can also be a significant compliance risk. Compliance training costs can rise dramatically if turnover of staff within the firm increases. Not only are more induction seminars required but also a confirmation of compliance philosophy of the firm must be made on a more frequent basis. Staff turnover in the compliance department is a particular concern as the firm loses both past knowledge of compliance business decisions and potentially loses its compliance equilibrium. A stable compliance department will enable business management to become familiar with and to understand compliance decisions. In contrast, the compliance department that changes its staff on a frequent basis is likely to frustrate the business and may provide conflicting signals as to the acceptability of products and practices. A further compliance risk to the firm in relation to staff turnover is the loss of knowledgeable staff within the regulator. Although it is inevitable that good staff in the regulator will receive approaches from industry, there is the real disadvantage to the industry in the loss of skills and business awareness especially when this is in the supervision or enforcement departments.

Regulatory risk assessment

1.26 The regulators' assessment of the firm's risks is today fundamental in managing the relationship between the firm and regulators. As noted above, there can be a lack of understanding of the business by the regulators due to a variety of reasons. It is clearly in the firm's interest to dispel any misunderstanding that exists and to ensure that the regulator understands the firm's business imperatives. Good communication with the regulator is clearly key to solving this potential problem and considerable effort should be put into opening and maintaining various channels of communication with the regulator. However, in a large firm there is also a risk that the regulator could be confused by too many contacts. In such circumstances it is normal to ensure that any staff member contacting the regulator is aware of and understands any previous dialogue with the regulator. Similar points also apply to the rating agencies' assessment of the firm's risks.

Documentation versus speed of decisions

1.27 Compliance departments frequently experience conflicts in the need to document all decisions with the need to make speedy decisions. It is important to ensure that all decisions of note, particularly those with regard to products, clients or policies, are documented for use both in training and for referral when similar decisions are required in the future. However, there is occasionally the need to make a decision on a product or client rapidly and before full documentation can be made. In the circumstances, the training of compliance staff will help to ensure that the details of the decision are not lost as the documentation can be carried out immediately after the decision-making process.

Staff training

1.28 Training of staff, both in the compliance department and in the company, can also sometimes be perceived as getting in the way of speedy decision-making. This is rarely the case as a trainer generally has the authority to make a decision which can then be explained to the staff being trained. Ensuring that all staff understand the logic and reasoning behind compliance decisions is of vital importance in ensuring a cohesive and well understood compliance framework around the firm.

Compliance framework

1.29 The ethical/regulatory/compliance perspective of the firm must be understood by all stakeholders of the firm, for example Board of Directors, external auditors, regulators, shareholders, customers. Reference to the compliance culture in all external documents (eg the annual report, product sales leaflets) is helpful in making clear the firm's position with regard to compliance. Internally, the inclusion of a compliance report in regular Audit Committee or Risk Committee documents helps to ensure the widespread dissemination of compliance information at a senior level. The compliance framework of the firm should be set by the Board of Directors on recommendation from the Audit or the Risk Committees.

Meeting attendance

1.30 The inclusion of members of the compliance department in regular meetings will do much to enhance compliance awareness around firm. Examples are various front office meetings such as sales and research, various departmental and interdepartmental administration meetings, regulatory meetings and auditors' meetings (both internal and external). Compliance points are often raised at such meetings and the rapid resolution of such points will greatly assist in the positive perception of compliance in the firm.

Differing views of risk

1.31 However, the natural conflict of interest between compliance needs and the needs of other areas of the firm will also come into play. Different views of risk from those of compliance are taken by the legal department, the credit department, the internal audit department and risk management department. Whilst one control department may approve a product another may need a product to be modified. Additionally the largely profit-driven motivation of the trading, sales and research departments will also pose challenges for compliance. Training of compliance staff can again help in these areas. Formal training such as examinations with a regulatory, business or product focus and informal training such as weekly or monthly meetings of the compliance department and mentoring of senior members of the department are all helpful in raising the skills, knowledge base and awareness of compliance staff.

Secure area with the compliance department

1.32 The need for a secure area, sometimes called the control room or conflicts room, within the compliance department itself is another requirement of a well-organised compliance function. This area will ensure that matters such as inside information and staff personal account dealing are kept secure from even (most) compliance staff. This ensures that the minimum number of staff are aware of particular sensitive information and that such information can therefore be more effectively controlled. However, there is a business requirement to ensure that this area is always manned, is responsive and business aware, and is quick to answer e-mails and telephone calls. This business requirement is difficult to reconcile with the fact that the work flowing into the secure area is often sporadic and will, by its nature, have extremes of peaks and troughs. The regular rotation of compliance staff in the secure area will help reduce alternate boredom and exhaustion but will diminish the ability to strictly control information.

Telephone call taping

1.33 Another requirement both of good front office management and of the compliance department is to have taping of all telephone calls of all functions that have economic interaction with the world outside the firm. This will include the trading department, the sales and marketing departments, research department and the settlements desk in the operations department. There should be easy access to the facilities for compliance staff although two people should be present at all times when a tape is being replayed. Possible conflicts with human rights and/or privacy legislation in various parts of the world should be investigated and resolved.

Independent assurance for the Board

1.34 The Board of Directors needs to be assured that the compliance management procedures are functioning as approved. This task should fall to the internal audit department, which provides independent assurance to the Board on all management matters. Internal audit will independently assess the risks posed by and controlled by the compliance department. It will then carry out an independent review of those risks and controls, taking into account the compliance policies and procedures and monitoring mechanisms within the compliance area. The compliance monitoring programme is likely to be tested as is the firm's compliance with a number of compliance policies and procedures relating to all departments within the firm. Internal audit should then provide a report on those risks, processes and controls to the Board (or the Board's nominated agent such as an Audit Committee or the Audit Committee Chairman).

Management responsibility for breaches

1.35 There is a clear risk to the compliance officer that business management will hold compliance responsible for a regulatory breach. It must be recognised that the compliance function cannot be responsible for breaches made in other departments where the breaching department creates the risk that a breach might occur. Compliance is responsible, amongst other things, for ensuring that departments are aware of their regulatory responsibilities and the regulatory risks that the departments run and for monitoring the controls that manage and mitigate the regulatory risk. If the compliance department has not raised compliance awareness, perhaps through a lack of regulatory training or relevant memoranda, it should be held liable for the missing awareness. However, all staff are themselves responsible for ensuring that they each understand their regulatory responsibilities. Ignorance is rarely an excuse and even more rarely when working in a heavily regulated industry. Where the risks of a breach are

11

known to the line management it is iniquitous and unreasonable to hold compliance responsible.

New employees

1.36 Amongst many risks that employees can pose to a firm from the regulatory perspective, one of the most fundamental is that from a new employee. Joiners to a firm may be new to the industry and therefore have little awareness of regulation at all. This problem is relatively easily solved by compliance induction training followed up by regular compliance awareness seminars and notices. The new employee may, however, have worked in the industry for a number of years but be imbued with a different compliance philosophy. To change a person's understanding of compliance ethics is a considerable task that can be started with an induction seminar but will require regular and frequent monitoring (and probably corrective action) even in a firm that has a positive view of compliance.

CHAPTER 2

Risk analysis and surveying

Summary

2.1 Compliance risk analysis and surveying has developed significantly in recent years with a number of tools becoming commonplace. Methodologies for identifying risks and their mitigating controls are now used by compliance managers. Frameworks for managing compliance risk and the use of action plans to improve the framework elements are increasingly employed. However, the specialised needs of compliance managers must continue to be taken into account and the issues raised embraced by line management.

Introduction

2.2 Managing and mitigating the compliance risk of an organisation is probably the most difficult challenge facing compliance managers. Compliance risk is a very wide category of risk bounded only by subjects such as Murphy's Law, the imagination of employees and, sometimes, external events completely beyond management's control.

2.3 Over recent years compliance risks have become more and more prominent partly as a result of changes in many sectors of the financial services industry, for example:

- The boundaries of existing business processes have been stretched by a continuing need to innovate through new product launches, the use of more complex investment instruments and the use of increasingly complex structures. The compliance responses to these have ranged from increasing compliance awareness through training to simple changes to existing processes, that in some cases can be manually intensive and lack the appropriate systems support. The increased use of 'manual workarounds', which are neither efficient nor scaleable, must necessarily increase the risk of compliance problems.

13

- Consolidation within industries has resulted in many institutions being exposed to the risks associated with the integration of business and operational processes including compliance risk. This can involve extended periods of operating parallel compliance processes and systems throughout the organisation, coupled with the migration of compliance data and management processes from pre-merger to post-merger systems. Accordingly, the potential frequency and complexity of problems must ordinarily increase.
- The extent of publicity given to both compliance and organisational failures has increased the realisation by management that compliance failures and the adverse shareholder value consequences could easily have happened in their own organisations. A scan through the press over recent years will reveal examples of compliance errors to which even the more 'robust' institutions are exposed. In some instances, these have resulted in both direct and indirect financial loss.

Building a systematic approach to compliance risk analysis and surveying

2.4   The key to developing an effective compliance risk process is the degree of consistency embedded within the process. This consistency can be achieved by systematically combining the identification of current key control weaknesses and the development of a framework to monitor the nature and extent of compliance risk and control throughout the organisation, on a continual basis. The process can be successfully applied to all types of business.

2.5   The first step in this systematic approach is to perform a current state assessment of the compliance risk and control environment. The compliance risk within each process should be identified and the key control processes analysed from both a performance and design perspective. Comparing the key control processes against industry good practice will often provide a useful benchmark when determining areas of potential control weaknesses.

2.6   In conjunction with this current state assessment, external and internal loss databases can be used to map errors and near misses against processes (providing a basis for detailed root cause analysis to identify further potential control weaknesses).

2.7   To add further value an institution could then consider the use of modelling techniques which allow a management to assess a value for the risks faced by the institution. Such a model could combine the output from self-assessments with key indicator and external loss data or may simply use self-assessment information. Either way, the modelling of compliance risk data can provide a significant extension to the metrics available for the management of compliance risk.

2.8　As a result of the changes highlighted at para **2.3**, many institutions have a range of current and planned change projects. Assessing the potential impact of these initiatives on the identified compliance risks provides an insight into the residual risks not being addressed. The identification of both the residual risks and any interim risk exposures (the risk the organisation is exposed to today, and until the project addressing the risk is implemented) allows management to determine whether additional or short-term actions are required to reduce the compliance risk associated with change to an acceptable level.

2.9　The systematic approach must provide more than a 'snap shot' of the level of compliance risk in the organisation. To maintain an up to date assessment, there is a need to develop a framework to monitor regularly the nature and extent of risk throughout the organisation. This framework should combine a continuous assessment of the level of compliance risk by individual business areas and information from key risk indicators to continually monitor and identify the level of compliance risk within critical business processes.

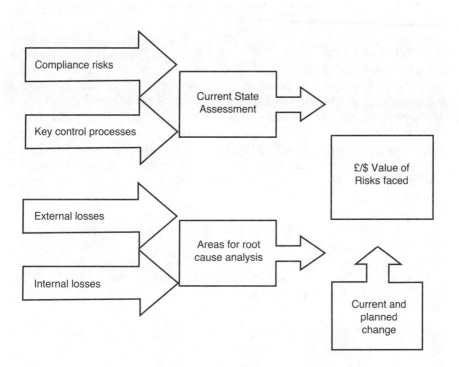

Tools to use in compliance risk analysis and surveying

2.10   There are number of tools available for use in risk analysis and which are suitable for compliance risk analysis and surveying including:
• self-assessment;
• risk maps and process flows;
• key indicators;
• escalation triggers;
• breach logs and near miss logs; and
• internal audit reports.

2.11   Each tool is valuable in its own right although no single tool is sufficient to provide an adequate compliance analysis. Using a number of tools together will mitigate the limitations of each one.

Self-assessment

2.12   This is probably the most widely used tool and emphasises the primary responsibility which senior line management carries in relation to the proper management and mitigation of compliance risk. Self-assessment, as its name suggests, is carried out in the department giving rise to the risk. Assistance and facilitation from compliance professionals is of course also required. Surveys, questionnaires, facilitated workshops and, occasionally, independent assessments are used.

2.13   The technique can be readily used for the development of day-to-day mitigation procedures and is generally carried out on an infrequent periodic basis for bottom-up assessments. A key advantage of self-assessment is that it raises compliance awareness within the business units that are undertaking it. It enables management of the business units to identify compliance issues and it achieves, in a natural way, recognition that the business unit itself creates and should, at least initially, manage and mitigate compliance risk. The reflective technique naturally employed when using this tool is also useful in building empathy between the business unit and compliance department.

2.14   A variation on self-assessment is a top-down assessment. More frequent reviews are possible with this technique as the business unit is less involved. However, the potential remoteness of a top-down assessment from day-to-day processes must be recognised and both variations should be used in order to ensure that the assessments remain in touch with each business unit's senior management and with the everyday needs of the business.

Risk maps and process flows

2.15 These two tools are widely used by internal audit and they can be very useful for reviewing compliance risk. Given their likely existing use by internal audit it is probable that the organisation will already have a number of risk maps and process flows. Reviews of these by compliance will enable compliance risks to be identified and appropriate mitigation procedures to be implemented. Risk maps will also assist in developing suitable procedures and mitigation measures for the risks identified.

2.16 Similar methodologies to self-assessment are used for creating risk maps and process flows although the focus tends to be more on interviews and focus groups. The functional heart of the tool is centred on processes and flow of risks rather than on the business unit and it therefore covers more departments although in a narrower band. These tools are helpful at a detailed level as they define the key risk and control points as well as responsibilities and accountabilities at each step of the process. However, this is also a key disadvantage of these tools as they tend to be very detailed and therefore inappropriate for senior management reporting.

2.17 A similar increase of compliance awareness is achieved compared to self-assessment although this tends to transcend the business unit as the whole process flow is covered. Risk maps and process flows can also be alternative outputs from self-assessments.

Key indicators

2.18 This tool can often use existing reports and systems and is therefore easily and quickly implemented. The firm will already be measuring many key compliance indicators such as volume of trades or sales, new clients and new employees. It is possible to develop a scorecard of risk metrics that will enable the head of compliance to use actual figures from the organisation rather than solely relying on a qualitative assessment. Management familiarity with the indicators will also assist in developing empathy with the compliance department. Key indicators can also provide an insight on the effectiveness of compliance procedures.

2.19 The widely differing frequencies of key indicators should be borne in mind when constructing uses for them. Although compliance indicators enable trend analysis to be performed they are unlikely by themselves to yield useful procedures for mitigating compliance risk. However, they do facilitate decision-making and often enable preventative actions to take place. A detailed awareness of each business unit's sensitivities is necessary for the indicators to be fully useful as the degree of applicability of each indicator will vary with the sensitivity of each business unit.

2.20 Many institutions use a combination of key risk indicators and key control indicators to monitor operational efficiency and the effectiveness of controls. Key risk indicators (KRIs) are simply metrics that can be used to monitor risks relating to the efficiency and performance of a process or business and can include transaction turnover, staff turnover, market volumes, price movements and systems downtime. Key control indicators demonstrate the effectiveness of controls. By combining the monitoring of risk and control indicators, an organisation can establish a process to monitor key performance indicators – interpreting lagging indicators to provide a leading indicator of failure or possible breach.

Examples of KRIs in wholesale operations	*Examples of KRIs in retail operations*
• Age and number of outstanding personal registrations • Age and number of unconfirmed trades • Market volumes • Price movements • Transaction turnover	• % Rejected Fact Finds • Product mix of individual's sales • Number of complaints by product, by salesperson, be product • Persistency of sales • Time for individuals to reach competent standards

Escalation triggers

2.21 These are fundamental to the reporting of potential compliance problems to higher levels of management. They can provide an early warning of an increase in compliance risk or a potential breach in regulatory requirements. A set of compliance indicators that have previously been agreed with business unit management and compliance management are a necessary prerequisite of escalation triggers. When the trigger level is reached the indicators are highlighted and given to predetermined senior management.

2.22 Escalation trigger points can be set at differing levels, which may vary over time. For example, trigger levels for a new product may initially be set at a very high level that may be decreased as the compliance department and business management gain familiarity with, and experience of, the compliance risks identified. Escalation triggers can also be set at levels that accord with a firm's compliance risk appetite. The advantage of escalation triggers is that they allow management by exception and, therefore, in theory, efficient management. However, it should be noted that it is possible for indicators to run at a level just beneath the trigger for a considerable time if too much attention is paid to the trigger levels per se.

> ## Example: Setting trigger points for the introduction of a new retail product
>
> - Set a high pass mark for any assessment of the training for individuals
> - Set low trigger points for business review, for example you may want to review all cases during the first month decreasing the sample as results show that the product is sold correctly
> - Set a high short-term persistency rate to ensure that a high level of cancellations in the small numbers of new products are not obscured by the mass of normal sales

Breach logs and near miss logs

2.23 Keeping a log of regulatory breaches and near misses can be instructive if used positively. Care must be taken to learn lessons from such logs rather than merely apportion blame. Analysis of the logs can assist assessment of current mitigation policies and controls and senior management can gain comfort on the effectiveness of the compliance risk policies. Such logs can also be helpful in identifying trends and in assisting in focusing resources. However, practitioners will have concerns that a regulator could use such logs inappropriately.

Internal audit reports

2.24 Although internal audit reports contain elements of an independent self-assessment, a breach log and a near miss log, they are themselves vital tools in surveying compliance risk. The internal audit department is perhaps the nearest department to the compliance department in having a broad functional control nature. Additionally, internal audit will often use compliance procedures and manuals as a starting point for its own risk assessment and procedures. There is therefore great value to the head of compliance in reviewing audit reports and extracting the relevant elements of risk from those reports.

Practical process

2.25 Whichever selection of tools is used there are three discrete steps in risk analysis and surveying. The first step is to formulate a framework within which the tools will be used. A coherent methodology designed in a collaborative fashion between compliance and the department/business being surveyed and analysed is essential for the successful use of the tools. Thought and time applied at this step will pay significant dividends in the subsequent steps. It is likely that a relatively small number of senior, experienced managers will be involved in this strategic design phase.

2.26 Secondly, the tool must be developed and tested in a pilot area before being fully disseminated. This allows the fine-tuning of the tool to the individual characteristics of each department/business and also allows for feedback to be easily taken into account so that the third step can be delivered efficiently. A larger but still small number of staff will be involved at this stage.

2.27 Once the development and testing in one area or unit has taken place, the tools can be rolled out to the department/business. The amount of support required should not be underestimated for this stage. Unless the tools have been constructed so that they are very intuitive, a significant amount of training may also be required. A helpdesk might be needed and e-mail support will almost certainly be required. It can be expected that a significant number of staff will be involved at this stage although most of the staff will be part-time only.

2.28 The involvement of a significant number of line staff will assist the buy-in process and will disseminate the executive management's view on the identification, measuring and management of compliance risk. The advantage to the organisation of this point cannot be overstated. The process of using a risk management tool will focus the attention of large numbers of staff on potential compliance risks and will significantly increase the education and awareness of such risks in the organisation. This will considerably reinforce compliance procedures and lead directly to a more compliant organisation. A welcome by-product for executive management is likely to be a more relaxed regulatory attitude to the firm.

Risk identification

2.29 Before managing the compliance risk to an institution, its management must first identify the elements from which the institution is most at risk and then find a method of monitoring the risks. Only when an institution's compliance risk profile has been identified and is being monitored can its compliance management hope to begin serious efforts to manage and then mitigate the compliance risks.

2.30 The identification of the compliance risks facing an institution can be carried out in a variety of ways. Typically, interviews and/or workshops of senior managers and compliance executives explore the compliance objectives of the institution and the possible causes that will prevent the institution from reaching those objectives. Alternatively, compliance processes may be identified and the risks to those processes considered by the managers and supervisors most familiar with the process.

2.31 Both the objectives and the process can be high-level strategic ones affecting the entire institution or can equally be part of a detailed compliance procedure specific to a department. The identification of the compliance objectives (or the process) is a necessary first step without which the risks subsequently explored will have no context. Without boundaries it is very difficult to determine at what level the risks should properly be analysed and the development of an appropriate compliance risk profile becomes much more problematic.

Risk analysis: ownership

2.32 The monitoring of compliance risks is assisted by an analysis of each risk into the owner of the risk, the risk's impact on an organisation and the likelihood that it will happen. The identification of a risk owner is to ensure that a specific person (or sometimes a committee) takes responsibility for the risk and therefore for its management and mitigation, where possible. Risk owners are not identified in order to generate (or perpetuate) a blame culture and the institution's senior management must be fully committed to the responsibility approach in order for the institution to benefit from the management and mitigation of its risk. Without a commitment to the responsibility approach for risk ownership (rather than the blame approach) there will be many fewer risks identified and much less enthusiasm by management and supervisors to be conscious of the risks faced by an organisation (and the reduction of those risks).

Risk analysis: components

2.33 Typically, the impact of a risk on an organisation is initially evaluated as a high, medium or low impact. However, this often rapidly becomes a monetary value and generally is viewed from a value perspective once the management of risk has been embedded in an organisation. Similarly, the likelihood that a risk will happen to an organisation is also often initially evaluated on a high, medium or low basis. This also tends to transform into a percentage likelihood or a time value (such as once every three months) as the managers become more familiar with risk management.

2.34 Many of the previously manual approaches to self-assessment are increasingly being automated to provide a more proactive method of monitoring compliance risk. The implementation and operation of an effective compliance control and risk self-assessment process can provide valuable management information on both the level of risk and the adequacy of the control responses to those risks. There are several critical factors that can be used to guide the success of a compliance self-assessment process including senior management sponsorship for the process, a focus on the development of action plans to address key weaknesses (rather than a focus on the existence of the weakness) and the willingness of senior and middle management to own and drive compliance risk and control accountability through the organisation.

Control identification

2.35 The same process applied to each control yields the beginnings of a tool to manage (and mitigate) compliance risk. The control owner should be identified as the person who is responsible for the control operating effectively. The control's importance and effectiveness are also assessed, during either interviews or workshops.

2.36 The importance of a control gives management the ability to judge whether a control is fundamental to mitigating the inherent compliance risk, is important to the mitigation or is one of perhaps a suite of controls, no single one of which by itself will prevent a risk from occurring. The effectiveness of a control is its ability to mitigate the risk based on the control's design and on how the control is carried out in practice.

2.37 Alternatively, the controls' design and performance could be analysed. The design of a control is the inherent mitigation of the risk by that control and often reflects the adequacy of processes and IT systems relating to the control. Its performance is the adequacy of the carrying out of the control and this is mainly reflected by the people and systems used in the control.

Example suite of controls

Compliance Risk: Mis-selling by new retail sales staff

	Control	Criteria	KPI
Level 1	Recruitment Standards	Minimum standards reached	% pass on recruitment assessment
Level 2	Induction and competence assessment	Minimum standards met	% pass internal and external exams
Level 3	Supervision	All business counter checked	% reject level for new staff
Level 4	Sign off as competent	All examinations and worksite assessments passed	Days/months to achieve sign off

Risk and control monitoring

2.38 With the above risk and control analysis an institution's senior management is equipped to start monitoring and managing its compliance risks. At an early stage the institution will probably monitor its risks once every quarter in order to begin monitoring trends in the risks. Ideally, the process of identifying the compliance risks and controls will be embedded in the institution and its compliance risk awareness will have been enhanced considerably. In these circumstances, new compliance risks to an institution and the appropriate controls will be identified as they first occur at the latest (or are first perceived at best) and will be added to the institution's compliance risk inventory (which, when displayed graphically, is sometimes called a risk map).

2.39 It is also important to review the compliance risk inventory to ensure that risks that are no longer applicable to an institution are removed and that the associated controls are not carried out (thus saving costs). However, it must be noted that a control often mitigates more than one compliance risk and, therefore, stopping a control should only be done after a full review of the design of the control (both the original design and how it works in practice).

2.40 Many varied methods are employed to monitor risk ranging from using periodic reviews of both risks and controls to the continuous real-time monitoring of both qualitative and quantitative risk indicators. A recent development in monitoring risk is the use of internal loss databases to monitor errors and near misses.

2.41 The reporting, escalation and analysis of compliance errors and breaches can be used to reinforce the diligence and thoroughness of individuals responsible for compliance risk and/or control within the business. Proactive compliance risk management functions are using these loss databases to provide a basis for detailed root cause analysis to ensure that key learning points are identified and escalated throughout the business, in order to reduce the likelihood of repeated errors.

Risk and control framework

2.42 A comprehensive compliance risk control framework is comprised of a number of different layers all working in conjunction to either prevent errors and breaches from occurring in the first place or, should a failure occur, limit either the direct or indirect exposure of the firm.

Front-line prevent controls

2.43 The first layer of control can be considered to be front-line prevent controls which are used to ensure that things go right in the first place and operate as the foundation for the business process as a whole. These commonly include: clarity of roles and responsibilities, access to accurate, timely and clear management information (eg inside information flowing into the firm) and establishing processes with minimal manual interfaces and intervention (eg automated trade generation, capture, recording and reporting mechanisms).

Processes prevent controls

2.44 A second level of prevent controls can be defined as those controls embedded within processes that are used to catch errors prior to and at the time of execution of a contract. As the name suggests the controls are designed to prevent problems and can include automated controls to prevent the entry of a prohibited trade into the firm's system.

Detect controls

2.45 Detect controls can be used to detect rather than prevent problems. Many front-line detect controls are designed to detect operational problems on the same day or, at the very least, on the next day in an effort to limit the potential impact of the problem – either operational or financial. These controls can include an end of day review. A secondary level of detect controls can be designed to detect errors on a less time critical basis (for example 2–5 days) and are particularly of use where the nature of any financial impact would not support investment in more expensive prevent type controls.

Back-stop detect controls

2.46 Back-stop detect controls can be designed to limit the financial loss associated with any errors. These controls are typically performed on a less timely basis (for example on a monthly basis).

Examples: risk and control framework

Front Line Prevent Controls	• Clear responsibility and accountability for risk areas • Prompt and pertinent MI • Clear governance for decision making affecting risk
Processes Prevent Controls	• Automatic rejection of imperfect/incomplete applications not meeting pre-determined criteria • Pre-checking of documentation before submission
Detect Controls	• End of day balancing of trading • Manual weekly check on outstanding issues
Back stop Detect Controls	• Review of MI trends at executive meetings • Quarterly Compliance inspections

Relative cost of different controls

2.47   Placing the emphasis of control on automated front-line prevent controls and process prevent controls, with an objective of 'getting things right first time', reduces the likelihood of compliance breaches. There is, however, a price for this – preventative controls are the most expensive controls to establish and maintain as they tend to be more transaction related.

2.48   Heavy reliance on manual control processes, particularly where these processes are focused on the detection of operational errors after the point of contract execution, can increase the likelihood of delayed detection and more serious compliance problems. Not only is the organisation exposed longer to the underlying risk for which the control is designed but also to a longer period for the potential failure of the control. Untimely detection of errors can expose the organisation to adverse market movements, may exacerbate the potential financial loss and is very likely to increase the regulatory exposure. Intuitively, the timely detection of compliance errors can be a key to effective risk mitigation.

Use of technology

2.49   Leading institutions have used the implementation of new IT systems to develop a more 'straight through' process to improve efficiency where compliance risk mitigation relies on manual processes and to address key compliance risks. In many cases, enhanced process automation and the re-designing of key processes can provide the opportunity to reduce, and even eliminate, some compliance risks. In addition, it can also help to shift the emphasis of control from manual detect to automated prevent controls.

2.50 A current trend is to develop an organisation's capability to provide greater and more timely management information to support and enhance the control framework. Re-cycling management information from the administration area to the front office on a real-time basis not only ensures that decisions are based on a complete and up-to-date view but also increases the likelihood of any errors or breaches being detected quickly.

2.51 The introduction of a risk function within the compliance department, responsible for identifying and monitoring compliance risk and key indicators, can provide the firm's management with a 'dashboard' to measure compliance risk and the effectiveness of the controls in place to manage those risks. These metrics can help to shift compliance risk management from being a reactive after-the-event activity to a more predictive before-the-event activity.

Action plans

2.52 Concrete steps to reduce the institution's compliance risk profile or appetite can also be taken. Both the inherent compliance risk and the current residual risk can be evaluated when the mitigation of the relevant controls, as believed by the management, is known. Action plans can be drawn up for any control which is deemed insufficient and for any residual risk which is deemed to be beyond the institution's risk appetite.

2.53 The action plans will be to enhance the existing controls, add further controls and further mitigate the risks. As a minimum, the owner of the action plan, a target date for completion and a brief description of the action plan will be drawn up. Deliverables by which the plan will be judged as completed are also often included.

2.54 It is essential that action plans are followed up on a regular basis to assess progress. The failure to do so will result in the likely event of the action plan not being followed through, with the institution losing its compliance risk momentum and requiring considerably more effort when re-evaluating its risk and control assessment in the future. However, if action plans are carried through, the institution will achieve a higher compliance risk awareness coupled with a usefully lower compliance risk profile. The natural next step in this case is to re-evaluate the compliance risks and controls for the next set of action plans, thus creating a virtuous circle of compliance risk management and mitigation.

2.55 With control owners identified, it will be possible to investigate likely groupings of potential control failures and their impact on compliance risk occurrences. Groupings of risk owners can also be useful in identifying clusters of risks and therefore susceptibility to risk cascade (ie the occurrence of one risk leading to a greater likelihood of the occurrence of other risks within the risk group).

External risk data

2.56 There are a number of compliance risks that occur only infrequently and therefore, by nature, are difficult to validate and verify independently. To counter the problems of data collection, the extreme values of certain risks could be derived from external loss databases. Such collections of data are useful in allowing an institution to place a value on a risk that has not happened to it (and may be extremely unlikely to happen).

2.57 The relevance of external data needs to be questioned closely so that the risk (and the loss amount derived from the external database) is appropriate to the institution. For example, a compliance breach incurred by a commercial bank may not be relevant to a retail bank and the loss may therefore need to be multiplied by a percentage reflecting the relevance of the breach to that particular firm. A loss may also require scaling for the size of the institution wishing to use the data (against the size of the institution incurring the breach). Another area of caution with regard to external data is to ensure that the institution's view of a particular breach is the same as the database provider's view.

2.58 Subject to the above, loss data from an external database should prove useful in assisting compliance management in determining more accurate values for low likelihood risks than solely relying on management's perception of the possible loss.

Measurement

2.59 The reporting of data to the compliance department is fundamental to the proper continuing analysis of compliance risk. The reporting must be both timely and accurate. Timescales that are viewed as realistic by the supplying department as well as the compliance department should be agreed. There should also be an escalation procedure to senior management of both compliance and the supplying department if data is not supplied within the timescales. This will safeguard against circumstances where the data shows unacceptable compliance risk and the supplying department wishes, for whatever reason, to withhold such data. Additionally, it is useful to have a feedback mechanism so that unusual data can be easily and rapidly questioned and amended or actioned as appropriate.

2.60   The compliance department will wish to review different data at different intervals, for example:

- daily: trading tickets;
- weekly: temporary joiners and leavers;
- monthly: permanent joiners and leavers;
- quarterly: personal registrations; and
- annually: authorised scope of the business.

2.61   It is likely that the compliance department will wish to keep data on its management of compliance risks for a number of years in order to assist on potential investigations and to demonstrate a history of risk surveying to the regulators. However, the compliance department should also recognise that some data may be regarded as sensitive by the supplying department and clear assurances must therefore be given with regard to who will be allowed access to the data and any conclusions drawn from it. An example of sensitive data would be salaries and bonuses.

Line management of compliance risk

2.62   The tools used above will lead to the enhancement of each department's compliance policies and procedures. The review of such policies and procedures from time to time by senior management assists the executive in remaining aware of the compliance programme throughout the firm. A rolling programme of review and reporting to a committee such as the audit committee or the risk management committee will enable a senior management review process to be conducted efficiently and effectively. Detailed reviews will also be carried out periodically by the compliance department, the line department involved and possibly by internal audit.

Special areas of compliance risk

2.63   There are certain special areas of compliance risk that span a number of departments or businesses. Whilst the tools described above are just as applicable to these areas, a different approach is required. It will be necessary in the design phase to gather together specialists from the various line departments and businesses involved so that a methodology can be worked out which will cover the needs of each department or business. The special areas of compliance risk include, but are not limited to:

- insider dealing;
- money laundering;
- senior management responsibility;
- training and competence;

- advertising;
- compliance fatigue/forgetfulness;
- ethical creep; and
- new staff (contract, temporary and permanent).

2.64 Although the above risks are narrower in perspective than the compliance risks applicable to an entire business or department, they are also more complex and will require considerably more input from the compliance manager. The resulting procedures following the analysis will also require much wider dissemination, typically across the entire organisation. Where compliance procedures cover a number of departments it is appropriate for an executive, or more likely a committee, that covers all those departments to provide a final review and approval before full implementation.

Training and competence

2.65 The FSMA 2000 and the revised rules and guidance issued by the FSA have increased the scope of the training and competence regime to encompass everyone who is involved, directly or indirectly, in regulated business. In the words of Principle 3 a firm should make 'proper arrangements for any employee associated with a regulated activity carried on by the firm to achieve, maintain and enhance competence'.

2.66 In particular, the competence of senior managers appointed to take responsibility for controlled functions, is included within the scope of these rules and evidence of their benchmark competence and continuing maintenance of those competencies is required.

2.67 Regardless of where in the organisation the responsibility sits for establishing, maintaining and supervising the scheme for the training and competence arrangements, the compliance department should consider two sets of risks when reviewing which rules are being met:

- outputs from the scheme, that is the competence standards being achieved, robustness of sign-off of individuals as competent, actual maintenance of competence etc; and
- inputs to the scheme, that is the monitoring and control regime within the training area that governs the robustness of the scheme.

2.68 In the past the industry has incurred disciplinary action arising from failures in this area, which is viewed as a key protection for investors. Common problems arise from failure to monitor the inputs. Examples would include:

- individuals' records can be incomplete or incorrect and under weak control which undermines the entire scheme;

- internal assessment standards are not monitored leading to very high numbers (99%) of pass rates and question banks are not updated to reflect internal and external changes; and
- training modules are developed without business approval and trained face to face according to the individual delivering the training without any consistency check.

Change

2.69   Probably the most difficult area of risk arises from change. This can be either a fundamental shift in the strategy of the business and/or a comparatively small change in an IT system on which a structure of compliance risk monitoring has been built. Sometimes changes are developed and implemented without those involved appreciating that there is any need to consider compliance.

2.70   To avoid the possibility of this risk, it is appropriate for the organisation's project management procedures to contain a step that requires sign-off by compliance of the change proposals regardless of the nature of the change. Periodic reviews by compliance of all change projects underway (perhaps quarterly) are desirable.

CHAPTER 3

Fashioning compliance systems

Summary

Framework

3.1   Compliance systems need a framework before they can be developed. The framework within which any system is developed will include a vision, principles and an oversight structure. The framework will also include comments on the current environment and the intended future environment as well as how the compliance department integrates with core business processes including performance measurement, planning and budgeting. There may also be commentary on the sustainability of the compliance department including its attitude to continuous improvement and training and education.

Vision

3.2   This will include comments on the governance of the department such as the expectations of the board. Additionally, the compliance department may have a mission statement or, potentially, its own vision statement. Guiding principles may be laid down together with goals and objectives for the department. The organisation structure of the firm and the compliance department's position within it will be spelt out.

Common language

3.3   The framework will make clear the common language to be used throughout the organisation with regard to compliance. This will enable the organisation to participate in compliance work with a single view of the meaning of compliance terms.

Oversight structure

3.4   The roles and responsibilities of each of the control departments within the firm with respect to compliance will be made clear in this chapter. This will include responsibilities of the Board of Directors and senior management as well as staff responsibilities. Reporting processes and escalation triggers will be detailed. How the compliance department will achieve quality assurance and quality control will also be articulated. The staffing and management of the department together with its interaction and integration with other departments of the firm will be mentioned.

Change management

3.5   It is also helpful for the framework to make clear how the compliance department can create a positive environment to support sustainable change including, where necessary, new processes, new organisational structures and new technologies. The executive sponsorship of compliance should be clear as should the value created by the department through activities such as proactive assistance to new business initiatives. The commitment of the firm to integrating the compliance with all of the firm's processes through training and education should be explicit.

3.6   With an overarching compliance framework in place it is easier to set about fashioning compliance systems. Given the new regulatory push towards risk-based compliance a good place to start is with the development of a risk policy for compliance.

Policy

3.7   The risk policy of a compliance department must identify what risks are covered and those responsible as well as several other fundamental and necessary topics, listed below.

What risks should be covered?

3.8   It is natural for a compliance manager to wish to identify the risks that fall within the purview of his department. However, such a list is likely to be extensive unless the work of a compliance department is very clearly defined. A restrictive description of compliance risks is likely to hinder the effectiveness of a compliance function. Many of the cross-departmental advantages that a compliance department can bring to a firm will be lost if its boundaries are too clearly circumscribed. Whilst all departments need to communicate and take into account the risks lying within other areas of an institution, a compliance department is more functional in nature than most other departments. Although this inevitably leads to a blurring of where compliance risks end and other risks begin, there are clear benefits (as well as some disadvantages) to a firm if the management cadre is able and willing to work with a risk model which does not inhibit the natural tendency to enquire what should exist within a compliance department.

3.9   Such comments also apply, of course, to other departments of a functional and control nature such as internal audit, legal and risk management. If properly implemented and managed, the above risk model will ensure an overlapping of risk reviews and should increase significantly the protection afforded to the firm by all risk control departments. However, the human element within this risk model is difficult to manage and can become unworkable unless the risk philosophy is shared by all management from the CEO downwards.

3.10   The compliance risk policy will cover the firm breaching regulatory requirements due to inadequate or failed processes, people and systems or due to external events. These should include, but in accordance with para **3.9**, should not be limited to:

- Processes:

    (a) third-party risks such as money-laundering;
    (b) business resumption risks such as insurance;
    (c) client risks such as suitability, capacity, sales practices and client identification;
    (d) employee risks such as wrongful trading, collusion, trading limits and delegation of duties;
    (e) management risks such as control, valuation and audit;
    (f) product risks such as complexity, internal disclosure and external disclosure; and
    (g) strategic risks such as corporate governance, reputation, new markets, new products and acquisition and disposal.

- People:

    (a) employee failure risks such as malice, fraud, negligence, information misuse and morals;
    (b) employee proficiency risks such as competence and training;
    (c) employer failure risks such as disciplinary, turnover, morals and negligence;
    (d) inappropriate culture risks such as whistle blowing, morale and control culture; and
    (e) conflict of interest risk.

- Systems:

    (a) communications risk such as availability;
    (b) data risks such as quality, integrity and model risk;

    (c) hardware risks such as failure, integrity and security; and

    (d) software risks such as programming errors, security and capacity.

- External:

    (a) government risks such as a change in the political environment or government;

    (b) industry-linked risks such as changes in regulatory standards and policies;

    (c) physical risks such as physical security and natural disasters; and

    (d) terrorism risks.

3.11   An alternative overview of compliance risks at a strategic level could be with regard to the FSA principles and would be likely to include the following:

- observance of high standards of conduct and integrity by the firm;
- sufficient information for and about customers;
- avoidance where possible and minimisation where appropriate of conflicts of interest;
- safeguarding of customers' assets;
- appropriate review of the firm's internal controls; and
- openness with regulators.

3.12   A major concern with the above list would be the very broad nature of risks identified. The compliance manager responsible for covering the risks identified at para **3.11** would have a very wide functional responsibility that may not fit with the management philosophy of the firm. However, the regulators do require a firm to address the risks inherent in the above points and, as an arm of the CEO's control function, it could be argued that the compliance department should take the lead in addressing these points.

3.13   The wide-ranging nature of the risks also opens the compliance manager to considerable personal exposure unless the function of the compliance department is understood by the firm to be that of a messenger rather than an enforcer. This is not to say that the compliance manager should not be responsible for monitoring and reporting the risks but rather that (having identified, measured, managed and reported them) the highest levels of management firm must ultimately take responsibility.

3.14   A further alternative could include reference to appropriate and adequate risk management of the following compliance risks:

- authorisation and registration including staff as well as the firm;
- client money and other assets including collateral and credit management policy;
- customer interests including types of customer, agreements, confirmations and suitability;

- advertising and promotion including unsolicited calls;
- collective investment schemes and packaged products;
- order execution including allocation and aggregation;
- insider dealing;
- stabilisation;
- transaction reporting including record-keeping;
- personal account dealing;
- complaints; and
- relationship with regulators.

3.15 The advantage of the above list is that the compliance risks are clearly spelled out (albeit in a broad manner) and can be clearly seen to relate to specific matters that are of concern to a regulator. Whilst the points will undoubtedly impact upon and cause interaction with many other departments in a firm, they are all obviously connected with compliance and regulation. It is therefore likely that turf wars can be avoided and co-operation of other departments obtained in what appear to be legitimate areas of interest for the compliance department.

Who is responsible?

3.16 Ultimately the CEO and Board of Directors must be responsible for the compliance culture within an organisation. However, the compliance department functions as an arm of the CEO's control function that also includes departments such as credit management, internal audit and risk management. Although the CEO takes ultimate responsibility he delegates day-to-day identification, measurement, management and reporting of compliance risks to compliance. This delegation is directly comparable to that given to the credit department who are responsible for identifying, measuring, managing and reporting credit risks to which the institution is exposed.

3.17 The compliance risk policy must be clear on where the head of compliance's responsibilities begin and end. In particular, it must be clear that, having reported compliance risks and made recommendations to the senior management, it becomes the responsibility of the management cadre to direct action relating to those risks. Periodic reports to compliance to assist monitoring greatly helps in this matter.

3.18 Additionally, the risk policy should acknowledge the responsibility of departmental and line managers in complying with compliance policies and procedures. Although the compliance risk analysis and surveying process (and subsequent identification, measurement, management and reporting of the risks) will be led by the compliance department, the continuing mitigation of the risks identified through compliance with agreed procedures remains the primary responsibility of the line and department in which the risks are generated. It must be clear that the line and departmental managers cannot abrogate their responsibilities for compliance risks to the compliance department and that the compliance department has not and will not take first-line responsibility for the day-to-day mitigation of the compliance risks. Each manager in the firm must be responsible for ensuring that each department uses the appropriate agreed compliance procedures and thereby avoids breaching regulations.

Policy statement or overview

3.19   The compliance risk policy statement must contain an overview or clear, short and concise statement as to the nature of compliance risks acknowledged by the organisation to be covered by the compliance department. This is likely to refer to the risk of the firm breaching regulatory requirements or perhaps, more positively, to broad regulatory principles (such as those in the UK). The policy statement can also be seen as a mission statement for the compliance department although this will only be helpful if other similar departments also have similar statements.

Relationships and lines of communication

3.20   Although the responsibilities of the compliance department (and where they end) will be made clear in the compliance risk policy statement, it is also important to document the relationship that compliance department will have with all other departments and what lines of formal communication will exist. There will be various compliance functions that are most efficiently carried out within the line departments responsible for the risk, eg transaction reporting by the operations or administration department. These functions must be clearly documented so that the appropriate managers are fully aware of their responsibilities. Each line manager concerned must of course first agree such delegation and responsibility for such functions. It is also important to make clear how the compliance department interacts with other departments and, in particular, trading, sales and research departments.

3.21   Communication is the lifeblood of a compliance department and lines of formal communication, such as the receipt of reports from other departments, should also be documented. This will include agreed and acceptable timescales within which such reports must be submitted and the minimum amount of information required that enables the compliance department to perform its functions efficiently. Relationships and lines of communication are often best illustrated diagrammatically.

Timescales

3.22 There should be a commitment on the part of the compliance management to appropriate timescales within which to identify, measure, monitor and report compliance risks. Although new compliance risks will continue to appear, the senior management must be given an assurance that such risks will be properly identified, measurement processes set up, control procedures implemented and reporting started within acceptable timescales. Timescales should take account of the skill sets and staffing within the compliance department but must not be so long as to expose the firm to unnecessary compliance risk.

Staffing requirements

3.23 Risks cannot be properly identified or functionally managed with inappropriate staff. Both the skill sets and numbers in the compliance department must match the existing and projected complexity of the firm. The staffing requirements of the compliance department must be made explicit in the policy statement and reviewed periodically, ie at least annually, to ensure that the correct quality and numbers of compliance staff are available to the firm. Staffing requirements should take account of training time needed by staff in order to stay abreast of product and regulatory developments as well as the peaks and troughs of workflow in certain types of firms.

Reporting requirements

3.24 A fundamental part of a compliance department's responsibility is reporting on compliance risk. Just as a compliance department requires communication to it in order to function so it must communicate with senior management in order to ensure that risks are properly highlighted and that appropriate levels of management are aware of the compliance risks to which the organisation is exposed. The policy statement should include when, to whom and how often reports are made on compliance risk. At a minimum, the compliance department staff should make monthly reports to the head of compliance who should then report to the senior management, including the CEO and a high-level committee of executive management. Additionally, a quarterly compliance report to the Board of Directors or a suitable subcommittee such as a Board audit committee should also be made. Such reports will ensure the correct level of senior management attention to compliance risks and will help establish an appropriate compliance culture within the firm.

Reporting lines

3.25   Another fundamental part of the compliance risk policy statement is the clear identification of reporting lines for the compliance department and the head of compliance. If the head of compliance does not report directly to the CEO, the policy statement must make clear that a functional reporting line, ie a dotted line, exists between the head of compliance and the CEO. For line management purposes, it may be appropriate for the head of compliance to report to the head of administration or the head of legal although the manager of the head of compliance should freely acknowledge that a functional line responsibility exists directly to the CEO (or another appropriate channel such as to the chairman of the Board audit committee).

Documentation

3.26   The resulting compliance systems need to be well documented and well understood. The systems must be agreed with each relevant head of department or business head and, additionally, with the appropriate executive committees and, at a summary level, the Board of Directors. Whilst the documentation relating to the systems will generally be A4 in size, account should be taken of the use to which the documentation will be put, eg sales and marketing staff may find an A5 booklet or binder a more useful size for carrying around with them when visiting clients.

Understanding

3.27   Following on from good documentation is good understanding of documentation. Many large organisations today have specialist compliance training managers and this move underlines the importance of explaining fully and applying consistently the compliance procedures. Seminars, workshops, and acted scenarios are all useful in emphasising different points relating to the compliance systems. Although seminars can be useful for the dissemination of information, workshops where the audience fully participates are far more effective in assisting the long-term absorption of compliance procedures. The person that participates in a workshop will be far more likely to remember a workshop than one who is merely receiving a lecture. If the audience is very participatory, the acting out of a scenario (or role play) can be introduced. This is extremely effective as the audience and the actors tend to take ownership of the training session. At the other end of the scale, but nevertheless still essential, is the sign-off form which formally commits an individual to complying with the procedures and systems in the spirit as well as the letter of the documentation.

Rule review

3.28   The survey and analysis of the risks must of course take into account the rules and regulations imposed upon the firm. An essential part of the compliance risk analysis is undertaken by the compliance department itself. This involves the review of every rule and part of every rule in order to consider whether it is or can be applicable to the institution. If it is not applicable then a reason must be noted why it is not applicable. If it is applicable a procedure must be written to cover the rule that will tie in with the procedures generated from the other part of the risk survey and analysis.

Consolidated procedures

3.29   When the risk surveys and analyses have been completed an overall compliance procedures manual will be needed which pulls together all the compliance procedures into one volume. The single volume should then be reviewed for consistency of approach and procedures.

Monitoring procedures

3.30   A compliance department monitoring procedures manual can then be prepared which will monitor the procedures that have evolved from the risk analyses and surveys. The monitoring procedures will detail clearly how the compliance procedures are to be tested in order to assist senior management in gaining confidence that risk-based compliance is operating such that a breach of regulatory requirements will be detected.

Cross-reference documents

3.31   An essential document can then be prepared which cross-references all rules to the compliance and monitoring procedures. This document will provide comfort to management and appropriate regulators that every applicable rule and sub-rule has a compliance procedure and that the procedure is monitored according to the effect that a breach of the rules will have on the firm's compliance objectives. It will contain the following:

- the number of every rule and sub-rule;
- a brief description of the rule or sub-rule;
- whether it is applicable or not to the firm;
- the owner of the rule breach risk;
- an assessment of the likelihood and impact of the rule being breached;
- the applicable compliance procedure reference or the reason why the rule is not applicable;

- the primary department and person responsible for carrying out the compliance procedure;
- an assessment of the design and performance of the compliance procedure;
- the monitoring procedure reference;
- the frequency at which the monitoring procedure should be carried out;
- the frequency at which the rule should be reviewed for applicability;
- the frequency at which the procedure should be reviewed (if different); and
- any cross-references to either procedure.

3.32 However, it is also necessary to provide internal comfort to the executive management, the business management and the compliance department itself that all compliance procedures are necessary and that there are no redundant procedures. A further document containing similar information to the above but listing all procedures will give this comfort. Additionally, this document will provide confirmation that the compliance department monitors all compliance procedures, as every compliance procedure will have a monitoring procedure reference. The document will contain:

- every compliance procedure reference;
- a brief description of the compliance procedure;
- the primary department responsible for carrying out the compliance procedure;
- the reason why the procedure is necessary including the rule reference where applicable;
- an assessment of the design and performance of the compliance procedure;
- the monitoring procedure reference;
- the frequency at which the monitoring procedure should be carried out;
- the frequency at which the procedure should be reviewed; and
- any cross-references to either procedure.

Procedures manual

3.33 For the purpose of controlling the company procedures manual it is a useful discipline to ensure that all copies are version controlled and properly dated. This will allow monitoring of amendments and additional materials by reference to the date that they were published. In time compliance departments may find that procedures and procedures manuals are called into question and even litigated upon. It is essential to determine which version of the procedures manual was in force at any particular time. A reference number and publication date printed at the foot of each page is perhaps the simplest method of controlling documentation.

The compliance department

3.34   In fashioning an internal compliance system it is important to consider the role that the compliance department will play in an organisation. Organisations will wish to establish compliance departments that are best suited to the business model of the firm. There are many disciplines contained within compliance. Some or perhaps all of these can be catered for within the compliance department. Others, depending on the type of organisation, may be best dealt with in other departments. In this event, compliance systems should take into account that the central compliance department may wish to exercise oversight or a monitoring activity over these other functional areas. The firm should consider the following responsibilities and where they are best placed within an organisation:

- Complaints handling and responsibilities for receipt, investigation and reporting of complaints received within the firm.
- Monitoring programmes by which the firm monitors the activities of the company. These may range from daily or weekly monitoring activities through to monitoring of activities on a less frequent basis. The firm should identify those areas that are of a higher risk to ensure they are monitored more frequently.
- Advice and guidance:

  Provision should be made for compliance functions to provide advice and guidance to the organisation about the application of regulators' rules and the firm's compliance procedures. This should be offered on a proactive basis in response to any issue the compliance department identifies during its monitoring of activities and also in response to any specific queries the firm may have. Certainly a compliance department that operates an open-door policy towards such queries is likely to engender an improved compliance culture within the firm.

- Controls and approvals:

  Provision should be made for an area of the firm, possibly the compliance department, to be responsible for control and approvals of any advertising or promotional materials. The extent to which the firm advertises and conducts financial promotion will be determined by the type of business the firm conducts. Certainly product providers will issue routinely promotional materials for their products which will require close scrutiny to ensure compliance with applicable rules. Brokerage houses may be involved in public offerings and securities which will require specialist compliance input and smaller brokerage houses, possibly independent financial advisers, are likely to advertise their services which again will require compliance approval. The compliance systems necessary to support, control and approve promotional materials should ensure that appropriate expertise is devoted to the process of granting approval. The person appointed within the firm to approve material must be able to ensure that all necessary regulatory requirements are catered for and the firm must grant authority to the person responsible for advertising approvals to prevent publication where an item is considered to be non-compliant.

In addition, systems should ensure that appropriate records are maintained to demonstrate that an item has been submitted for approval, approval has been granted and that a record of the final copy of the item is maintained.

- Investigations:

  The firm may wish to devote a specific resource for the conduct of compliance investigations. These may be necessary where either a complaint has been made against the firm and the investigation of that individual complaint suggests that failings within the firm may be more widespread and require detailed consideration. Moreover, where the compliance department, through its monitoring activities, identifies that a particular problem may exist within an organisation and, again, specialised resources should be devoted to the matter.

- Enforcement:

  Chapter 8 deals with issues of enforcement in more detail. However, in establishing compliance systems for an organisation, firms should consider whether it is necessary to make provisions for compliance enforcement measures in response to identified breaches. Enforcement mechanisms can be dealt with in a variety of different ways. It may be the designated responsibility of a firm's human resources department, line management or the compliance department. The firm should consider which is the appropriate method to deal with enforcement measures in the context of the business it operates and an objective of creating an appropriate compliance culture for the organisation.

- Money laundering prevention:

  Measures to prevent a firm from being used as a vehicle for laundering the proceeds of crime should be taken into account. Indeed, the FSMA 2000, s 6 provides the FSA with the obligation to reduce financial crime. As a consequence, the FSA now has the responsibility for the monitoring of money laundering prevention procedures within authorised firms. A firm may consider that it is appropriate for an anti money laundering function to be the responsibility of its central compliance department or placed elsewhere within the organisation. Larger firms often take the decision to create a centralised anti money laundering department responsible for monitoring compliance with money laundering regulations, liaising with the NCIS in respect of suspicious money laundering activities (where such other law enforcement agencies will apply in local jurisdiction) and providing training in anti money laundering measures for the company. The issue of money laundering is considered in full in **Chapter 6**.

- Oversight and internal audit:

> Finally, it should be taken into account that in larger, complex organisations that compliance arrangements maintained by the compliance department will benefit from an oversight review. These may by conducted by an internal audit department. That epartment should be encouraged to develop an internal audit or oversight plan, committing them to devote regular time in the compliance department each year to reviewing their functions to ensure they are being maintained correctly. This does not necessarily give rise to the requirement to ensure that the internal audit department is familiar with the regulatory arrangements in the jurisdiction in which the compliance department operates. However, It may be necessary in larger organisations for a member of the internal audit department to be a specialist in regulatory and compliance issues.

Training and experience of compliance staff

3.35 It is appropriate to ensure that all staff responsible for compliance functions have the appropriate expertise and skill to fulfil their responsibilities. Under the Financial Services Authority Approved Persons Regime it will certainly be the case that one or more members of the compliance department will be exercising a controlled function and will therefore need to be an approved person before they can commence their duties. Not all compliance functions carry identical skills requirements. Therefore, it is important to take into account that different areas of the compliance function will require different skills sets. For example, those persons engaged in daily monitoring activities will be better equipped to discharge their responsibilities if they have experience or background in audit as well as technical experience of the products and investments which they may be monitoring. Whereas those persons engaged in the area of providing interpretation, rules analysis or control and approval functions are more likely to be able to discharge their responsibilities if they have legal drafting, opinion writing skills as well as knowledge of the products and investments that they may be asked to comment on or approve. In addition, the compliance department should also consider the extent to which its staff should be managed or supervised to ensure that appropriate and consistent standards are maintained and whether complex areas of regulation should be escalated to a more senior or experienced member of the compliance department.

3.36 It certainly is the case that members of the compliance team should be subject to a continued education programme to ensure that their knowledge and skills are up to date. A regular approach to identifying development needs for the compliance team should be undertaken to allow any weaknesses in compliance staffs' skills sets to be identified and acted upon accordingly. For example, it may be necessary to ensure that compliance staff engaged in monitoring activities receive training prior to any new product launch. This will allow them to understand the new product or investment to such an extent that allows them to monitor the sales or transactions of that product and feedback responses to the organisation. All necessary steps should be taken to ensure that the compliance staff are not exposed to a situation where they are expected to be involved in a matter which they have little or no experience of, thus finding themselves at a disadvantage to other areas within an organisation.

CHAPTER 4

The complaints process and internal complaints investigations

Introduction

4.1   Greater numbers of people are aware of their rights as consumers and are prepared to ensure their rights are respected. Consumers regularly resort to the law wherever they consider use of the legal system is the best method to uphold their rights. As a result, case numbers in the courts are high which, in turn, can contribute towards delay. By way of example, in 2000, 1,631,966 money claims were issued in county courts in England and Wales and the average waiting period for a trial was 74 weeks.

4.2   This rise in court proceedings may be due partly to increased awareness of the rights of consumers. Organisations, such as the Consumers Association, undertake a valuable role in ensuring the general public is aware of the standard of service they should expect to receive when purchasing goods and services. In its annual report for 1999/2000 the consumers association reported:

> 'Challenging the government to deliver a Financial Services and Markets Bill with consumer interests at its core has been the main thrust of our personal finance campaign this year. We ensured that two of the Bill's statutory objectives – protection and education – are consumer-driven. We successfully supported an amendment on the regulation of long-term care insurance, and ensured that the Consumer Panel, which advises the Financial Services Authority, exists on a statutory, rather than just a discretionary basis. We also played a part in the creation of a single Financial Service Ombudsman and in securing commitment to regulation which focuses on products as well as procedures.'

4.3   The Financial Ombudsman Service in its Plan and Budget for 2001/2002 estimates in that year that the existing Ombudsman schemes will handle a total of 38,000 complaints, broken down as follows:

- insurance: 7,200
- banking: 6,800
- investment: 24,000

and that it will receive 375,000 initial contacts from customers.

4.4 Understanding the standard and level of service to expect of a financial services firm can be problematic for the non-professional investor. The nature of intangible products such as stocks, bonds and packaged products cause difficulties for the investor wishing to determine whether an acceptable level of service has or has not been received. Compare this to a consumer purchasing a new domestic appliance. The consumer will know very soon whether the item is defective. It may not operate at all or only in part, and the consumer will be in a position to develop an appreciation of what to expect from the product by reference to whether it does the job it is described as being able to perform. Consumers will carry out their own immediate assessment of the product in comparison to this information and use their own knowledge and experience to determine the value of what they have received.

4.5 Investment products, however, can be complex. Whilst consumers may assess their value (although this may not always be possible in the case of many packaged products), they may not always be in a position to determine easily whether they have received suitable advice if the investment has been sold as part of a complex financial planning exercise. For example, many investors were unable to determine that they had been inappropriately advised, when being advised to opt out or not join their employers' occupational pension schemes in preference to a personal pension.

4.6 For consumers that have suffered a disadvantage at the hands of a financial adviser or an investment firm, resorting to law can be a costly and time consuming exercise. In addition, the tactics of delay often encountered during a litigation can cause anxiety and distress and even consumers with good prospects of success will give up their case, or settle their claims at a level they feel unsatisfied with.

What the legislation states

4.7 The FSMA 2000 makes provision for the establishment of a single complaints resolution scheme covering all authorised activities under the Act. The outlined framework for the scheme is contained within ss 225–234 and Appendix 17 to the Act.

4.8 FSMA 2000, s 225 (1) sets out certain objectives for the scheme. These state that the scheme relates to certain disputes. It will resolve them quickly with the minimum of formality and by an independent person. It should also be noted that the scheme is administered by a body corporate, known as the Financial Ombudsman Service.

4.9 The legislation provides for two parts to the scheme. The first relating to complaints over which it has compulsory jurisdiction and the second to complaints over which it has voluntary jurisdiction. The compulsory jurisdiction requires authorised forms to submit to the jurisdiction of the scheme for resolution of any complaints made against it by its customers. The voluntary jurisdiction allows firms to participate in the ombudsman scheme where they are not authorised by the FSA, or in respect of activities falling outside the compulsory scheme.

The compulsory scheme

4.10 The main thrust of the scheme is that of its compulsory jurisdiction. The compulsory elements relate to complaints where certain conditions apply. These conditions are:

- the complainant is an eligible complainant;
- the complainant wishes to have their complaint dealt with under the scheme;
- the respondent to the complainant is an authorised person at the time of the act or admission complained of; and
- the act or admission occurred at a time when the compulsory jurisdiction rules were in force in relation to the activity complained of.

The voluntary scheme

4.11 The schemes' voluntary jurisdiction will only apply where certain conditions are met, namely:

- the complainant must be an eligible complainant;
- the complainant wishes to have their complaint dealt with under the scheme;
- at the time of the act or admission complained of, the respondent was participating in the scheme;
- the respondent has not withdrawn from the scheme at the time the complaint is made;
- the act or admission complained of occurred at a time when the voluntary jurisdiction rules were in force in relation to the activity in question; and
- the complaint had not been dealt with under the scheme's compulsory jurisdiction.

4.12 The Act gives the FSA the authority and power to make rules relating to the way in which firms handle complaints and to share responsibility with the Financial Ombudsman Service. It should be noted that the rules relating to the operation of the scheme require the approval of the FSA. Although the provisions relating to the compulsory and voluntary jurisdiction schemes derive from different sections of the FSMA 2000, an attempt has been made to co-ordinate the scheme rules wherever possible so that the process to follow by both consumers and authorised firms, whether they are dealing with the compulsory or voluntary jurisdiction complaint, are identical.

4.13   The Ombudsman Service has identified its scheme as having the following objectives[1]:

- provide consumers with a free one-stop service for dealing with disputes about financial services;
- resolve disputes quickly and with minimum formality;
- offer user-friendly information as well as adjudication and promote avoidance of disputes as well as their resolution;
- take decisions which are consistent, fair and reasonable;
- be cost-effective and efficient and be seen as being good value;
- be accessible to disadvantaged and vulnerable people;
- be forward-looking, adaptable and flexible, making effective use of new technology; and
- be trusted and respected by consumers, the industry and other interested parties.

1   First Financial Ombudsman Scheme annual report, 1999/2000.

4.14   For potential Complainants the Ombudsman service has published 7 points they recommend must take into account when making a complaint:

1. It's usually best to complain to the firm in writing. But if you phone, ask for the name of the person you speak to. Keep a note of this information, with the date and time of your call – and what was said. You may need to refer to this later.
2. Try to stay calm and polite, however angry or upset you are, that way you're more likely to explain your complaint clearly and effectively.
3. If possible, start by contacting the person you originally dealt with. If they can't help, say you want to take matters further. Ask for details of the firm's complaints procedure.
4. If you don't get the information you need, or you're not happy with the way your complaint is being dealt with, contact the most senior person in the firm. This will usually be the CEO.
5. When you write a letter of complaint, set out the facts as clearly as possible. This will make it easier for the firm to start putting things right.
6. Write down the facts in a logical order and stick to what is relevant. Remember to include important details like your customer number or your policy or account number. Put these details at the top of your letter.
7. Keep a copy of your letter. You may need to refer to it later.

Internal complaints procedures

4.15 Under s 138 and para 13 of Sch 17 to the FSMA 2000, rules have been made requiring authorised firms to establish internal complaints rules to deal with complaints made against the firm. Schedule 17, para 13(4) requires an authorised person who may become subject to the compulsory jurisdiction as a respondent, to establish such procedures as the authority considers appropriate for the resolution of complaints.

4.16 The rules made by the authority are set out in its Handbook of rules, entitled 'Dispute Resolution: Complaints'. Rule 1.2.1 states that a firm must have in place, and operate, appropriate and effective procedures (which must be in writing) for handling complaints about any expression of dissatisfaction, whether oral or written, and whether justified or not, about a service or activity relating to financial services offered, provided or withheld by that firm.

4.17 The Rules set out certain guidance to assist firms in designing their complaints systems. In particular, it specifies that the firm's complaints handling procedures should make provisions for receiving complaints, responding to complaints and, where a complaint cannot be resolved on the spot, the appropriate investigation of complaints. Guidance in the Rules also go on to suggest that when designing complaint handling procedures, firms should have regard to the type of business they undertake, the nature and complexity of the complaints they are likely to receive, the likely number of complaints and the size and organisational structure of the firm.

4.18 Firms, therefore, are required to have in place complaints handling procedures whether or not they expect to receive complaints from their customers. They should design their procedures in relation to the style and model of their business, the manner in which the organisation of their business is structured and the potential complexity of the complaints they are likely to receive.

4.19 Guidance rule 1.2.4(1)G states that the rules should make provision for how complaints are received. This is an important step for an organisation. Complaints can be received in many parts of a large business, whether in the front office by a trader or broker, the back office by an operations or administration department or even at more senior levels, for example by the firm's chief executive officer. The internal procedure should therefore, ensure that all members of staff and departments are aware how they should deal with complaints when they are received and, also, how they can identify whether an item of correspondence or telephone call is in fact a complaint. It is not only a question of establishing internal rules to cover this point, but also to ensure that members of staff are adequately trained to be able to identify complaints when they are received. It should be noted that the FSA's own rules specify that complaints handling procedures are required when handling complaints about 'any expression of dissatisfaction'. It should, therefore, give proper consideration to ensuring that internal procedures not only deal with complaints alleging financial loss, but also where customers are dissatisfied about the firm's service.

4.20   Firms should consider the following:

- Should all complaints or expressions of dissatisfaction be referred immediately to a compliance department?
- Is it feasible within the structure of the firm for complaints to be handled, in the first instance, by a customer services or operations department, and only if those complaints cannot be resolved, then escalated to a compliance department?

4.21   In considering this, firms should also consider the rule 1.2.16, which states that a firm must, wherever possible, make provisions for complaints to be handled or reviewed by a member of staff with sufficient competence and authority who is not directly involved in the matter which is the subject of the complaint, although, in the guidance to that rule, the FSA state that they will take into account the size and nature of the firm when applying compliance with this rule. Firms should always attempt to ensure that, in order to avoid any conflict of interest, the complaint should never be investigated by a person implicated, either directly or indirectly, in the matter complained of.

4.22   The complaints rules make provision for requirements that must be met within a firm's complaints handling procedures. Some elements of these requirements will be new to participants in previous complaints handling schemes. Requirements can be divided into the following three areas:

- disclosure of the firm's complaints handling procedures;
- awareness of the firm's complaints handling procedures; and
- the firm's management of its complaint handling procedures.

Complaints disclosure

4.23   Rule 1.2.9(1) requires that the firm must publicise, in all of its official stationery and marketing literature, that it is subject to the Financial Ombudsman Service. Compliance with this rule will require, in addition, disclosure to a regulatory authorisation that a firm is 'subject to the Financial Ombudsman Service'.

4.24   In addition, the firm is required to publish at the point of sale of a product, or when it first provides customers with documentation, details of the availability of its own internal complaints handling procedures.

Moreover, when it is requested to do, or unless it can resolve a complaint immediately upon it being received, it must supply details of its compliant handling procedures to a complainant.

4.25 Guidance on this rule from the FSA, suggests the firm may wish to publicise the availability of its internal complaints procedures and it being subject to the Financial Ombudsman Service by displaying a notice to that effect in all of its branches, on a website and in advertising materials.

Staff knowledge of complaints procedures

4.26 The FSA requires that all relevant staff within a firm, including appointed representatives of that firm, are aware of internal complaints handling procedures. It goes on to state that firms should also endeavour to ensure that those persons act in accordance with the procedures. It is suggested that mere publicity within the firm of complaint procedures is not sufficient to ensure awareness. The firm should consider providing training to staff on how the procedures operate and who in the firm is responsible for complaint investigation and resolution. This training requirement is particularly important for new members of staff within a firm. It is possible that any member of staff on their first day at the firm could receive correspondence or a telephone call, which contains an expression of dissatisfaction. The member of staff must be able to know how to deal with that in accordance with the firm's internal procedures.

Identifying trends from complaints

4.27 Rule 1.2.22 deals with the management control and manner in which complaints are handled internally. In particular, it is concerned with the fairness, consistency and promptness with which complaints are handled. It goes on to require that procedures also identify and remedy any recurring or systemic problems, as well as any specific problems identified by the complainant. The latter point in this rules goes to the very root of risk-based compliance. Given that complaints received in a firm can be a clear indication to the firm of where its standards of compliance are falling down, it is imperative that complaint procedures do not only deal with complaints in isolation. A firm should consider whether a complaint is indicative of a systemic problem within a firm, and arrangements should be available to escalate the complaint's investigation above the individual circumstances of the complaint. However, a fair balance must be made between considering wider issues of the firm and dealing with the complainant's individual concerns. The firm, therefore, should ensure that its procedures allow for the complainant's individual concern to be dealt with promptly and if the complaint has identified more widespread failings within the firm, that they be pursued separately from the individual complaint investigation but nonetheless seriously.

A consistent approach to complaints

4.28 It is also essential for firms to ensure that their internal procedures allow for similar complaints to be dealt with in a consistent manner. It is therefore vital that two or more complaints, whenever they are received highlighting identical or similar situations, are resolved in a consistent manner. It is the complainant's legal rights and appropriate remedies that should be observed, not necessarily the interest of the firm or the individual interest of a member of staff that may be implicated by the complaint. It would therefore be inappropriate and non-compliant for two similar complaints to be resolved differently. For example, a complaint made against an area of a firm's business, which is less productive, should not be resolved in the same manner as a complaint against an area of a firm which is highly successful. It is not appropriate for the first complaint to be dealt with more favourably towards a customer with the second dealt with in favour of the firm, merely to support the interest of the individual member of staff. Rule 1.2.22 addresses specifically the procedures required to ensure consistency. It also goes hand in hand with rule 1.2.16, which provides that the complaint should be handled or reviewed by members of staff who have sufficient experience, competence and authority as well as not being directly involved in the matter subject to the complaint. Those charged with the responsibility of complaints investigations within the firm should have sufficient authority to be able to make independent and objective decisions without fear of criticism from senior management. It would be acceptable to specify to complaints investigators that complaints must be dealt with in accordance with basic concepts of law. However, it is wholly inappropriate for a firm to place conditions on a complaints investigator's role by specifying that the primary objective is to defend the firm by attempting to find or develop a defence wherever possible. To place an investigator under the pressure of their employment if the manner in which they conclude complaints is against the firm's interest.

The complaint investigation

4.29 Firms should give careful consideration to the level of authority at which complaint investigators deal with complaints. It is clearly acceptable, by reference to guidance rule 1.2.5, that the firm's procedures can take into account the nature and complexity of the complaints likely to be received. Rule 1.2.22 states that a firm must have in place appropriate management control over the complaints. This would allow the conclusion of complaints investigation and authority levels to be limited for some investigators. It may be the case that in a larger firm, the investigator should refer a complex or sizeable complaint to his department manager for final approval, or indeed, to the CEO.

4.30   To ensure a prompt conclusion to complaints a firm's procedure should provide clear levels of authority to compliance staff allowing them to conclude complaints without the need for onward referral.

4.31   In conclusion, however, the rules are quite clear that no matter who is involved in a complaints investigation, they must remain sufficiently objective and independent of the matter to ensure that the firm's response addresses adequately the subject matter of the complaint.

Complaints investigations: acknowledgements and time limits

4.32   The complaint rules specify specific time limits within which complaints should be actioned or concluded. The first stage of dealing with any complaint is that, if the complaint cannot be resolved immediately, then a written acknowledgement should be sent to the complainant. That acknowledgement must include the name or job title of the person within the firm with whom the complainant should have contact, together with details of the firm's internal complaints procedures (rule 1.4.1).

Acknowledgements

4.33   In addition, the FSA recommend that if the complaint is made orally, the firm should try and confirm its understanding of the complaint. Some firms may choose also to have the customer sign, to acknowledge that the understanding of the complaint is correct. However, as the rules make it clear that complaints may be made in writing or orally, it does not seem acceptable for a firm to insist that such a written confirmation is a requirement for a complaint investigation to commence. The guidance also specifies that if a complaint is received by the firm via e-mail, the acknowledgement may also be transmitted by e-mail.

4.34   Guidance to rule 1.4.1 states that the firm should aim to resolve complaints at the earliest possible stage. The FSA does however, in rule 1.4.4, go on to state that a complainant must receive no later than four weeks from making a complaint, one of the following:

- a final response, which either accepts the complaint and, where appropriate, offers redress;
- an offer of redress, but without accepting the complaint; and
- a rejection of the complaint with reasons for doing so.

Complex complaints

4.35 Particularly complex complaints may require longer than four weeks to be concluded (see para **4.42** setting out suggested methods of complaint investigation). Rule 1.4.5 takes this into account. It states that at the four-week point, a holding response explaining why the firm is not yet in a position to resolve the complaint should be provided and this should give an indication of when the firm will make further contact with the complainant. The rule goes on to state that the further contact must be within eight weeks of original receipt of the complaint.

4.36 The next time requirement arises no later than eight weeks following receipt of the complaint. These requirements also apply where the complainant receives final responses. The requirements are:

- If the complaint remains outstanding at this point, the firm must provide the complainant with written reasons for the further delay, indicating when the firm will provide a written response.
- The complainant must be informed that it may refer the complaint to the Financial Ombudsman Service if it remains dissatisfied.
- The complainant must be informed that, if they wish to do so, they must complain to the Financial Ombudsman Service within six months.
- The complainant should be sent an explanatory leaflet regarding the Financial Ombudsman Service.

4.37 In addition, further restrictions for time limits within which complainants may refer their complaints to the Financial Ombudsman Service are retained within the rules (see para **4.38** below).

Offers of redress

4.38 Rule 1.2.17 makes it clear that a firm must, where it considers that redress is appropriate, provide a complainant with fair compensation. There is no specific guidance in the rules as to what constitutes redress. The guidance in rule 1.2.19 states that, where redress is appropriate, a firm should aim to provide fair compensation for any acts or admissions for which it was responsible and the redress may include a reasonable rate of interest based on UK current rates.

4.39 Logic dictates that at this stage, as the courts are not involved, it is open for a firm, subject to compliance with other areas of the rules, to offer redress in such manner as it considers appropriate. Remedies that may be acceptable to complainants may or may not be those which would be enforceable in the courts. This could include, for example, methods such as reinvesting customer's monies, the repurchasing of investments on dates or at rates that are favourable to the customer, offering ex gratia payments, gifts or tokens as a method of compensating a customer for inconvenience. Indeed it is clear from the rules (see rule 3.9.1) that the Ombudsman Service can, if it finds in the complainant's favour, direct the firm to take such step in relation to the complaint as considered appropriate, whether or not a court could order those steps to be taken.

4.40 The FSMA 2000, s 2.2.9(2)(b) reflects the above mentioned approach and states that, in determining the complaint, the ombudsman may make a direction that the respondent takes such steps in relation to the complainant as the ombudsman considers appropriate (whether or not a court could order those steps to be taken). Furthermore, s 2.2.9(9) provides that compliance with the direction under sub-s 2(b) is enforceable by injunction.

Enforcement

4.41 It is likely, however, that the majority of complex and serious complaints will require conventional monetary compensation. Such compensation should be calculated in accordance with general principles of damages. The FSMA 2000, s 2.2.9(8) states that a monetary award is enforceable by the complainant in accordance with Sch 17, Pt III. Schedule 17, para 16 provides in essence that a monetary award, including any interest may, if a county court orders in England and Wales, be recovered by execution issued from the county court as if it were payable under an order of that court.

Compliance officer and complaints management

4.42 Notwithstanding the regulatory requirements to comply with the FSA's complaint handling rules, it is important for a compliance officer and the firm to consider the practical aspects of handling complaints received from customers. All expressions of dissatisfaction received by the firm can be used by the firm to assess the level and acceptability of the service that the firm is providing to its customers. A complaint may not only be an important indicator of compliance and regulatory issues but is also an excellent mechanism by which the firm can measure the failures in its service standards. It would, therefore, seem essential for a firm to attempt to keep not only for the purpose of compliance with its regulatory compliance but, for general assessment of service levels, statistics of all complaints received categorising those into complaint types.

4.43 In addition to using complaints as a method of measuring success, it is important that all customer complaints and expressions of dissatisfaction are handled promptly. It is often the case with customers that prevention is better that cure, and, if at all possible, it is better for the purpose of customer relations if a potential complaint is defused before the matter becomes out of hand. Not only do the rules require that complaints be handled as promptly as possible, so does common sense. If a customer is of the opinion that they have a legitimate complaint, they are more likely to remain a loyal customer if they feel their complaint has been dealt with promptly, fairly and objectively than if they feel the matter has been subject to considerable delay and defensiveness.

4.44   In the event that a complaint arises that does require investigation, then some key principles may be used by the complaints investigator.

Scope of investigation

4.45   It is essential for the complaints investigator to understand exactly the nature of the complaint and what it is they are investigating. The length of time taken to investigate a complaint will be considerably extended if the investigator goes on a fishing expedition without any clear understanding, scope or limitation to their investigation.

4.46   It may be worthwhile at the stage of receiving a complaint, which is broadly drafted by the complainant by letter or expressed during a telephone call, to agree with the complainant the precise matters to be investigated.

4.47   To assist case management, the investigator may consider the benefit of specifying the scope of the investigation, and identifying areas of the firm's practice which are to be reviewed, the individuals they wish to speak to, the documents they are going to examine and the regulatory rules and practices they may wish to analyse. The investigator should record the scope of the investigation by keeping it on file and reviewing it periodically during the investigation to ensure that they remain focused and on track.

4.48   Many complaints investigations require a significant assessment of evidential matters. They may either be a case of an allegation of what one person has said in terms of describing or disclosing the features of an investment, or require some analysis of documentation supplied to an investor. The investigator should, as early as possible, identify those documents that are critical to the investigation and those persons he or she wishes to interview.

Interviews

4.49   As part of the investigation into the complaint it may be necessary to speak to members of staff that have been involved in the subject matter of the complaint. Complaints of a technical nature may merely require an analysis of documents. However, typically, complaints made against the manner in which an investment has been sold, require an investigation that goes beyond a document analysis. Whilst a copy of the firm's 'Know Your Customer' or 'Factfind' information may demonstrate what the firm knew about the customer and record why the investment may have been suitable, it will often be of great assistance to the investigation if the broker or salesperson can explain the thinking behind the advice.

4.50   Often, a complaint may allege matters which are not recorded anywhere on file. In these circumstances it is imperative that the brokers report on the matter to be obtained.

4.51   The investigator should consider whether the interview should be conducted face to face or by telephone. Indeed, with simple interviews it may be possible to send to the interviewee a set of questions and have the interviewee respond in writing.

4.52   The investigator will find it beneficial to consider the scope of their interview in advance, planning the questions that need to be raised and answered. In this way, the interview can be much more focused and concentrate on the fundamental issues.

4.53   Consideration should also be given to the recording of the answers during the interview. This will ensure that a contemporaneous note of the interview is taken which can be referred to later, and provide the interviewee with an opportunity to check and confirm that the interviewer's understanding of the answers is correct. Lastly, it may be appropriate with some complaints, to put the interviewee's answers to the complainant for comment.

Analysis of documents

4.54   As part of the scope of the investigation, the investigator should identify those documents that need to be gathered and analysed. Many organisations arrange their record keeping in different ways to other firms. Therefore, it should not be assumed that all documents relating to the subject matter of the complaint will be present on the customer's file. By way of example, the customer may make allegations regarding the manner in which a product is sold. Not only should the adviser be interviewed, but it may be appropriate to analyse the product's materials and brochures.

4.55   Almost as a matter of course for every investment-related complaint, the investigator should review the company's terms of business to establish whether the subject matter of the complaint is within the responsibility of the company. This should also include an analysis of any terms or conditions relating to the investment sold, key feature documents, illustrations and suitability letters for packaged products.

4.56 It should also become standard practice for the investigator to consider the firm's compliance obligations both contained within the FSA rules and also the firm's compliance manual. The investigator should seek to establish whether the firm has operated in a compliant manner in relation to the matter complained of. It should be remembered that under the FSMA 2000, s 150, a contravention of a rule by an authorised person is actionable by a private person who has suffered loss as a result of the contravention.

Obtaining expertise

4.57 In many cases, the person appointed to conduct the investigation will not be an expert in all matters material to the complaint. Provided the investigator appreciates this, it should in no way hinder the investigation. The investigator should be able to call upon impartial expertise to assist during the investigation. In this event, the investigator may wish to obtain a report or opinion from an expert. The expert may be found from within the organisation or, in very special cases, could be obtained from outside.

4.58 The investigator may also, during the investigation, consider it necessary to obtain external legal advice on aspects of the law affecting the subject matter of the complaint. It would be dangerous for the firm to assume that, simply because its practice is one which has been followed for a number of years, and has not been the subject of a previous complaint, that it is a practice which will be upheld by the courts.

Balancing the evidence obtained

4.59 Once the investigator has completed their enquiries and obtained all the necessary comments and documentation, it will be necessary to balance the evidence obtained. Where there is indisputable documented proof to support the company's point of view or, conversely, the complainant's point of view, then this task is a relatively simple one.

4.60 The process, however, becomes more complicated where the investigator is dealing with a situation of one person's word against another or where there is conflicting documentation.

4.61 The investigator should firstly consider some basic legal concepts:

• Who has the obligation to prove their case? In the majority of matters, the concept of 'he who asserts must prove' will operate. This means that the complainant must be able to prove their case if they are to be successful.

- Civil law matters – for a complainant to be successful, they must prove their case on a balance of probabilities. That is, is it more probable than not, that the alleged matters are accurate? This is a much lower standard of proof than the criminal one of 'beyond reasonable doubt'.

Complaints conclusion

4.62 Once the complaints investigation has been completed and a decision reached, it is sensible practice for the investigator to write up a report on the matter, justifying their decision. This will be a useful document to remain on file, as it will justify the thought processes behind the decision and evidence obtained. It will become a permanent record on a complaints file and can be used in the event of either regulatory scrutiny of the complaints investigation or if the matter is referred further on to the Financial Service Ombudsman.

Post-investigation matters

4.63 It is imperative that all individual actions to compensate or deal with individual complainants are dealt with. Any action taken within a firm either to adjust procedures or protect the firm's own position or deal with any rule breaches must not be conducted in a manner which prejudices the interest of the customer.

Complaint trends

4.64 An analysis of the firm's complaints experience provides a valuable opportunity for the firm to analyse regulatory risks it is facing when transacting business. It is vital, therefore, that the firm whether through its compliance or complaints departments maintains a central record of all complaints received and analyses these regularly to identify complaint trends. That central record can be as simple or as complex as the firm considers necessary. However, it should at the very least contain the following vital information:

- The date the complaint was received:

  This will allow the firm to identify whether any compliance problems are date specific and may result from a particular action of the firm occurring at around that date.

- The name of the complainant.
- The product or investment held by the complainant:

Once again, this will allow the firm to identify whether any particular compliance problem relates to specific investments or products that have been sold by the company.

- The person in the firm against whom the complaint is made:

  This will allow the firm to identify whether any particular compliance problems are being presented by an individual employee or broker or an appointed representative.

- A summary of the complaint allegations made:

  If the complaint analysis log is to be a useful tool, the firm should attempt to keep this summary as succinctly as possible. Once again, this will allow an analysis of various complaint types for the purpose of establishing whether a particular trend or pattern is emerging within the firm.

- Whether the complaint has been upheld in favour of the customer, defended, or whether the firm has decided to make an ex gratia offer to the customer without admitting liability.

4.65   The compliance department should determine the frequency at which complaints records are analysed. It may be that is appropriate to analyse them as frequently as once a day, particularly if the firm is a large organisation, where complaints numbers may be quite high. This will allow the firm to respond immediately to any patterns or trends that emerge. Smaller firms may determine that their complaints records can be analysed less frequently. No matter the frequency, the firm should always ensure that appropriate actions are taken. Those actions can relate to an individual employee concerned or company wide if complaints patterns suggest that a widespread failing is occurring. It should also be remembered that all records of complaints, whether they have been upheld in favour of the customer or not, can be a useful way to measure regulatory performance. Even a series of defended complaints relating to the same matter can identify a pattern of problems. For example, if a number of customers have complained about the manner in which a particular product has been described when it has been sold. Although the company may have determined, as a result of its complaints investigation, that it has no liability to the customer, the pattern of allegations may suggest that, in future, further care should be taken in a manner in which correct details are explained.

Complaints and staff education

4.66   The compliance department should also consider the method in which it communicates complaints trends to the organisation. It may be that details of complaints should be reported to the company's senior management or possibly directly to the training department. No matter what method the company considers to be the most appropriate, it can be a useful compliance tool if details of these communications and the manner in which the company agrees to act in relation to any compliance trends are recorded as evidence of the action the company has taken.

4.67 At a more serious level, if the trends identified in the complaints record reveal that there is a widespread failing in relation to the sale of a particular product or conduct of the company, the company should, determine that a thorough review of that entire sales process should be undertaken. This may result in individual customers being contacted for the purpose of identifying whether the company has created a liability for them. Although such a method of approach may be contentious and certainly should be managed very carefully within the firm, it does provide an early opportunity for the company to eliminate and manage any compliance breaches that have occurred early as opposed to allowing those breaches to go unattended. Thus, over time, reducing any potential liability that the company may have.

4.68 The manner in which such broader reviews may be undertaken and the obligation the company may have to report such matters to the regulator is explored in more detail in **Chapter 10**.

Notification to professional indemnity insurers

4.69 Many firms will maintain professional indemnity insurance which provides cover for liability caused by the company's acts or omissions. Where such indemnity insurance provides cover in relation to losses arising from investors' complaints, it is essential that the insurers are notified of the potential claim before any admission of liability by the firm. The firm should consider approaching a professional indemnity insurer in advance of any complaints investigations with the view to agreeing with the insurer the firm's internal complaints process and the manner in which complaints investigations and correspondence should be managed. Certainly, where a larger volume of complaints is experienced, such prior agreement with insurers will ensure that individual complaints investigations can be concluded expeditiously. Where the firm maintains a good relationship with its professional indemnity insurer it may be the case that that insurer will allow the firm to conclude the investigation and accept liability without prior reference to the insurer. This should, of course, always be checked in advance with the professional indemnity insurance company.

4.70 Where fewer volumes of complaints are experienced, it will certainly be the case that the professional indemnity insurer will require notice of the potential claim in advance and will want to agree the outcome before there is any offer made to the complainant. If this is the case, then this should be considered to be an element of the compliance process and should be built into the firm's written complaints procedures.

Conclusion

4.71   The firm's complaints procedures are an essential element of compliance procedure within the firm and provide a window for the compliance department to view any problems being created by the company in relation to the conduct of its business. The manner in which the firm manages its investigation of individual complaints will certainly reflect on its commitment to its customers and, if those complaints are handled properly in a large number of cases, the complaining clients will remain a client of the firm.

4.72   Regulators will expect to see firms taking their complaints investigation responsibilities seriously and will take action against firms that do not deal with complaints in an appropriate manner.

CHAPTER 5

Relevant provisions in the Financial Services and Markets Act 2000

The new regulatory structure

5.1   The main purpose of the regulatory restructuring which is a consequence of the Act is to create a single system of regulation with the FSA regulating virtually the entire financial services industry. This process had already started with the passing of the Bank of England Act 1998 which transferred the regulation of banks from the Bank of England to the FSA. The rest of the new regime consists of the FSA being responsible for the regulation of: investment business, banks, building societies, friendly societies, credit unions, insurance companies and the Lloyd's insurance market.

5.2   The other regulators will be abolished as the new Act comes into force with the exception of the Bank of England which continues to exist but with a more limited remit (see para **5.16** below). The regulators which are disappearing are the self-regulating organisations (PIA, IMRO and the SFA), the Bank of England (surveillance and supervision only), the Building Societies Commission, the Insurance Directorate of the Treasury, the Friendly Societies Commission and the Registry of Friendly Societies.

The Financial Services Authority

5.3   The Act provides the FSA with the power to regulate the categories of financial business and also the competent authority for official listing of securities which will entail, inter alia, specifying the requirements to be complied with for listing. The FSA is responsible for maintaining the official list and applications for listing have to be made to them. The Treasury maintain the capacity under s 95 to keep the FSA's performance under review. A detailed analysis of the listing rules is, however, beyond the scope of this book.

5.4   The purpose of the listing rules is to provide a regulatory framework for the issuing of new (primary) securities and the selling of existing (secondary) ones. The aim of the regulations is to keep a balance between the interests of those in industry who wish to raise capital and those of the public at large who may wish to subscribe. Securities will only be admitted to listing if the applicant is suitable and it is appropriate for the securities concerned to be publicly held and traded. They must be brought to the market in a way that is appropriate to their nature and number and which will facilitate an open and efficient market for trading in those securities. Issuers must make full and timely disclosures about themselves and the listed securities both at the time of issue and afterwards. The continuing obligations imposed on issuers are designed to promote investor confidence in standards of disclosure, in the conduct of listed companies' affairs and in the market as a whole. Holders of equity securities must be given adequate opportunity to consider in advance and vote upon major changes in the company's management and constitution.

5.5   The other ingredients of the FSA's powers are:

- controlling insurance business and banking transfers;
- overseeing the regulation of Lloyd's of London;
- combating market abuse;
- recognising and supervising investment exchange and clearing houses;
- overseeing the compensation scheme; and
- overseeing the ombudsman scheme.

5.6   The FSA is placed in a different position to its predecessor, the SIB, in that the FSA has the power to issue rules that will, as far as those affected by them are concerned, have force of law.

5.7   The Act also sets out the FSA's objectives. These are:

- the maintenance of confidence in the UK financial system[1];
- the promotion of public understanding of the financial system[2]. This objective involves the promotion of public awareness of the risks and benefits of investment and financial dealing and also making available the necessary information and advice for the public to be able to do this;
- to secure an appropriate degree of protection for consumers[3]. In considering what to provide in this context, the FSA must consider both the degree of risk and experience that consumers may possess, as well as their need for accurate information;
- the reduction of the extent to which it is possible for financial services business to be used to facilitate financial crime[4]. The FSA is required to make sure that regulated businesses are aware of the risk of their business being used in connection with the commission of financial crime and to make sure that the necessary steps are taken to monitor, detect and prevent financial crime. The main target in this area is money laundering (see **Chapter 6** below).

1   FSMA 2000, s 3.
2   FSMA 2000, s 4.
3   FSMA 2000, s 5.
4   FSMA 2000, s 6.

5.8   Although this appears to leave the FSA with an enormous degree of power they are scrutinised by Parliamentary Committee and the Treasury.

Regulation

5.9   All 'approved persons' must be accepted for registration by the FSA to enable themselves and their firms to carry on the specified activities in relation to investments. In the case of those firms and individuals currently regulated, the process will normally involve their existing regulation being transferred.

FSA Principles for Business

5.10   These are the initial part of the rules and, in many respects, the most important. The Principles overarch the various detailed regulations and a breach of either can potentially lead to disciplinary steps being taken by the FSA, though a breach of the Principles will not in themselves give rise to potential civil action by clients. This is in contrast to the FSA rules which can give rise to civil liability where the action is at the suit of a private person[1]. The Principles are widely worded and thus can represent an opportunity for the FSA to bring proceedings where the regulations do not themselves deal precisely with the issue that has arisen. In practice, however, the vast majority of disciplinary actions for breach of a Principle are likely to involve clear breaches of the other rules.

1   FSMA 2000, s 150(1).

The eleven FSA Principles

5.11   The eleven FSA Principles are as follows:

1. *Integrity.* A firm must conduct its business with integrity.
2. *Skill, care and diligence.* A firm must conduct its business with due skill, care and diligence.
3. *Management and control.* A firm must take reasonable care to organise and control its affairs responsibly and effectively, with adequate risk management systems.
4. *Financial prudence.* A firm must maintain adequate financial resources.
5. *Market conduct.* A firm must observe proper standards of market conduct.
6. *Customers' interests.* A firm must pay due regard to the interests of its customers and treat them fairly.
7. *Communications with customers.* A firm must pay due regard to the information needs of its customers and communicate information to them in a way which is clear, fair and not misleading.

8. *Conflicts of interest.* A firm must manage conflicts of interest fairly, both between itself and its customers and between one customer and another.

9. *Customers' relationships of trust.* A firm must take reasonable care to ensure the suitability of its advice and discretionary decisions for any customer who is entitled to rely upon its judgment.

10. *Customers' assets.* A firm must arrange adequate protection for customers' assets when it is responsible for them.

11. *Relations with regulators.* A firm must deal with its regulator in an open and co-operative way, and must inform the FSA promptly of anything relating to the firm of which the FSA would reasonably expect notice.

Approved persons

5.12 All significant individuals involved in a business that requires authorisation from the FSA must be 'authorised'. This means that the FSA must be convinced that the person concerned has suitable abilities, relevant qualifications and/or experience and an appropriate level of honesty and integrity. The people concerned fall into two main groups: those who carry on controlled functions themselves, such as by advising clients or arranging contracts and those who manage them, the other group are those who are in such senior positions that the FSA need to be satisfied that they are suitable. Examples are: the chief executive, directors, partners (if relevant), senior managers, compliance officers, money laundering reporting officer and finance officer.

5.13 Despite this the regulated firm remains primarily responsible for compliance with the regulations. There is however a Code of Practice affecting approved persons that sets out the conduct expected of them. Its main purpose is to make sure that those people realise the legal obligations being imposed on them in the area of risk based compliance.

5.14 In addition to the firms being subject to general Principles in addition to the rules, the approved persons are also subject to a series of ongoing requirements in the form of general principles. Principles 5–7 only apply to those in positions of significant influence whereas the first four apply to all approved persons.

Statements of principle for approved persons

5.15 The Principles themselves are:

1. An Approved Person must act with integrity in carrying out his controlled function.

2. An Approved Person must act with due skill, care and diligence in carrying out his controlled function.
3. An Approved Person must observe proper standards of market conduct in carrying out his controlled function.
4. An Approved Person must deal with the FSA and with other regulators in an open and co-operative way and must disclose appropriately any information of which the FSA would reasonably expect notice.
5. An Approved Person performing a significant influence function must take reasonable steps to ensure that the business of the firm for which he is responsible in his controlled function is organised so that it can be controlled effectively.
6. An Approved Person performing a significant influence function must exercise due skill, care and diligence in managing the business of the firm for which he is responsible in his controlled function.
7. An Approved Person performing a significant influence function must take reasonable steps to ensure that the business of the firm for which he is responsible in his controlled function complies with the regulatory requirements imposed on that business.

Relevant bodies other than the FSA

The Bank of England

5.16   Since the Bank of England Act 1998 the Bank's main role has been that of central bank to the UK whose functions are:

- setting interest rates for sterling;
- advising the government on economic and monetary policy and implementing agreed monetary policy decisions, mainly through the bank's operations in the markets;
- promoting an efficient and competitive framework for financial activity in the UK, particularly through its involvement in payments and settlements systems;
- responsibility for note issue;
- acting as banker to the commercial banks and to the government;
- acting at its discretion to provide assistance to the money market when it is short of funds, both directly and through the discount houses;
- advising on and managing the government's short and long-term borrowings, for which it acts as registrar; and
- managing, on behalf of the Treasury, the nation's gold and foreign currency reserves.

5.17   The Bank's involvement in payment and settlement systems includes membership of APACS (the Association of Payment Clearing Services), active participation in the development of new real-time payment procedures, as well as the provision of the Central Gilts Office and the Central Moneymarkets Office services which provide on-line settlement facilities for gilts and money market instruments.

The London Stock Exchange

5.18 Since the FSMA 2000 made the FSA the official listing authority, the Exchange's primary role is now in relation to trading equities already in existence. The Board is the governing body of the Exchange and has power to manage the property and affairs of the Stock Exchange. Most importantly, it governs strategic policy direction and is currently discussing the possibility of a merger with LIFFE. It also has the power to determine the use of the Exchange's facilities and to manage property belonging to the Exchange, including its acquisition, disposal and letting, borrowing money and the investment of surplus funds. Applicants for membership must have obtained appropriate authorisation to carry on investment business from the FSA, unless they are exempt or in some way excluded from the requirement. Special requirements apply to EU and certain other overseas businesses. Branch membership of the Exchange is permitted and is available to any office that is not the main office of the relevant business, where either the company operating the branch, or another company in its group, is a member of another appropriate investment exchange.

5.19 Settlement of transactions in gilt-edged securities is effected either on the basis of payment against documents of title and transfers or through the Central Gilts Office (CGO Service). This operates on a cash against delivery basis and incorporates a system of assured payments, by which each member procures that a settlement bank acting on its behalf undertakes to pay, at the end of each business day, the amounts due in respect of securities transferred to that member through the CGO Service on that day.

5.20 London traded options are settled through a clearing house or houses provided by the Council. The current clearing houses are the London Options Clearing House (LOCH), (a wholly-owned subsidiary of the Stock Exchange), which clears all options except currency options and the International Commodities Clearing House (ICCH) which clears currency options.

Lloyd's

5.21 Lloyd's is a society, incorporated by statute, which provides the facilities for the Lloyd's market to carry on business. In so doing it is overseen by the FSA for regulatory purposes. The members are syndicates managed by a managing agent. The members of the syndicates who are provided with financial backing by names who are fully liable for their share of the accepted risk in the case of individuals and to the extent of their accepted risk in the case of limited company names. The insurance business itself falls into four main categories: marine, aviation, non-marine and motor.

5.22 The members do not deal directly with the public. Those requiring insurance will approach a Lloyd's broker. They place business both with Lloyd's syndicates and insurance companies. If it is placed at Lloyd's, the broker will first approach a lead underwriter and then follow up by approaching other underwriters to take a share.

5.23 Lloyd's is now a part of the FSA regulatory regime. Lloyd's syndicate capacity and syndicate membership are specified investments and advising a person to become or cease to be a member of a Lloyd's syndicate, managing the underwriting capacity of a Lloyd's syndicate as a managing agent or arranging deals in contracts of insurance written at Lloyd's, are specified activities. The Council of Lloyd's retains the capacity to make rules regulating the market and has responsibility for the functioning of it.

5.24 In addition, it requires[1] the FSA to keep itself informed about the way in which Lloyd's Council supervises and regulates Lloyd's market and the way in which regulated activities are being carried out there. The FSA's concern will be twofold: protecting policy holders and protecting the members who underwrite the policies. The Society of Lloyd's has been made an authorised person[2] and, consequently, has authority to carry out its basic market activity, namely arranging deals in contracts of insurance on the Lloyd's market. The relationship between the parties can be varied[3] where the FSA believes that the Society is failing to satisfy its threshold conditions, has failed to carry on a regulated activity for at least one year, or where the FSA believe it is necessary in the interests of consumers. The FSA can also apply the FSMA 2000 to a member of Lloyd's or its Society[4] by applying a general prohibition or a core provision[5] to the carrying on of an insurance market activity or give a direction to the Council or Society of Lloyd's[6].

1　FSMA 2000, s 314.
2　FSMA 2000, s 315.
3　FSMA 2000, s 45.
4　FSMA 2000, s 316(1).
5　FSMA 2000, s 317.
6　FSMA 2000, s 318.

5.25 In addition to the FSA Principles and the Principles for Approved Persons, there are also a set of Lloyd's Core Principles for underwriting agents. These can be obtained from the FSA website[1].

1　http://www.fsa.gov.uk

The derivatives exchanges

5.26 There are three main derivatives exchanges in London: LIFFE, the London Metals Exchange and the International Petroleum Exchange.

5.27 LIFFE provides exchange facilities to deal in a range of financial futures contracts and options on futures. Both types of contract are traded in relation to a range of currencies, the FTSE 100 index and the FTSE 250 index. Futures contracts alone are traded in relation to Japanese government bonds and stop futures in short equities are available in a range of Spanish, Italian, German and UK contracts. Options alone are traded in: FTSE 100 American style, European style and FLEX together with a range of equities. LIFFE also trades commodity products, both as futures and options covering cocoa, robusta coffee, potatoes, wheat, barley and white sugar.

5.28 The London Metal Exchange provides a market for futures and options contracts for aluminium (both alloy and prime grade), copper, lead, nickel, silver, tin and zinc. It administers its own functions and formulates the regulations governing trading, investigates complaints, settles disputes and provides conciliation and arbitration facilities for disputes in respect of transactions relating to the Exchange.

5.29 The International Petroleum Exchange administers the International Petroleum Exchange in London. The contracts traded are: Gas Oil Futures, Gas Oil Traded Options, Brent Crude Oil Futures, Brent Crude Oil Traded Options, Natural Gas Futures and Electricity Backload Futures.

London Clearing House

5.30 This primarily exists to provide independent central clearing services to London-based futures, options and securities markets. It does so for all three of the above exchanges. It also provides clearing for a range of OTC derivatives[1]. In so doing it carries on the business of a commercial clearing house to regulate and assist the smooth running of the contracts traded. It also affords facilities to secure the performance of these contracts and to ensure the performance of registered contracts following default by a member.

1   US$, euros, yen and sterling.

5.31 A key element of this clearing process is that it guarantees the performance of the contracts concerned. The contractual process involves a two-stage contract of novation: the first of which involves the seller transferring ownership to the Clearing House and the second involving the Clearing House in transferring title to the buyer. The process involves the Clearing House guaranteeing the contract by taking cover and other security from members and taking margin payments by way of security from parties to contracts being registered. The guarantees are also supported by the Clearing Houses' own capital reserves.

EEA authorities

5.32 Businesses established in another EEA Member State and who have their head office there, who are recognised by that state as one of their nationals and who do not carry on investment business from a permanent place of business in the UK are treated as authorised to the extent that the investment laws of that state afford protection to investors equivalent to that afforded in this country. Whether such a state of affairs exists will normally be determined by the Chancellor issuing a certificate to that effect. Passport rights are governed by FSMA 2000, Sch 3 and, in this context, 'EEA firm' means one of the following, where it does not have its head office in the UK[1]:

- an investment firm[2] authorised by its home state regulator[3];
- a credit institution[4] authorised[5] by its home state regulator;
- a financial institution[6] which is a subsidiary[7]; and
- an undertaking pursuing the activity of direct insurance[8] which is authorised[9] by its home state regulator.

1   FSMA 2000, Sch 3, para 5.
2   As defined by the Investment Services Directive, art 1.2.
3   The Investment Services Directive, art 3.
4   As defined in the First Banking Co-ordination Directive, art 1.
5   See also the First Banking Co-ordination Directive, art 1.
6   The Second Banking Co-ordination Directive, art 1.
7   A 'subsidiary' of the type mentioned in the Second Banking Co-ordination Directive, art 18.2 which fulfils the conditions in art 18.
8   Within the meaning of the First Life Insurance Directive, art 1 or of the First Non-Life Insurance Directive.
9   Under the First Life Insurance Directive, art 6.

Wholesale market activities

The Inter-Professionals Code and the London Code of Conduct

5.33 From 2002/3 the London Code of Conduct will be replaced by the Code on Inter-Professional Conduct (IPC) which is already available in the form of a consultation paper1. In due course, it will form a chapter of the Market Conduct Sourcebook within the FSA Handbook of Rules and Guidance. It is primarily aimed at market professionals with a view to promoting market confidence and standards of market conduct in an environment that will remain primarily self-disciplining. In addition, it sets out the transitional arrangements for the Training and Competence regime for 's 43 brokers'. These are brokers and listed money market institutions who, together with their employers, were exempt from the financial services regime provided the firm was on a list issued by the regulator. As this was authorised by the Financial Services Act 1986, s 43 it became known as the s 43 list.

1   FSA Consultation Paper 83.

5.34   The two main categories of institution operating in the money markets are brokers and market makers. Brokers are those who act to bring together the independent counterparties to a transaction. Market makers, as their name implies, hold themselves out as being willing to make prices in the instruments concerned on a continual basis. There is, however, no legal commitment on market makers in the wholesale markets to make prices regardless of conditions in the market. Most of these need to be authorised by the FSA as they take deposits. However, not all of them are banks.

5.35   The IPC will also govern wholesale counterparties, who are those who have entered into a transaction above the minimum limits within the last 18 months, with, or as a result of, arrangements by a firm on the FSA list. Such a transaction must be on one of the instruments listed in paragraphs 6–13 of the London Code of Conduct. A wholesale counterparty cannot be a listed institution.

5.36   Most of the instruments traded on the wholesale markets are short term and all such instruments are covered by the IPC. However, the FSA are not responsible for supervising transactions in instruments traded by a recognised investment exchange. The rules of the exchange and the Principles, subject to those rules apply. In addition, the FSA could become involved primarily in the field of market abuse.

5.37   There are other transactions which are exempt on the grounds that the parties need no protection. These are transactions of over £100,000 for debentures, loan stock and sale and repurchase agreements, and of over £500,000 in the case of forward rate agreements, options, futures and contracts for differences are exempt from the London Code of Conduct. This is expected to remain the case.

5.38   Smaller transactions are also exempt where:

- both parties are wholesale counterparties; or
- both are on the s 43 list; or
- one is a listed institution and the other is a wholesale counterparty.

5.39   For a sale and repurchase agreement to be exempt, both counterparties must be listed institutions and acting as principal.

5.40   Turning to a comparison of the new IPC with the old London Code of Conduct, a number of points become apparent. The main one is that the IPC guidance is less prescriptive and less detailed. For example, the guidance on quotes and on brokers visiting each other's dealing rooms and sharing confidential and/or market sensitive information. However, the essential behavioural requirements remain essentially the same. A key factor here will be FSA Principles 1 and 5 which, together with a degree of guidance in the IPC, will control the giving of gifts. The new approach no longer involves specific guidance on dealing mandates and prompt payment of brokerage. There is also a less detailed approach to confirmations and how often they should be checked. There is a slight change in the approach to taping. Currently, relevant data must be taped and retained for two months. Under the IPC it should be done where necessary to provide a record and then kept as such. This may involve tapes being kept for up to three years. Market practice is reflected in a level playing field being applied between OTC and on exchange transactions. Activities on exchanges are, however, stated to be governed by the FSA Principles, subject to the exchange rules. The FSA have indicated that isolated departures from the IPC will not normally cause FSA action, though that would, of course, be determined by what exactly the departure consisted of.

Investment business in the UK

Specified investments

5.41   The Financial Services and Markets Act 2000 (Regulated Activities) Order 2001[1] provides full definitions of specified investments and activities. It should, however, be borne in mind that the distinctions that currently exist between the FSMA 2000 regime and the Investment Services Directive still survive[2]. Thus, a firm that is qualified under the Directive must be congniscent of the Directive as well, in particular with regard to any exclusions that might apply[3].

1   SI 2001/544, Pts II and III.
2   Financial Services and Markets Bill, Regulated Activities – consultation document, February 1999, part three, p 1, HM Treasury.
3   FSMA 2000, Sch 3.

5.42   As far as the Order is concerned, the investments that are specified are as follows.

Deposits

5.43   The investment itself is effectively left undefined but there is a definition of 'accepting deposits' at para **5.71** below.

Contracts of insurance

5.44 These are defined in Sch 1 to the Instrument. The definition covers the following categories of insurance policy: accident, sickness, land vehicles, railway rolling stock, aircraft, ships, goods in transit, fire and natural forces, damage to property, motor vehicle liability, aircraft liability, liability of ships, general liability, credit, suretyship, miscellaneous financial loss, legal expenses, travel assistance, life and annuity, marriage and birth, linked long term, permanent health, tontines, capital redemption contracts, pension fund management, collective insurance contracts and social insurance.

Shares

5.45 This is widely defined as 'shares or stock in the share capital of:

(a) any body corporate (wherever incorporated), and
(b) any unincorporated body constituted under the law of a country or territory outside the United Kingdom[1].'

1 Para 76.

5.46 It also includes deferred shares within the meaning of the Building Societies Act 1986, s 119 and any transferable shares in a body incorporated under the UK law relating to industrial and provident societies or credit unions, or under equivalent laws in other EEA states.

5.47 Shares were defined by Farwell J as being 'the interest of a shareholder in the company measured by a sum of money, for the purpose of liability in the first place, and of interest in the second, but also consisting of a series of mutual covenants entered into by all the shareholders *inter se*[1].' The definition appears to extend to stock[2].

1 *Borland's Trustee v Steel Bros & Co Ltd* [1901] 1 Ch 279 at 288.
2 Companies Act 1985, s 744.

5.48 The Instrument's definition excludes shares in open-ended investment companies, building societies, industrial and provident societies, credit unions or an equivalent entity in another EEA jurisdiction.

Instruments creating or acknowledging indebtedness

5.49 The definition of debentures is a wide one as was that in the Building Societies Act 1986, Sch 1 and, in addition to normal debentures, loan stock and bonds, it includes certificates of deposit and any other instrument creating or acknowledging indebtedness.

5.50 It is generally accepted that 'debenture' has never been properly defined[1]. The most widely accepted definition is that of Chitty J[2], who described a debenture as being ' a document which either creates a debt or acknowledges it'. This is the wording adopted by the Instrument and, as a result of it being so wide, certain other financial instruments are excluded, namely:

- an instrument acknowledging indebtedness for money borrowed to provide the cost of goods or services;
- cheques, bills of exchange, bank drafts and letters of credit, but not a bill of exchange accepted by a banker;
- bank notes and bank statements, a lease or other disposition of property or a heritable security; and
- contracts of insurance.

1 See, for example, Dine *Company Law*, 2nd edn, p 262 and Simon Morris *Financial Services: Regulating Investment Business* 1st edn, p 128, Sweet & Maxwell.
2 *Levy v Abercorris Slate and Slab Co* (1887) 37 Ch D 260.

Government and public securities

5.51 This covers loan stock, bonds and other instruments issued by central, regional and local government in the EEA. Excluded are those instruments excluded under 'debentures' at para **5.50** above and instruments issued by the National Savings Bank and under the National Loans Act 1968 and the National Debt Act 1972, s 11(3).

Warrants

5.52 The definition applies regardless of whether the instrument relates to something that is or is not already in existence. They have been defined as[1] 'transferable option certificates issued by companies and trusts which entitle the holder to buy a specific number of shares in that company at a specific price... at a specific time in the future'. As is made clear in the definition, this state of affairs applies regardless of whether the shares are already in existence.

1 McHattie *The Investor's Guide to Warrants* (Pitman Publishing) 1st edn, 1992.

Certificates representing securities

5.53 Certificates providing contractual rights in respect of shares, instruments creating or acknowledging indebtedness, government and public securities and warrants where the interest is held by someone other than the person on whom the rights are conferred and where the transfer can be carried out without the consent of that person. This paragraph effectively debars the creation of investments which amount to an indirect interest so as to facilitate carrying on business in such investments outside the jurisdiction of the FSA regime.

5.54 Excluded are instruments conferring rights in respect of two or more investments issued by different persons, or in respect of two or more types of government or public security issued by the same person. The first of these exclusions covers legal and equitable mortgages because such an arrangement involves a transfer of property interest from the party granting the mortgage to that receiving it[1].

1   A charge on the other hand only amounts to a proprietary interest.

Units in collective investment schemes

5.55   Such schemes are defined in FSMA 2000, s 235 as:

'(1)...any arrangements with respect to property of any description, including money, the purpose or effect of which is to enable persons taking part...(whether by becoming owners of the property or any part of it or otherwise) to participate in or receive profits or income arising from the acquisition, holding, management or disposal of the property or sums paid out of such profits or income.

(2)   The arrangements must be such that the persons who are to participate ...do not have day-to-day control over the management of the property, whether they have the right to be consulted or give directions.

(3)   The arrangements must also have either or both of the following characteristics:

    (a) the contributions of the participants and the profits or income out of which payments are to be made to them are pooled;

    (b) the property is managed as a whole by or on behalf of the operator of the scheme.'

5.56   If the property is held on trust for the participants the fund will be known as a unit trust[1]. An open-ended investment company on the other hand is a collective investment scheme where the property concerned belongs beneficially to and is managed by or on behalf of a body corporate[2]. The aim of such a scheme must be to spread investment risk and give the members the benefit. The investment must, however, appear to a reasonable investor to be one from which he can realise the investment within a reasonable period and be satisfied that the value of that investment would be calculated by reference to the value of property into which the scheme has invested.

1   FSMA 2000, s 237.
2   FSMA 2000, s 236.

Rights under stakeholder pension schemes

5.57   These are defined by the Welfare Reform and Pensions Act 1999, s 1 which, in essence, states that such a scheme is one which is registered with OPRA and meets a series of conditions which are set out in s 1(2)–(9) and any others that may be added by statutory instrument.

Options

5.58   The definition covers options to buy or sell:

- a security or contractually based investment;
- UK or foreign currency; or
- palladium, platinum, gold or silver.

5.59   There are two main categories: put options, which involve the party paying a deposit acquiring the right to sell one of the above commodities whilst the counterparty takes on the obligation to buy, and call options which operate in reverse. The party paying a deposit acquires a right to buy whilst the counterparty must sell. In each instance the party who has the right to perform can also decide to walk away from the contract and the only cost to them will be the loss of the deposit. Their counterparty has no such right.

Futures

5.60   This covers rights under a contract to sell a commodity or property where the price is agreed now but delivery is in the future where such an agreement is made for an investment rather than a commercial purpose. A contract will be regarded as being for investment purposes if it is traded on a recognised investment exchange or where it is not but is expressed to be traded as such. A contract will be regarded as being for commercial purposes if delivery is to be made within seven days or where one of the parties is a producer of the commodity or property or uses it in their business, or where delivery is intended.

5.61   The contract must be for sale, hire, loan or bailment. In practice, it is usually a contract for sale. The definition has been widened, for example to cover a weakness in the previous definition that did not clearly cover futures contracts in indexes[1].

1   Compare the Financial Services and Markets Act 2000 (Regulated Activities) Order 2001, art 84(3) and (7) with the Financial Services Act 1986, Sch 1, para 8.

Contracts for differences

5.62   This covers agreements the aim of which is to secure a profit or avoid a loss by either or both of the parties by reference to fluctuations in the value of property or an index or other factor. There are two types of contract which would potentially appear to be caught by this wording: swaps and forward rate agreements.

5.63   Swap contracts exist in a number of forms, but essentially, they all consist of a contractual arrangement whereby two counterparties will agree to notionally swap similar or dissimilar assets or debts. The original type – currency swaps – evolved as a method of circumventing exchange control restrictions prior to their suspension in 1979[1]. Rather than use traditional methods, such as parallel and back-to-back loans, the parties would enter into a spot exchange transaction to sell one currency and use a forward exchange contract to reverse the original contract. As loans were not being made as such it did not constitute borrowing and the transaction could be omitted from the balance sheet. Any necessary payments between the parties were then made on a net basis, commonly every six months. The net major development was the emergence of the interest rate swap, where one party who had a greater quantity of fixed rate debt that they wished to retain arranged with a counterparty who had a surplus of floating rate debt, to 'swap' the respective debts. The arrangement did not consist of a transference of the legal title to the debts but the periodic payment of net amounts needed to place the parties in the financial position they would have been in had the legal transfer of the debt taken place. Recent years have seen the emergence of a wide range of swap contracts, the most important of which are credit swaps where one party exchanges an income stream against another's equity holdings. This can facilitate a transfer of risk that better suits the respective parties' financial needs.

1   Haynes and Penn *The Law and Practice of International Banking*, 2nd edn, Sweet & Maxwell, 2002, chapter 9.

5.64   Excluded by the Instrument are contracts under which delivery is going to take place to one of the parties, and contracts in relation to money deposits where interest or another return will be paid by reference to fluctuations in an index or other factor. Also excluded are contracts in relation to deposits at the National Savings Bank or money raised under the National Loans Act 1968 or under the National Debt Act 1972, s 11(3).

Lloyd's syndicate capacity and syndicate membership

5.65   Lloyd's is an insurance underwriting market. Those who underwrite risks are the underwriters who work in syndicates to spread the risk between them. They do not carry all this risk themselves but spread it to 'names' in return for passing them a share of the premium. These names fall into two categories. The traditional names who are wealthy individuals who risk all their assets in return for a premium income and the corporate names who take on limited liability in return for premium income on behalf of their shareholders. Syndicate capacity and membership are specified investments.

5.66   Largely as a consequence of the problems that beset Lloyd's in the 1990s the Council of Lloyd's that traditionally ran the market is now subject to oversight by the FSA. The FSMA 2000, s 314 requires the FSA to keep itself informed about the Council's running of Lloyd's and the manner in which regulated activities are being carried out with a view to exercising their own powers if necessary.

Funeral plan contracts

5.67   This issue is discussed below at para **5.92**.

Regulated mortgage contracts

5.68   This is arguably the most important addition to the range of investments covered by the financial services regulatory regime. It is for most people the largest or second largest financial investment they make. Although the banks and other main lending institutions had adopted a code of practice with regard to mortgage lending, the involvement of the FSA now means that tighter control can be taken of advice given to those taking out one of the various types of mortgage contract now available.

Rights or interests in investments

5.69   Essentially, this covers any right or interest in the above-mentioned investments. Excluded are interests under trusts of an occupational pension scheme and certain interests in contracts of insurance or under certain trusts. This is effectively a safety net provision to catch instruments that would otherwise have been covered by one of the above but are technically outside it, for example because the beneficiary of the investment has a legal or equitable charge or mortgage over the property or a beneficial interest in a trust rather than a direct involvement with the investment.

Specified activities

5.70   The Financial Services and Markets Act 2000 (Regulated Activities) Order 2001 also defines the activities that are regulated in the new regime where they relate to specified investments. These activities are listed as follows.

Accepting deposits

5.71   This covers the receipt of deposits that will be repaid, either with or without interest, and either on demand or at another time agreed by the parties. It does not cover payments referable to the provision of property other than currency, or services or giving security. There are a range of exclusions, namely sums paid by:

- central banks in Europe;
- an authorised person who has permission to accept deposits;
- EEA authorised firms;
- the National Savings Bank;
- a municipal bank;
- Keesler Federal Credit Union;
- a certified school bank;

- local authorities;
- a body which is enacted to issue a precept to local authorities in England and Wales or by requisition in Scotland;
- the European Community, European Atomic Energy Community or European Coal and Steel Community;
- the European Investment Bank;
- the International Bank for Reconstruction and Development;
- the International Finance Corporation;
- the International Monetary Fund;
- the African Development Bank;
- the Asian Development Bank;
- the Caribbean Development Bank;
- the inter-American Development Bank;
- the European Bank for Reconstruction and Development; and
- the Council of Europe Resettlement Fund

5.72 Also, sums paid by any other party in the course of wholly or significantly carrying on the business of money lending; sums paid by one company to another where they are both members of the same group or when the same individual is a majority shareholder in both of them; or the making of a payment by a person who is a close relative of the person receiving it or who is a close relative of a director or manager of that person or a partner in it. Likewise, a sum received by a solicitor, or anyone dealing in investments, acting as agent in relation to investments, arranging deals in investments, managing investments, or establishing, operating or winding up a collective investment scheme or stakeholder pension scheme. Also excluded are sums received in consideration of the issue of debt securities.

Insurance

5.73 This covers both effecting and carrying out a contract of insurance. Excluded from this are where such contracts are effected or carried out by an EEA firm falling within the FSMA 2000, Sch 3, para 5(d) and motor vehicle breakdown insurance. Contracts of insurance are defined in Sch 1 to the Instrument in two main categories – general and long-term insurance. These are explained at para **5.44** above.

Dealing in investments as principal

5.74 This covers buying, selling, subscribing for or underwriting securities or contractually based investments (other than funeral plan contracts and rights to, or interests in, investments). Excluded are situations where the person concerned holds themselves out as willing to deal at prices determined by him generally and continuously or holds themselves out as engaging in the business of buying or underwriting investments of the type concerned. Also excluded are those who hold over 20% of the shares in a company and who seek to buy the shares of other shareholders or sell those shares to them, or someone acting on behalf of such a person. Finally, there is a general exception for those whose head office is outside the UK and whose ordinary business consists of dealing as principal or agent, arranging, managing, safeguarding and administering investments and advising on investments. Likewise those who are establishing, running or winding up a collective investment scheme or stakeholder pension scheme, and, where relevant, those agreeing to carry on any of these.

5.75   This category does not extend to those who:

- enter into contractually based transactions with or through an authorised or exempt person;
- accept instruments creating or acknowledging indebtedness;
- are companies issuing shares or share warrants;
- are contracting as principal in relation to options and contracts for differences where the counterparties are not individuals and the principal is contracting with a view to limiting an identifiable business risk other than one arising as a result of regulated activities (or matters that would be regulated activities but for the exclusions in Part III of the Instrument).
- trustees;
- contracts for the sale of goods and supply of services;
- groups and joint enterprises;
- sale of a body corporate; and
- overseas persons.

Dealing in investments as agent

5.76   This covers buying, selling, subscribing for or underwriting securities or contractually-based investments (other than funeral plan contracts and rights or interests in specified investments) as agent.

5.77   The exclusions are:

- dealing through authorised persons where the transaction is entered into or the advice given to the client by an authorised person or where it is clear that the client is not seeking and has not sought advice from the agent regarding the transaction. This exclusion does not apply if the agent receives payment from anyone other than the client, for which he does not account to the client;
- transactions relating to options, contracts for differences or rights or interests in either of those, between parties who are not individuals where the sole or main purpose is that of limiting the extent to which the business may be affected by an identifiable risk other than one arising as a result of carrying on a regulated activity;
- activities carried on in the course of a professional or non-investment business;
- activities carried on in connection with the sale of goods or supply of services;

- groups and joint enterprises;
- activities carried on in connection with the sale of a body corporate;
- activities carried on in connection with employee share schemes; and
- overseas persons.

Arranging deals in investments

5.78 This covers the making of arrangements for another person to buy, sell, subscribe for or underwrite investments which are either a security, a contractually-based investment, an interest in investments or syndicate capacity or membership of Lloyd's. It also extends to making such arrangements with a view to someone participating. It does not extend to merely introducing someone to another party unless it is done for a fee or on a recurrent basis. The wording is clearer here than in the previous legislation[1] in that it makes overt that the act of arranging must be a causative element in the transaction following[2].

1   Financial Services Act 1986, Sch 1, Pt II, para 2.
2   Financial Services and Markets Bill, Regulated Activities – a consultative document, February 1999, part three, p 2, HM Treasury.

5.79 The exclusions are:

- arrangements which would not bring about the transaction;
- merely providing the means of communication;
- where the person entering into the contract does so as principal or as agent for another;
- arranging deals through authorised persons where the client is acting on the advice of an authorised person, or where it is clear that the client is not seeking advice from the person acting (or if he has and it has been refused and the client advised to seek advice from an appropriate person);
- arranging transactions in connection with lending on the security of insurance policies;
- arranging the acceptance of debentures in connection with loans;
- providing finance to enable a person to buy, sell, subscribe for or underwrite investments;
- introducing persons to either an authorised person, an exempt person acting in the course of a regulated activity for which he is exempt, or someone who is lawfully dealing, dealing as agent, arranging, managing, safeguarding and administering investments, sending dematerialised securities, establishing, operating or winding up a collective investment scheme or stakeholder pensions scheme or advising. The introduction must be made with a view to the provision of independent advice;
- arrangements for the issue of shares, share warrants, debentures or debenture warrants by the company issuing them;
- international securities self-regulating organisations who have been approved as such by the Treasury;
- trustees;

- activities carried on in the course of a professional or non-investment business;
- activities carried on in connection with the sale of goods or supply of services;
- groups and joint enterprises;
- sale of a body corporate;
- employee share schemes; and
- overseas persons.

Managing investments

5.80 This is a specified activity if the assets concerned consist of or include an investment which is a security or a contractually-based investment. It is limited to discretionary management. If there is no discretion it would normally then be covered by 'arranging deals in investments' at para **5.78** above.

5.81 The exclusions are:

- where the assets are being managed under a power of attorney and all day-to-day decisions are taken by an authorised person acting within the scope of
- their authorisation;
- trustees;
- activities carried on in connection with the sale of goods or supply of services; and
- groups and joint enterprises.

Safeguarding and administering assets

5.82 This category applies regardless of whether the securities are held in a certified form.

5.83 The exclusions are:

- where responsibility has been accepted by a qualified third party;
- making introductions to a qualified custodian;
- providing information as to the units or value of assets held, converting currency or receiving documents relating to an investment solely for the purpose of onward transmission to, from, or at the direction of the person to whom it belongs;
- trustees;
- activities carried on in connection with professional or non-investment business;
- activities carried on in connection with the sale of goods or supply of services;
- groups and joint enterprises; and
- employee share schemes.

Sending dematerialised instructions

5.84   The exclusions here are:

- acting on behalf of a participating issuer within the meaning of the 1995 regulations;
- acting on behalf of settlement banks;
- instructions in connection with takeover offers;
- instructions in the course of providing a network;
- trustees; and
- groups and joint enterprises.

Establishing, operating or winding up a collective investment scheme

5.85   The definition of 'collective investments schemes' is considered at para **5.55** above.

Establishing, operating or winding up a stakeholder pension scheme

5.86   The definition of 'stakeholder pension schemes' is considered at para **5.57** above.

Advising on investments

5.87   This covers giving advice to an investor or prospective investor on the merits of buying, selling, subscribing for or underwriting an investment which is a security or a contractually- based investment or exercising any right conferred by such an investment. It applies whether the advice is given to someone in their own capacity or as agent or another. However, generic advice is not covered so, for example, it is possible to advise on the relative merits of direct and indirect investments or of investments of a particular nature.

5.88   The exclusions are:

- advice given in newspapers, journals or broadcast transmissions where that media is neither essentially giving advice or leading or enabling people to buy, sell, subscribe for or underwrite securities or contractually based investments;
- trustees;
- activities carried on in connection with professional or non-investment business;
- activities carried on in connection with the sale of goods or supply of services;
- sale of a body corporate; and
- overseas persons.

Lloyd's

5.89   This covers advising a person to become or to cease to be a member of a Lloyd's syndicate; managing the underwriting capacity of a Lloyd's syndicate as a managing agent or arranging deals in contracts of insurance written at Lloyd's. The background to this is discussed at para **5.65** above. The Society of Lloyd's itself is an authorised person[1] and has permission to carry on the following regulated activities[2]:

- arranging deals in insurance written at Lloyd's (basic market activity);
- arranging deals in participation in Lloyd's syndicates (secondary market activity); and
- activities carried on in connection with basic and primary market activities.

1   FSMA 2000, s 315(1).
2   FSMA 2000, s 315(2).

5.90   However, the FSA retains the legal capacity to involve itself by applying core provisions of the Act[1] to a member of Lloyd's or the Society of Lloyd's generally if it thinks so fit bearing in mind the interests of policyholders and potential policyholders[2]. The FSA can do this either by giving a direction to the Council of Lloyd's or to the Society acting through the Council[3].

1   These are FSMA 2000, Pts V, X, XI, XII, XIV, XV, XVI, XXII and XXIV, ss 384 to 386 and Pt XXVI.
2   FSMA 2000, s 316(1) and (3).
3   FSMA 2000, s 318(1).

5.91   Former underwriting members can carry out each contract of insurance that they have underwritten at Lloyd's whether or not they are authorised[1]. However, the FSA can impose on them such requirements as the FSA thinks fit to protect policyholders against the risk that the underwriter may not be able to meet their liabilities[2].

1   FSMA 2000, s 320(1).
2   FSMA 2000, s 320(3).

Funeral plan contracts

5.92   This covers contracts under which one person makes payments to another in return for the provision of a funeral on the first person's death provided it is not expected to occur within the first month.

5.93   The exclusion is that of plans covered by insurance or trust arrangements.

Regulated mortgage contracts

5.94   This covers entering into or administering a regulated mortgage contract. Such an arrangement arises where a lender provides the credit to an individual or trustee in return for an obligation to repay which is secured by a first legal mortgage on land in the UK, at least 40% of which is to be used as a dwelling by the borrower or, if it is the beneficiary of a trust the beneficiary, or a related person. In this context administering means notifying the borrower of changes in interest rates on payments due and taking any necessary steps to collect or recover payments from the borrower. Merely exercising the right to take action does not amount to administering.

5.95   Exclusions cover arranging administration by an authorised person or pursuant to an agreement with one.

Agreeing to carry on activities

5.96   Agreeing to carry on any other specified activity other than accepting deposits, effecting and carrying out contracts of insurance, or establishing, operating or winding up a collective investment scheme or stakeholder pension scheme.

Gaming

5.97   Traditionally, gaming contracts were unenforceable as being for an illegal consideration[1] and any monies loaned to another person with the intention that the borrower shall use those monies for gambling is also an unenforceable debt[2]. This gave rise to problems with the increased use of derivative contracts (ie futures, options and contracts for differences) which could, in some instances be viewed as having similar characteristics to gaming contracts. Indeed, this misconception is reflected in part in Lord Wilberforce's judgment in *Hazell v Hammersmith and Fulham London Borough Council*[3] where he stated:

> 'A swap contract based on a notional principal sum of £1 million under which the local authority promises to pay the bank £10,000 if LIBOR rises by 1% and the bank promises to pay the local authority £10,000 if LIBOR falls by 1% is more akin to gambling than insurance'.

1   Gaming Act 1845, s 18.
2   Gaming Act 1892, s 1.
3   [1991] 1 All ER 545 at page 559, para b.

5.98   Hopefully, the greater understanding of derivative instruments and their usage that now exists will debar this judicial approach in the future. In any event to stop contracts of such financial importance being rendered unenforceable the FSMA 2000 largely reproduces the provisions of the old Act[1] as s 412 which states that:

> '(1) No contract to which this section applies is void or unenforceable because of:
>
> (a) section 18 of the Gaming Act 1845, section 1 of the Gaming Act 1892 or Article 170 of the Betting, Gaming, Lotteries and

Amusements (Northern Ireland) Order 1985, SI 1985/1204 (NI 11); or

(b) any rule of the law of Scotland under which a contract by way of gaming or wagering is not legally enforceable.

(2) This section applies to a contract if:

(a) it is entered into by either or each party by way of business;
(b) the entering into or performance of it by either party constitutes an activity of a specified kind or one which falls within a specified class of activity; and
(c) it relates to an investment of a specified kind or one which falls within a specified class of investment.'

1   The Financial Services Act 1986, s 63.

5.99   The case law following the Financial Services Act 1986 would still seem applicable to the new section. In particular, *Morgan Grenfell & Co Ltd v Welwyn Hatfield District Council*[1] where the judge made clear that in this context 'business' would be very widely interpreted and cover any situation where one of the parties was entering into the arrangement for other than recreational purposes.

1   [1995] 1 All ER 1.

5.100   The definition of 'contracts for differences' (see para 5.62 above) is extremely wide and should thus continue the tradition already seen in *City Index Ltd v Leslie*[1] where it was held that a contract in relation to stock market index movements was not a gaming contract and could be enforced as it fell within the definition of 'contracts for differences' and the party seeking to enforce it was properly authorised to carry on the relevant category of investment business. Indeed the definition of 'contracts for differences' in Article 85 of the Instrument appears wide enough to cover most spread betting.

1   [1992] QB 98.

5.101   Perhaps the other issue is that of speculative forex trading which had been suggested as being at risk from the gaming laws[1]. This risk appears to remain as exemption under s 412 only exists where the activity involves a specified investment. This could give rise to problems as forex contracts do not fall within any of the 16 categories.

1   See SIB Guidance Release 1/96 at p 16.

CHAPTER 6

Special compliance obligations: money laundering

Introduction

6.1 Money Laundering has been defined as[1]:

'...the process by which criminals attempt to conceal the true origin and ownership of their criminal activities. If undertaken successfully, it also allows them to maintain control over those proceeds and, ultimately, to provide a legitimate cover for their source of income.'

1   Joint Money Laundering Steering Group: Guidance Notes for the Financial Sector, at 1.03.

6.2 Another, briefer definition was[1]:

' rendering the proceeds of crime unrecognisable as such.'

1   Simon Gleason 'The Involuntary Launderer' in *Laundering and Tracing*, Clarendon Press, Oxford, 1995.

6.3 The increased problems caused by organised crime in general and, in particular, the drugs trade has given rise to a succession of increases in the obligations imposed on those involved professionally with money to report transactions that appear to be suspicious to the relevant authority. More recently, the publicity given to the corruption of certain governments and the tendency of their rulers to both steal money intended as aid and take bribes in return for business contracts has added a new dimension to the laundering problem. Much of the drugs trade laundering commences with cash which has to be placed into the financial system. From here further laundering will need to take place. In the case of corrupt government officials, the money will already be in the financial system at the outset. Thus, not all laundering will be of the same nature.

6.4 However, the Joint Money Laundering Steering Committee Guidelines adopt a common mistake which provides false security in many of the larger laundering operations, in other words:

'Criminally earned money is invariably transient in nature.'

6.5 This will often be the case as the criminal concerned will be in need of the funds as soon as possible. However, the vast increases in wealth available to the larger organised crime groups in recent years, and possibly some of the smaller ones, means that it may be possible for them to tie up some of their funds for significant periods of time as part of the laundering process[1].

1   A Haynes 'Secondary securitisation and money laundering', *Journal of Money Laundering Control*, vol 1, no 2, p 148, 1997.

6.6 The range of methods that can be utilised to launder money are enormous and anyone needing to have a clear understanding of the subject should read widely and keep abreast of changes in laundering patterns. The commonest vehicles for laundering are those where large amounts of cash or liquid investments of assets are handled. In the financial markets banks and investment business firms are the most heavily used. In the commercial field businesses dealing in high value goods can prove attractive as they provide the opportunity for moving money around by dealing in expensive goods, often across international boundaries. Another development, and one that has become more heavily utilised as banks and other financial businesses have attempted to tighten their anti-money laundering operations, is to include a firm of solicitors, accountants or other professionals in what appears to be a bona fide scheme to invest or transact money[1]. This provides the attraction of feeding money through a professional's client account to mask the arrangement with a veneer of respectability. There have been recent suggestions by the National Criminal Intelligence Service that some of these firms have been assisting criminal clients by knowingly laundering money[2] though, at the time of writing, there have been no arrests. It seems unlikely that many professional firms would take such a risk. A particular problem in spotting laundering is that most of those with large amounts of money to launder can construct their operations intelligently enough to avoid it looking suspicious. In almost all instances of large movements of laundered money the criminals will be employing experts to advise and assist them.

1   Financial Action Task Force, 1996 update on the 40 recommendations.
2   Robert Mendick 'Police probe City firms links to organised crime', *The Lawyer*, 24 November 1998, p 1; Richard Tyler 'City accusations send sparks flying', *The Lawyer*, 1 December 1998, p 11 and 'Law Society laundering reaction will not wash', Comment and Analysis, *The Lawyer*, 1 December 1998, p 16.

6.7 The legislation and guidelines follow from the UN Convention on the subject[1] and thus focus primarily on laundering the proceeds of drug sales. A consequence of this is that they are not of great assistance in picking up terrorist monies. In the UK in particular a dissimilarity arises between the patterns of terrorist money and many of the other laundering schemes. There is also a dissimilarity in the legislation in that it is necessary to report the movement of monies which may be utilised to commit a criminal act by a proscribed organisation rather than money simply being moved after a crime. This issue is examined more closely at para **6.18** below.

1   UN Convention on Psychotropic Drugs and Narcotic Substances, 1988.

6.8 The imposition of money laundering obligations on financial institutions and certain professionals has created a situation where those parties must ascertain whether a particular transaction is 'suspicious' and, if so, potential reporting issues arise. This chapter will consider what circumstances should arouse suspicion, what reporting issues then arise and what to do in borderline situations.

The criminal offences – laundering drug proceeds and the profits of crime

Concealing or transferring the proceeds of drug trafficking

6.9   It is an offence for someone to transfer property, convert it or remove it from the jurisdiction to avoid criminal proceedings or to conceal or disguise it if there are reasonable grounds to suppose that it is the proceeds of another's drug trafficking or criminal offence. In this context 'criminal offence' includes a confiscation order[1].

1   Drug Trafficking Act 1994, s 49 and Criminal Justice Act 1988, s 93A.

Assisting another to retain the benefit

6.10   It is an offence to assist someone in retaining the proceeds of drug trafficking or other crime or to place the proceeds of crime so that the criminal can gain access to them. Likewise, it is a crime to assist someone in utilising the proceeds of crime to acquire property. The person facilitating the crime must know or suspect that the money is either the proceeds of drug trafficking or other crime[1]. Thus, the offences do not appear to extend to innocent involvement in commercial investment to protect or increase the value of the money concerned[2].

1   Drug Trafficking Act 1994, s 50 and Criminal Justice Act 1988, s 93C.
2   See comments to the Criminal Justice Act, s 51 in *Current Law Statutes*, Sweet & Maxwell, London, 1993.

Disclosure

6.11   Anyone making a disclosure to 'a constable' is protected[1]. In the case of suspected laundering of drug proceeds, the recipient of the disclosure would normally be the National Criminal Intelligence Service (NCIS). In the case of other general crime, the local fraud squad would be more appropriate. However, in the vast majority of cases the person spotting a suspicious transaction is unlikely to have any idea as to the nature of the original crime. Thus, a report to NCIS is generally the best option. The law also covers reports being made after the event as, in many instances, suspicion will only arise then. In such cases the party making the report is not committing a criminal offence by not having made a report earlier provided they did so as soon as was reasonable and on their own initiative[2].

1   Drug Trafficking Act 1994, s 50(3).
2   Drug Trafficking Act 1994, s 50(3)(b)(ii).

6.12   Such disclosures are not treated by the law as a breach of any statutory or common law duty of confidentiality or breach of contract or the laws of defamation. In other words, the party who makes the report need not fear civil proceedings as a consequence. In any event, it is extremely unlikely that the party to whom the disclosure referred would ever know that it had taken place.

Acquisition, possession or utilising the proceeds

6.13   It is a criminal offence to use or acquire property which the person concerned knows to represent the proceeds of drug trafficking, whether directly or indirectly[1]. If they have paid 'adequate consideration' for the property (ie consideration which is not 'significantly less than the value of the property') that person will have a defence. The accused would have to discharge the burden of proof in showing that adequate consideration had been paid were this defence to be pleaded.

1   Drug Trafficking Act 1994, s 51.

Failure to disclose suspicion

6.14   This is the one area where there is a significant difference between the law relating to drug money laundering and laundering the proceeds of crime. It is a criminal offence to fail to disclose to the police, in practice the NCIS, a suspicion that someone carrying on 'relevant financial business' (see para **6.21** below for a definition of this) is engaged in laundering the proceeds of drug sales[1]. The law only applies if the information came into that person's possession as a result of their trade, profession, business or employment. It does not extend to legal advisers obtaining such information in circumstances of professional privilege. The civil law protections mentioned above apply here as well.

1   Drug Trafficking Act 1994, s 52.

6.15   If the person concerned had a reasonable excuse for not disclosing the information, they have defence. Unfortunately, the Drug Trafficking Act 1994 does not explain what a reasonable excuse is and so far there have been no cases on the point.

Tipping off

6.16   It is a criminal offence to provide someone with information the nature of which is likely to obstruct a police investigation[1]. It is also an offence if, having disclosed information to the police or NCIS, further information is released which is likely to prejudice any investigation. Solicitors and barristers are excluded from this where they are giving legal advice in connection with legal proceedings.

1   Drug Trafficking Act 1994, s 53 and Criminal Justice Act 1988, s 93D.

Penalties

6.17   The offences relating to concealing, assisting or acquiring goods are punishable by a fine or up to six months' imprisonment on summary conviction or a fine or up to 14 years' imprisonment on indictment. The penalty for the offences of failing to disclose and tipping off is the same on summary conviction but falls to a fine or up to five years' imprisonment on indictment.

Terrorism

6.18   There are a separate set of laws that apply to terrorist money. These are determined by the Terrorism Act 2000 which, inter alia, creates a series of criminal offences relating to handling terrorist money. The most relevant criminal offences to those involved in the banking and financial services industries are as follows:

- to receive money or other property with the intention that it be used, or where there is reasonable cause to believe it will be used, for the purposes of terrorism[1];
- to become concerned in an arrangement which facilitates the retention or control of terrorist property by or on behalf of another, whether this be done by concealment, removal from the jurisdiction, transfer to nominees or in any other way[2];
- to fail to report to the police (in practice the NCIS) as soon as is reasonably practicable a suspicion that someone has committed a financial offence in relation to laundering where this information has come into their possession as part of their trade, profession, business or employment. They must also report the information on which their suspicion is based. There is a defence of having a 'reasonable excuse' for not making the disclosure[3]. Information obtained by a professional legal adviser is exempt if it is obtained in privileged circumstances[4]; or
- to disclose information to another which is likely to prejudice an investigation or interfere with material which is relevant to such an

investigation where there are reasonable grounds to suppose that the police are conducting, or proposing to conduct, a terrorist investigation.

1   Terrorism Act 2000, s 15(2).
2   Terrorism Act 2000, s 18.
3   Terrorism Act 2000, s 19(2).
4   Terrorism Act 2000, s 19(5).

6.19   Terrorist offences by their nature relate to terrorist organisations and the Terrorism Act 2000 provides a list of 14[1] who are all parties involved in the conflict in Northern Ireland. Since then a statutory instrument[2] has added a rather more cosmopolitan list of 21 additional organisations whose activities relate to overseas conflicts.

1   At Sch 2.
2   Terrorism Act (Proscribed Organisations) (Amendment) Order 2001, SI 2001/1261.

6.20   The penalties for non compliance are a fine or up to six months' imprisonment on summary conviction and a fine or up to 14 years' imprisonment on indictment[1].

1   Terrorism Act 2000, s 22.

Relevant parties

6.21   Not everyone is bound by the requirement to report suspicious transactions. Essentially those who are caught are those carrying on 'relevant financial business[1].' This covers[2]:

'(a) deposit taking business, carried on by a person who is for the time being authorised under the Banking Act 1987;

(b) acceptance by a building society of deposits made by any person (including the raising of money from members of the society by the issue of shares);

(c) business of the National Savings Bank;

(d) business carried on by a credit union within the meaning of the Credit Unions Act 1979 or the Credit Unions (Northern Ireland) Order 1985;

(e) any home regulated activity carried on by a European institution in respect of which the requirements of para 1 of Sch 2 to the Banking Co-ordination (Second Council Directive) Regulations 1992 have been complied with;

(f) specified investment activities within the meaning of the Financial Services and Markets Act 2000;

(g) any activity carried on for the purpose of raising money, authorised to be raised under the National Loans Act 1968, under the auspices of the Director of National Savings;

(h) any of the activities in points 1 to 12, or 14 of the Annex to the Second Banking Directive...; and

(i) insurance business carried on by a person who has received official authorisation under Article 6 or 27 of the First Life Directive.'

1   Money Laundering Regulations 1993, reg 4(1).
2   SI 1992/3218, annex to Sch 1.

6.22 Under reg 4(2), specifically excluded from being 'relevant financial business' are:

- the issue of withdrawable share capital within the limit set by the Industrial and Provident Societies Act 1986, s 6 if within the limits set by ss 6 and 7(3) respectively;
- the issue of withdrawable share capital within the limit set by the Industrial and Provident Societies Act (Northern Ireland) 1969, s 6 by a society registered under that Act;
- activities carried on by the Bank of England;
- the miscellaneous exceptions set out in the Financial Services and Markets Act 2000, of whom the bulk are the holders of certain judicial or other offices; and
- anyone who is the subject of a statutory instrument issued pursuant to the Financial Services Act 1986, s 46 made prior to 1 April 1994.

6.23 The Second Banking Directive, referred to at para **6.21** above, covers:

- acceptance of deposits and other repayable funds from the public;
- lending;
- financial leasing;
- money transmission services;
- issuing and administering means of payment (eg credit cards, travellers' cheques and bankers' drafts).
- guarantees and commitments;
- trading for own account or for account of customers in:
  (a) money market instruments (cheques, bills, CDs etc),
  (b) foreign exchange,
  (c) financial futures and options,
  (d) exchange and interest rate instruments,
  (e) transferable securities.
- participation in securities issues and the provision of services relating to such issues;
- advice to undertakings on capital structure, industrial strategy and related questions and advice and services relating to mergers and the purchase of undertakings;
- money broking;
- portfolio management and advice;

- safekeeping and administration of securities; and
- safe custody services.

6.24 A draft EU Directive will extend the application of the laws to professionals such as solicitors and accountants and others whose businesses render them particularly at risk as laundering vehicles, such as those owning casinos.

Checking identity

6.25 The Money Laundering Regulations 1993 require that the identity of a new client be checked in any of the following situations:

- where it has been decided that a business relationship should be formed with them;
- when the person dealing with the client has reason to suspect that a one-off transaction could be part of a money laundering operation;
- where a one-off transaction exceeds euro 15,000; and
- where there are a series of connected transactions exceeding euro 15,000 in total value.

6.26 It would be wise for most financial services firms to require that all new clients have their identity checked at the outset. Failure to do so could give rise to the risk of someone using the firm on an incremental basis and then getting round the identity checking requirement because staff do not remember to do so on breaching the euro 15,000 barrier. Generally speaking, the client's identity should be checked at the outset but the regulations do permit some variation in this, where the nature of the contact with the client may make this impossible, eg where they are in another country. In any event, it should always be done at the first reasonably possible time. If the person dealing with the financial institution appears to be acting for someone else, that person's identity must also be checked in the same way.

6.27 The regulations require that identity be checked by an approach that is 'reasonably capable of establishing that the applicant is the person he claims to be'. This means seeing original documents that prove that the person is who he claims to be and also that they live at the address they have provided. This will generally mean seeing more than one document. Documents that are useful to prove identity are:

- passport;
- driving licence;
- identity card (if from a country that has them); or
- references.

6.28   To prove that the person is resident where they claim to be it is useful to:

- see utility bills;
- check the electoral roll; or
- check the telephone directory.

6.29   Once both of these have been carried out and a photocopy of the document concerned has been placed on file the identity checking requirements have been met. However, it should be borne in mind that any criminal seeking to launder money will have no difficulty at all in satisfying the requirement that they produce such documents. They will either have fake or real documents in the name they are using. This is not a reason for being cavalier about checking identity, but it does mean that possession of 'proof' is not a reason to lower a firm's guard when it comes to suspicious activity by a client.

6.30   It is not necessary to check on identity where:

- there is clear evidence that another person, regulated by a financial services body in the EU has already done so;
- the applicant is someone who must themselves check clients' identity because they too are a regulated firm;
- it is a one-off transaction carried out via intermediaries who have themselves provided an assurance that their client's identity has been checked;
- the person who will receive the money will be re-investing it in another investment or transaction on their own behalf or for their benefit and proper records will be kept; and
- it is an insurance scheme with a single instalment that does not exceed euro 2,500 or with a periodic premium not exceeding euro 1,000.

What is 'suspicion'?

6.31   Unfortunately the statutes give no guidance on what 'suspicion' means. It probably relates to apprehension or mistrust considering the unusual nature or circumstances of the transaction or the person or group of persons with whom they are dealing. Whilst there is no case law in this country in the context of the legislation, there is case law on the nature of suspicion. In *Hussien v Chong Fook Kam*[1] Lord Devlin stated that:

'Suspicion in its ordinary meaning is a state of conjecture or surmise where proof is lacking.'

He added that:

'Suspicion can take into account matters that could not be put in evidence...Suspicion can take into account matters which, though admissible, could not form part of a prima facie case.'

1   [1970] AC 942.

6.32   The Money Laundering Guidance Notes[1] reinforce this[2]: 'Suspicion is personal and subjective and falls far short of proof based on firm evidence.' It goes on to say that 'a suspicious transaction will often be one which is inconsistent with a customer's known, legitimate business or personal activities or with the normal business for that type of account'.

1   Issued by the British Bankers Association.
2   At 6.01.

6.33   Given that the regulations require that those covered by them must 'know their customer' and are required to maintain an appropriate level of expertise, we are left with a situation in which the requirement begins to function in a manner much closer to an objective one than the subjective crime that the legislation provides. The Money Laundering Guidance Notes give assistance as to what can be regarded as suspicious. In part, however, there is also an element of common sense as to what looks unusual or abnormal.

6.34   Issues to consider would include:

- The speed with which cash is being transferred to another form of money and to another place. In particular is money, and, especially, cash paid into an account and then paid out at unusual speed?
- Does the routing of the funds involve a country with close contacts to drug production, processing or the laundering of proceeds?
- Is the arrangement one which does not make sense from a business point of view? In particular is it an arrangement that did not appear to be designed to make a profit. However, this is not always an element. Many criminal organisations now attempt to utilise the laundering process to make a profit, eg by utilising funds to buy goods which are then re-sold at a mark up.
- Does the arrangement involve offshore shell companies, trusts and tax haven banks when the purpose of their involvement does not fit in with normal business practice for the type of transaction taking place. Unfortunately, it often will as the criminals will have constructed their finances to optimise their tax position on an international basis after taking legal and financial advice. In reality, their transactions will tend to replicate legitimate ones.
- Does the transaction involve cash flows in and out of countries where the banking system is heavily permeated by organised crime, eg Russia? If it does careful note should be made of the exchange rates at which the currency concerned changes from one currency to another. If these appear to be other than market rates, the transaction should be regarded as particularly suspicious[1].

- Note should be taken of structures that seem to be designed to make it difficult for outsiders to ascertain exactly what is going on. An abnormally complex structure of companies should arouse suspicion.
- There may be aspects of the client that raise suspicion. This is only likely to occur with the less professional criminals. The rest will have little difficulty in maintaining a credible appearance.

1   Timor Sinuraya 'Integration of Criminal Capital from Russia into West European markets: An assessment of threat', *Journal of Money Laundering Control*, vol 1, no 1, p 32, 1997; V P Aksilenko 'Security Concerns', *Organized Crime Digest*, 27 September 1995, p 5; A Neshyadin 'Seraya ekonomika Rossii', *Izvestia*, 21 September 1994, p 9 and I Botovsky 'Koloss prestupnpsti podminaet gosudarstvo', *Pravda*, 1996, no 9, p 3.

Making a suspicious transaction report

6.35   Once a suspicious transaction report has been submitted, the NCIS (or, in the case of general money laundering, the local fraud squad) will then inform the person who has made the report whether it is acceptable to continue with the transaction. The NCIS normally prefer the transaction to continue to facilitate their observation of the transaction and to provide them with the opportunity to analyse the events concerned. It is necessary to obtain consent to act otherwise the party who made the report will almost certainly be committing a criminal offence, such as aiding and abetting or being an accessory after the fact. On the other hand, if the firm refused to continue to act for the client they could effectively be 'tipping off' because the client will then realise that the firm is suspicious and assume that a report has been filed (see also paras **6.57** and **6.58** below).

6.36   In cases where there are slight grounds for suspicion but the person concerned does not feel there is sufficient evidence to make a suspicious transaction report, it is a good idea to make a file note of the reasons for concern. It may be that as time goes by a succession of other minor issues may arise and eventually there may be sufficient grounds for making a report.

Civil law issues[1]

Introduction

6.37   It is not only the criminal law that poses a threat when an institution launders funds, there is also the potential threat of civil proceedings to recover the funds. For this to occur there must be a real owner of the money in pursuit of it. Two problems occur: the concept of real owner is widely defined and the area of law concerned seems to be going through a period of development, making it unclear.

1   For a detailed examination of this issue see Paula Reid 'The Civil Law and Money
     Laundering' in *The International Tracing of Assets*, Rides and Ashe, vol 1, Sweet & Maxwell,
     London, 1998.

6.38   The position is complicated by the doctrine of constructive trusts.
These occur where a court decides to determine after the event that a state of
affairs shall be treated as though the parties had set up a trust. Thus, the
obligations of trustee can be imposed on someone who had not thought of
themselves as being in that position. This was traditionally done where
someone was behaving in an illegal or immoral fashion. It has also been used
to create liability by creating a situation where the trustee is then held to have
knowingly assisted in breaching the trust or having knowingly been in receipt
of funds from one who has.

6.39   This issue often arises because of the doctrine of tracing. This is an
old rule of law that permits someone to pursue money they have lost through
the wrongful behaviour of another into the place where it now resides. The
common law rule of tracing is of limited use because of old case law that said
that once money that had been taken from you had been mixed by a
recipient with their own money in a purse, you could no longer use tracing
because it was no longer possible to tell which money was which. However,
equitable tracing got round this problem by applying relevant maxims of
equity which resulted in the court assuming that anyone in possession of the
property of another would act to try and repay it. Thus, any money they still
had should be the injured party's funds. Likewise, if they spent all the
money, the first money they received back would be held for the benefit of
the injured person. The only issue that defeated equitable tracing was where
the money had been paid through an overdrawn bank account as, in that
case, the bank would have been a creditor for the overdraft.

6.40   To obtain equitable tracing it is necessary to prove that the funds
were subject to a trust. Thus, those who have lost funds usually wish to try
and obtain a court declaration that the money was subject to a constructive
trust as it was not subject to one in an ordinary sense.

6.41   There is also a jurisdictional problem in that only those jurisdictions
that recognise trusts will allow equitable tracing into their jurisdiction. That
said, it is normally possible to trace through such a jurisdiction into one that
does recognise trusts. As a general rule, the common law countries (generally
ex-British Empire states) recognise the concept of trusts.

Grounds for constructive trusteeship

6.42   There are two basic grounds used by the courts:

- knowing receipt; and
- knowing assistance.

6.43 The classic exposition of English law on the point was stated by Selborone LC in *Barnes v Addy*[1]:

'strangers are not to be made constructive trustees...unless (they) receive and become chargeable with some part of the trust property or unless they assist with knowledge that it is a dishonest and fraudulent design on the part of the trustees.'

1   (1874) 9 Ch App 244.

6.44 Unfortunately the cases that have followed have left this area of law in an unclear state. Perhaps the crucial case is *Royal Brunei Airlines v Tan*[1]. Here the airline had appointed Borneo Leisure Travel as its agent for selling seats and cargo space on the airline. The contract stated that Borneo Leisure was to hold any money received on trust for the airline. However, instead of paying these funds into a trust account for their principal, Borneo Leisure paid funds received into their own account. The person controlling Borneo Leisure then allowed the company to use the money for its own purposes. Eventually the firm became insolvent and the airline appeared to have lost its money. It then brought legal proceedings against the managing director and main owner of Borneo Leisure alleging that he had knowingly assisted in breach of trust. He claimed that there was only mismanagement, which did not give rise to personal liability. The Privy Council stated that there were certain key issues:

- the liability of an accessory should apply regardless of whether the trustee and the third party have both displayed dishonesty or whether the trustee was innocent;
- that liability could be imposed regardless of whether the third party had procured the breach or dishonestly assisted in it; and
- that the key issue is the state of mind of the third party, not the trustee.

1   [1995] 3 All ER 97.

6.45 In other words, where someone interferes with a trust and deprives the beneficiary of some or all of their property, they should be able to get it back.

6.46 The Privy Council also approved some earlier cases which could be of particular concern for financial institutions who have laundered funds. One of these cases was *Fyler v Fyler*[1]. Here a firm of solicitors had put funds from a trust into an investment which was unauthorised. They were held liable even though they had believed that the investment would be of benefit to the beneficiary. The other was *Eaves v Hickson*[2]. Here the trustees made a payment on the basis of a forged document that was presented to them and which, according to the judge, would have fooled anyone not looking for forgery. The person who had produced the forgery was made liable to repay the money in priority to any claim being made against the trustees. However, had they not got the resources to pay, the trustees would then have been liable.

1   (1841) 3 Beav 550.
2   (1861) 30 Beav 136.

6.47   Liability was stated to arise where the person concerned was dishonest rather than unconscionable in their conduct. This consisted of not acting as an honest person would and the test was objective. Interestingly, negligence was held to be insufficient to create liability.

Knowing receipt

6.48   There is a dichotomy between two legal issues in many of the cases. This arises between knowing receipt of funds and liability for breach of fiduciary duty. Knowing receipt occurs when property has been received knowingly in breach of trust. Fiduciary duty is a generic term to cover one of a number of situations that occur where someone is held to have particular obligations to another party because of their relationship with them. There does not need to be a trust (though a trust does give rise to a fiduciary relationship) but similar obligations then occur. Again, a party who had laundered funds when a fiduciary relationship arose could find themselves faced with a civil claim. To provide such a right the courts have stretched the doctrine further and further over recent years although, surprisingly, a thief is not automatically a fiduciary of the true owner.

6.49   The legal consequences of the two states of affairs are different. In cases of knowing receipt an action in equity can be brought to recover the full amount including any capital growth that has occurred since the recipient received it. On the other hand, in cases of knowing assistance the liability is for the total amount lost plus simple interest.

6.50   Many of the issues were considered in *Lipkin Gorman v Karpnale*[1] where a solicitor became an obsessive gambler. He started gambling with clients' money. The firm's bank noticed that client account cheques were being paid to a casino but did nothing about it. A claim was brought for constructive trust, quasi-contract, negligence and conversion. The House of Lords held that a recipient of stolen money who was unjustly enriched was under an obligation to pay the same amount back to the victim. There is, however, a degree of protection for the recipient if he can show that his position had changed as a result of the arrangements and that he would lose out by having to pay the money back. This defence is of value to the financial extent of the change of position that has taken place. Unfortunately, the only issue that was considered on appeal to the House of Lords was a claim for money had and received. However, the Court of Appeal stated that a bank could not be liable to its customer as a constructive trustee unless it was in breach of its contractual duty of care to that customer.

1   [1992] 4 All ER 409.

6.51   In *Agip (Africa) Ltd v Jackson*[1] a firm of accountants had been acting for a fraudulent client. The accountants received funds from their clients and then passed them on as per instructions received. The true owners eventually appeared and claimed the funds back. As there was no financial sense in pursuing the clients, the wronged parties sued the accountants. It was held that they were not liable as they had not received the funds for their own benefit. However, it was stated that were a bank to receive funds to reduce an overdraft it would be receiving the funds for their own benefit.

1   [1992] 4 All ER 385.

6.52   In *Polly Peck International plc v Nadir (No 2)*[1] a claim for knowing receipt and knowing assistance was brought against Asil Nadir and the Central Bank of Northern Cyprus claiming that a huge amount of money had been wrongly transferred out of the company concerned. The Bank had received the funds for foreign currency contracts and, in the course of this, had not made enquiries about the source of the funds. The Turkish Cypriot bank concerned had £45m on deposit with Midland Bank in London. The company's administrator sought an order freezing the bank account. The court held that the key issue was whether or not the bank had been involved in any dishonesty or want of probity in that they had actual or constructive notice that they were receiving misapplied funds. The bank did not need to be shown to have been acting fraudulently. One of the judges felt that it was a case of knowing assistance and that the bank would only be liable if they received the money for their own use and benefit. As they received the money as agents and accounted for it to their principals, he did not believe that this requirement had been satisfied. Another of the judges however believed that most of the funds had been received as banker because the bank received the funds in their own right as a result of a currency transfer and therefore the issue was one of knowing receipt. The appropriate measure to apply was therefore whether there was knowledge that trust funds had been misapplied.

1   [1992] 4 All ER 769.

Holding property to the order of another

6.53   Sometimes called 'holding in a ministerial capacity' this arises when one person holds property belonging to someone else and mixes it with their own property. This is beyond 'knowing receipt' as discussed at para **6.48** ff above unless the agent is setting up their own title to the funds. Two issues arise here. The first is the principle that an agent who uses their principal's money in good faith to pay off a debt owed by the principal can rise the defence of 'payment over'. In *Holland v Russell*[1] an agent paid money to another as agent for a ship owner whose ship had sunk. It later transpired that the policy was void for non disclosure. By then the agent of the ship owner had paid some of the money over to his principal. The court held that the action would lie against the principal, not the agent, for this sum as the money had been properly paid over.

1   (1861) 1 B & S 424.

6.54   However, in *Springfield Acres v Abacus (Hong Kong) Ltd*[1] the defence failed. A company had successfully sued Springfield Acres for a large sum. Whilst the claim was waiting to be settled, the Springfield's assets were transferred to another company outside the jurisdiction. This money was then advanced to another company via a solicitor's trust account. These funds were then transferred to the defendant who in turn paid them on to other parties. In reality, these transactions were for the benefit of one man who was the major shareholder of Springfield and whose family were the beneficiaries of the trusts where the money ended up. The claim succeeded as the defendants were knowingly involved.

1   [1994] 3 NZLR 502.

6.55   In *El Ajou v Dollar Land Holdings plc (No 2)*[1] the plaintiff had been defrauded of money. The money concerned ended up being used as part finance for a building project in England and a claim was then brought against the building company claiming knowing receipt. It was held that a claim could only succeed if enquiry was not made in a situation where an honest and reasonable man would have done so.

1   [1995] 2 All ER 213.

6.56   In *Cowan de Groot Properties Ltd v Eagle Trust*[1] a claim was brought following an allegation that the directors of a company had sold some of its property at an undervalue. The purchaser was alleged to have been in knowing receipt. The case is not entirely in line with the others but it does appear to accept the doctrine that a defendant's knowledge will be determined on the basis of what a reasonable person would have learned.

1   [1992] 4 All ER 700.

Suspicious transaction reports and civil liability

6.57   When deciding on how to interpret suspicious behaviour there are problems in the context of civil liability. In theory it can depend on the party concerned failing to carry out a professional level of 'knowing their client' or failing to report suspicious transactions. In practice, we seem dangerously close to being in a situation where the courts impose a constructive trust wherever it suits them in order to recover illicit funds. The solution is for firms to be scrupulous in maintaining the requirements of the law and their professional bodies as minimum. Wherever they are in doubt as to whether to make a suspicious transaction report they should do so. From the point of view of both criminal liability and constructive trusteeship they should be safe. However this last issue can then arise in a secondary way.

6.58   A suspicious transaction report may have been made internally in a firm to its money laundering reporting officer, or an appropriate report made to either the NCIS or the fraud squad. Once this is done it could be argued that the firm is knowingly in receipt of illegal funds. Once a report has been made the firm will normally request permission from the body to whom they made that report before they act further. In most cases this will be the course of action which the criminal law enforcement bodies will prefer, so that they have the opportunity to observe the transaction and the client. There is no risk to the firm from the criminal courts in such cases, but neither is there a guarantee that the knowing receipt issue will cease to be a problem. It is possible that such a firm could still be held to be a constructive trustee, a risk exacerbated by the firm potentially ending up in a catch 22 situation. If they refuse to act on the client's instructions whilst waiting for confirmation from the criminal authorities that they can continue, they may be effectively tipping off the client. If, however, they act on such instructions they could well be held to be a constructive trustee. Rider suggests[1] that, in such cases, the safest approach would be to apply to the High Court for an Order 85 ruling.

1   BAK Rider 'The control of money laundering – a bridge too far?', *European Financial Services Law Review*, January/February 1998.

The role of the FSA

Introduction

6.59   In addition to the laws, regulations and guidance notes discussed above the FSA has also issued a set of rules which apply to those who are approved to carry on investment business and these operate in addition to the above. This has arisen as a result of the FSMA 2000 which, inter alia, gives the FSA the power to make rules in relation to the prevention and detection of money laundering in connection with the carrying on of regulated activities by authorised persons, with the objective of reducing financial crime[1]. In this context 'financial crime' is interpreted to mean:

'any offence …involving

(a) fraud or dishonesty;
(b) misconduct in, or misuse of information relating to, a financial market; or
(c) handling the proceeds of crime[2].'

1   FSMA 2000, ss 6 and 146.
2   FSMA 2000, s 6(3).

6.60   It is taken to cover any activity overseas which would have been an offence if it had taken place in the UK. In attempting to carry out its obligations in this respect, the FSMA 2000 requires the FSA to 'have regard to the desirability of:

(a) regulated persons being aware of the risk of their businesses being used in connection with the commission of financial crime;

(b) regulated persons taking appropriate measures (in relation to their administration and employment practices, the conduct of transactions by them...) to prevent financial crime, facilitate its detection and monitor its incidence;

(c) regulated persons devoting adequate resources to the matters mentioned[1].'

1   FSMA 2000, s 6(2).

6.61   Furthermore, FSMA 2000 also provides the FSA with the power to 'institute proceedings for an offence under prescribed regulations relating to money laundering[1].' This does not apply in Scotland. In addition, the FSA's suitability requirement for qualification for authorisation includes taking into account 'whether the firm has in place the appropriate money laundering systems and training, including identification, record-keeping and internal reporting procedures[2]'. Finally, the FSA's objectives include:

' 3. A firm must take reasonable care to organise and control its affairs responsibly and effectively, with adequate risk management systems.'

1   FSMA 2000, s 402(1)(b).
2   'The Qualifying Conditions for Authorisation', FSA Consultation Paper, March 1999.

6.62   The original draft version of this rule[1] added 'This will include...operating robust arrangements for meeting the standards and requirements of the regulatory system, and for guarding against involvement in market abuse or financial crime (including the detection and prevention of money laundering)'. In addition, Principle 1 states that 'A firm must conduct its business with integrity' and Principle 5 adds that 'A firm must observe proper standards of market conduct'. There is, therefore, no doubt as to the ability of the FSA to police the amended anti-money laundering regime they have created.

1   FSA Principles – Consultation Draft, September 1998, CP13.

6.63   The approach adopted has been heavily influenced by the Basle Committee on Banking Regulations and Supervisory Practices[1], and is therefore likely to be reflected by steps taken by regulators in other Basle countries. The FSA is passing a series of rules that will apply to all those whom it regulates. These will operate in addition to the statutes, regulations and guidance notes set out above. However, the FSA states that: 'firms whose systems and controls are already at acceptable levels will be able to comply with the proposed Rules with few changes or difficulties, if any[2].'

1　See the 'Prevention of Criminal Use of the Banking System for the Purpose of Money Laundering', Basle Committee, 1998.
2　FSA Consultation Paper 46, Executive Summary, p 1.

6.64　The purpose of the rules is stated to be to reduce the opportunities for laundering that are available to criminals through using the businesses of approved persons. They also assist in the promotion of market confidence, increasing public awareness, protecting consumers and combating organised crime.

6.65　The rules apply to 'relevant firms', which are firms engaged in regulated activities except those purely involved in general insurance or long-term insurance beyond the scope of the First Life Directive. The rules apply on a host state basis and therefore also impact on UK branches of firms established elsewhere in the EEA.

Money laundering duties

6.66　Relevant firms are expected to appoint a Money Laundering Reporting Officer. This is part of a wider duty whereby the firm and the Officer must make certain that the firm complies with the legal requirements regarding laundering, including the FSA rules. To deliver this, the Officer will need to keep himself up to date as to developments in laundering, arrange staff education as necessary, ensure that in-house systems function properly, receive internal reports from staff and send on information to the NCIS as appropriate. In addition, they must make an annual report to their own management. These requirements mean that the Money Laundering Reporting Officer must be of sufficient seniority and have the necessary resources to deliver this. As the role is a controlled function[1] their appointment will be subject to FSA approval. In a smaller firm the roles of Compliance Officer and Money Laundering Reporting Officer could be combined.

1　FSA Consultation Paper 46, annex A, p 22.

Customer identification

6.67　Regulated firms must not act without first identifying each customer (this has been discussed at para **6.27** above). This must be done prior to carrying out a transaction, or even reaching an agreement to do so in future. A 'customer' is defined as[1] 'a private customer, intermediate customer or a market counterparty engaged in, or who has had contact with that firm: (1)

on his own behalf; or (2) as agent for or on behalf of another'. 'Transaction' is also widely defined[2] as including 'the giving of advice and any other business or service which is within the scope of a regulated activity'. As with the regulations, identification procedures need not be used in cases that are below the financial limit of euro 15,000, where the person has been vouchsafed by someone else with a legal responsibility to do so and where the firm has no reason to be suspicious and is not in possession of knowledge that it is a laundering transaction. This is a development from the Regulations in that it extends to any member of staff being suspicious or in possession of knowledge. It appears to amount to strict liability and will apply whenever a firm or anyone within it is in breach, regardless of how thoroughly the firm has attempted to create a suitable anti-laundering regime. Two types of transaction are also exempt: where an isolated recorded transaction involves an investment that may only be re-invested in the client's name or be repaid directly to them, and certain transactions involving a long-term insurance contract below a de minimis figure or which is taken out as part of specified pension schemes.

1   FSA Consultation Paper 46, annex A, p 23.
2   FSA Consultation Paper 46, annex A, p 28.

6.68   The evidence that may be accepted regarding identity largely follows the lines of the guidance notes issued by the Joint Money Laundering Steering Group. A couple of points arise however. The first is the financial exclusion[1]. This permits firms to make allowance for the fact that some people do not have passports, driving licences or other documents that would satisfy the normal identity checking arrangements. In such instances, the firm may accept 'other evidence, such as a letter or statement from a person in a position of responsibility who knows the customer, sufficient to establish to the relevant firm's reasonable satisfaction that the customer is who he says he is, and to confirm his permanent address if he has one[2]'. This is unlikely to put the firm at risk given that the ease with which criminals can obtain false documentation means that they are unlikely to need to adopt this route[3]. The other is that there is no clear guidance on what to do when the client is a limited company or partnership. Such firms will therefore have to fall back on the JMLSC guidelines. In the case of listed public companies there is little risk as the Stock Exchange will have run extensive checks. In other instances it would be useful for the final version of the rules to suggest appropriate steps.

1   FSA Consultation Paper 46, 3.3.5.
2   FSA Consultation Paper 46, 3.3.6.
3   A Haynes 'Anti-Money Laundering Law' in *International Tracing of Assets*, p C1/8, Sweet & Maxwell, London, 1997.

6.69   Identification must be ascertained prior to carrying out a transaction or even reaching an agreement to do so in future.

Know your business

6.70 To try and increase the number of firms who spot suspicious transactions they are now required to utilise the information in their possession about clients to recognise transactions that are abnormal[1]. The rules provide that a firm may choose to establish an internal system to facilitate staff obtaining client information on request. Alternately, it is proposed that the firm could create a facility where further information would be made available to staff automatically under certain circumstances, such as unusual transactions or dealings.

1   FSA Consultation Paper 46 at rule 4.

Reporting

6.71 The reporting requirement is broken into two sub-sections; one dealing with internal reporting and one with external. The internal reporting requirement is that a suspicious member of staff must make a prompt report to the Money Laundering Reporting Officer. The firm is responsible for making sure that there is a system in place to facilitate this. There must be arrangements for taking disciplinary steps against anyone who has failed to do this without good reason.

6.72 The external reporting requirement is, as would be expected, that the Officer, once in possession of such a report, must promptly make a report to the NCIS if he believes that there are indeed grounds for suspicion. To facilitate this the firm should enable the Officer to access any information that could be relevant.

Using national and international findings on material deficiencies

6.73 Firms are required to make proper use of notices published by both the UK and international organisations of which the UK is a member, including the Financial Action Task Force. The notices concerned are those where there has been an examination of the anti-money laundering provisions in a state and that they have been found to be deficient. Proper use means, inter alia, applying that information in the contexts of introduction of a customer for an isolated transaction or the introduction by a customer of a person on whose behalf he is acting. It should be utilised as part of the 'know your customer' process and disseminated as part of staff awareness and training.

Awareness and training

6.74   The rules require that firms make sure that staff are aware of and given regular training in what is expected of them in relation to money laundering, the relevant law including the Money Laundering Regulations and the Sourcebook, the identity and responsibilities of the Money Laundering Reporting Officer and the nature of the consequences to the firm and themselves if they fail to meet the necessary requirements. In particular, the staff should be given information concerning the effect that facilitating a customer in laundering money can have on the firm's bank accounts and other assets. The rules state: '...in particular if a relevant firm decides it is unable to process transactions, because of the risk of committing a money laundering offence[1].' This is unfortunately worded. A firm should not decide not to process a transaction because it suspects it is a laundering operation. It should contact NCIS, report its suspicions, and ask for guidance from the NCIS as to whether to continue acting. The NCIS will usually want them to do so to facilitate watching the suspected laundering operation (this has been discussed at para **6.35** above).

1   FSA Consultation Paper 46 at 7.2.4.

6.75   Information relating to awareness and training need not be recorded in writing but it would be wise to do so, either by hard copy or electronic means, primarily so that the firm can show that the rules are being observed.

6.76   In addition, appropriate training must be given to those staff who handle money, or are managerially responsible for transactions which could be utilised to launder money. 'Substantially'[1], all staff should be covered by such training within a period of two years. Although this appears to provide some assistance for a firm that claims it has not been able to provide training for all relevant staff, it does appear to be at odds with the relevant law. There seems no sensible reason why appropriate training cannot be provided to all staff within a reasonable period of joining a firm or changing roles to one in which such training will be needed for the first time. Two years seems a very generous provision, and one without basis in the relevant legislation or statutory instruments. Likewise, the idea that 'substantially' all relevant staff should be so trained seems inadequate. It might satisfy the FSA: it might not satisfy a court.

1   FSA Consultation Paper 46 at 7.3.2(1)(c).

The money laundering reporting officer and compliance monitoring

6.77   The role of the money laundering reporting officer is one that must be filled. To facilitate his being able to do the job properly the person must be senior, free to act on his own authority, have sufficient resources, be based in the UK and within the firm, and be informed of any relevant knowledge or suspicion within that firm. It is his responsibility to pass on to the NCIS any suspicious transaction reports. It is this person who is also responsible for utilising the national and international information referred to at para **6.73** above. In addition, he is responsible for making sure that the awareness and training requirements are fulfilled and making an annual report to the firm's managers. The only exceptions to this requirement are sole traders, and incoming firms which only provide services in the UK from overseas.

6.78   The annual report must assess the firm's compliance with the sourcebook, show how any new findings under the requirement to learn from national and international findings have been put into effect and state how many internal reports of suspicious transactions have been made by staff to that officer. Internal reports should be broken down in a manner appropriate to the size and nature of the firm's business to facilitate discerning any patterns of reporting so that areas of inadequate reporting can be spotted. It is an obligation that the managers consider the report and take any necessary action to remedy deficiencies.

Record keeping

6.79   Firms must keep a copy of the client identification evidence on file or, where this cannot be done, a note must be kept on file of where that information can be obtained. It should be clear from where records can be obtained. Records must be kept of all regulated activity transactions. In addition, there must be records of any steps taken against insolvent clients to recover monies owed, and internal or external reporting and details of any action taken. This extends to keeping a record of any internal reports that the money laundering reporting officer decided not to act on.

6.80   Such records must be kept for five years. This time period starts to run with the termination of the firm's relationship with the firm, or the completion of the transaction, or the client's insolvency or the acquisition of the information leading to the creation of the record. In practice, most firms will keep files for at least six years as this will be the limitation period for any breach of contract or negligence action by a client. As the relevant information will normally be kept on client files, it will end up being retained as well.

6.81   There should also be records of the anti-money laundering training given (see para **6.74** ff above) including the names of the staff concerned. There should also be a record of consideration of internal reports of suspicion and any action taken.

Conclusions

6.82   The FSA requirements are not onerous and, in the case of those currently regulated by recognised professional bodies, only extend to relevant regulated activities. The extension of the role of the Money Laundering Reporting Officer is only bringing the requirement up to what many well run firms will already be doing. However, it is not clear whether the Money Laundering Reporting Officer and Head of Compliance can be carried out by the same person. The areas of operation clearly relate but, in large firms, it may be appropriate for the Money Laundering Reporting Officer to be someone who is less senior in rank than the Head of Compliance given that it is part of the latter's function to make sure that the anti-money laundering steps taken are, along with everything else, satisfying the firm's compliance requirements.

6.83   The requirements for staff training are, as discussed above, potentially less than many firms will currently feel they are required to provide to protect themselves, given the current legal situation.

6.84   There is a benefit to firms in the draft rules in that there is evidence that firms with tight anti-money laundering provisions tend to be better protected against fraud[1]. In addition, if it becomes entangled in a laundering operation the cost to a firm can be very high. Anything that reduces this risk has to be in the interests of the firm themselves. Nonetheless, there must be concerns that the approach adopted by the FSA has unnecessarily added an additional tier of regulation to those that are already in place. A simple obligation to satisfy the requirements of the relevant statutes and the Money Laundering Regulations might have been enough, possibly coupled with arrangements for the Regulations to be amended slightly. This could have achieved the same result more simply.

1   FSA Consultation Paper 46, annex B at B.34.

The Wolfsberg Principles

Why were they created?

6.85   A number of leading banks, acting in co-ordination with Transparency International, have agreed to take on board a set of general principles to facilitate improving the standards applied in combating money laundering where private banking relationships are concerned. They also accepted as a formal principle that the responsibility for this rested with the management of the banks concerned. The Principles (named after the town in Switzerland where the working sessions took place) have been issued in the hope that other financial institutions will follow them.

6.86   Banks and other financial institutions have become increasingly concerned that the enormous amount of money laundering currently taking place could pose a threat to them. This can come about as a result of bad publicity arising as a result of it becoming publicly known that the institution has been caught laundering money. Even where the bank concerned has maintained good standards, there is likely to be damage to reputation even where the regulator concerned does not believe that disciplinary steps are warranted. In many cases, however, they will. There are clear signs that the regulators are becoming both more assertive and more proactive in this field[1].

1   *Financial Times*, p 3, 24 March 2001.

6.87   The primary motivation in adopting the Principles has been a desire to create a new set of standards which it is hoped will become adopted by an increasing number of financial institutions. In the words of Dr Peter Eigen[1]:

> 'We fully expect that other banks will recognise these guidelines and volunteer to accept them…We believe it is essential that internationally active investment firms, brokerage houses, insurance companies, property and asset management firms, fully embrace standards similar to those being announced by the banks.'

1   Chairman, Transparency International, 30 October 2000: http://www.transparency.org

6.88   The Principles themselves are set out as follows.

Client acceptance: general guidelines

General

6.89   Bank policy will be to prevent the use of its worldwide operations for criminal purposes. The bank will endeavour to accept only those clients whose source of wealth and funds can be reasonably established to be legitimate. The primary responsibility for this lies with the private banker who sponsors the client for acceptance. Mere fulfilment of internal review procedures does not relieve the private banker of this basic responsibility.

The obvious aim of this is to deal with the issue of criminals in government who steal and then launder the assets of their country and hide them as a personal investment fund. In addition, there are others, particularly criminals involved in the drug trade, illegal arms dealing and people smuggling, to name the most remunerative. The Principle 1.1 has the weakness of only being aimed at private clients. In most instances those wishing to launder large amounts will have no difficulty in establishing a network of companies throughout the world and then getting the payments that hit the western banking system to be made out to companies in that group. In the case of corrupt government officials receiving bribes, the bribe will often be paid into a corporate bank account which appears to have no connection with the official in any event.

Identification

6.90   *The bank will take reasonable measures to establish the identity of its clients and beneficial owners and will only accept clients when this process has been completed.*

This is perhaps all that can reasonably be expected of a bank, but the effectiveness of such checks is rather limited due to the relative ease with which false documents and real documents in false names can be obtained (see para 6.29 above). In addition, how does a bank ascertain that the beneficial owner is who they appear to be? It is a relatively straightforward matter for one person to create a false identity or to hide behind the identity of another. A bank cannot become, nor be expected to become, a detective agency. The consequence of this is that Principle 1.2 may give a false sense of security to the bank which has taken this step and to others which deal with it.

Client

6.91   *Natural persons: identity will be established to the bank's satisfaction by reference to official identity papers or such other evidence as may be appropriate under the circumstances.*

The problem here is the general availability of good forged documents and the relative ease with which it is possible to obtain documents in the wrong name[1]. Apparently safe identity documents such as passports, national identity cards and driving licences are no real guide to identity. To give an idea of the scale of the problem, in the UK there are also estimated to be between one and a half million more national insurance numbers being used than should be the case.

1   A Haynes 'Anti-Money Laundering Law', p C1/7–1/9 in *International Tracing of Assets*, Ed Ashe and Rider, Sweet & Maxwell, London 1997.

6.92   *Corporations, partnerships, foundations: the bank will receive documentary evidence of the due organisation and existence.*

This will tend to reduce the number of off-the-shelf companies created specifically to launder money. However, it may well also accelerate the market in buying small, relatively dormant companies that are a number of years old and less likely to attract suspicion. There is evidence that this has been happening in the West Indies. Recent changes in ownership and radical changes in the financial behaviour of a company following acquisition should thus attract close investigation.

6.93   *Trusts: the bank will receive appropriate evidence of formation and existence along with the identity of the trustees.*

This is going to cause particular problems. It is never going to be possible to be certain whether the trustees are running the trust themselves or as a front for others. In some cases, for example the blind trusts available in Cyprus, the vehicle itself seems to have been designed to facilitate this very state of affairs.

6.94   *Identification documents must be current at the time of opening.*

Beneficial owner

6.95   *Beneficial ownership must be established for all accounts. Due diligence must be done on all principal beneficial owners identified in accordance with the following principles:*

> *Natural persons: when the account is in the name of an individual, the private banker must establish whether the client is acting on his/her own behalf. If doubt exists, the bank will establish the capacity in which and on whose behalf the account holder is acting.*

While this is an admirable sentiment it seems difficult to see how this is going to be achieved. Those with large amounts to launder should not find it difficult to hire people to front the transactions they need to engage in. Many of the points made above will also apply here.

> *Legal entities: where the client is a company, such as a private investment company, the private banker will understand the structure of the company sufficiently to determine the provider of funds, principal owner(s) of the shares and those who have control over the funds, eg the directors and those with the power to give direction to the directors of the company. With regard to other shareholders, the private banker will make a reasonable judgement as to the need for further due diligence. This principle applies regardless of whether the share capital is in registered or bearer form.*

Clearly this is an area where experience and staff training could make a vital difference. Does the client's corporate group structure make sense in terms of the business transactions being carried on? If not, may it be explicable in terms of the historical development of the corporate group? If neither is the case, then the reaction should be one of suspicion and the banker concerned should contact the money laundering reporting officer.

A more difficult problem will apply with investment companies. Namely, whose money is being invested? In the case of well-known fund managers and investment companies, 'know your client' provisions will normally suffice. However, in cases of firms who are not already known, 'know your client' is going to involve knowing your client's client; or at least being satisfied as to the intermediary's identity checking requirements.

115

Trusts: where the client is a trustee, the private banker will understand the structure of the trust sufficiently to determine the provider of funds (eg settlor), those who have control over the funds (eg trustees) and any persons or entities who have the power to remove the trustees. The private banker will make a reasonable judgement as to the need for further due diligence.

The points made above in relation to beneficial owners will apply here as well.

Unincorporated associations: the above principles apply to unincorporated associations.

This turns to the issues raised above concerning ascertaining who may be standing behind the party dealing with the bank. No guidance is given as to how this should be done. Indeed, the author has yet to come across guidelines issued by any state that have yet satisfactorily done this. It is perhaps a noble sentiment rather than a realisable objective.

Accounts held in the name of money managers and similar intermediaries

6.96   *The private banker will perform due diligence on the intermediary and establish that the intermediary has a due diligence process for its clients, or a regulatory obligation to conduct such due diligence, that is satisfactory to the bank.*

The comments made above in relation to investment companies will also apply here.

Powers of attorney/authorised signers

6.97   *Where the holder of a power of attorney or another authorised signer is appointed by a client, it is generally sufficient to do due diligence on the client.*

Practices for walk-in clients and electronic banking relationships

6.98   *A bank will determine whether walk-in clients or relationships initiated through electronic channels require a higher degree of due diligence prior to account opening.*

This remains a rather vague suggestion. It might be helpful if the banks could agree a clarification to this Principle to reach an agreed minimum standard. There are a number of variables here. How clearly can the proposed customer prove their identity? In regulatory terms, how safe is the country they are based in? In short, the fact that they contacted the bank by walking into the branch or by electronic contact is not of importance in itself. The key issue is the context and whether this explains the manner of contact. If it does then the degree of due diligence need not be higher than for other customers.

Due diligence

6.99   *It is essential to collect and record information covering the following categories:*

- purpose and reasons for opening the account;
- anticipated account activity;
- source of wealth (description of the economic activity which has generated the net worth);
- estimated net worth;
- source of funds (description of the origin and the means of transfer for monies that are accepted for the account opening);
- references or other sources to corroborate reputation information where available;
- unless other measures reasonably suffice to do the due diligence on a client (eg favourable and reliable references), a client will be met prior to account opening.

This could prove particularly helpful. It is unlikely to assist in spotting suspicious clients or funds at the outset unless the launderers are unusually obtuse. However, it will provide the bank concerned with a context into which to place the client's financial activities. It may well be that, in the longer term, apparently incongruous payments will be made and thus draw the bank's attention. 'Know your customer' has considerably more potential to lead to laundering being spotted than identity checking on opening an account.

Oversight responsibility

6.100   *There will be a requirement that all new clients and new accounts be approved by at least one person other than the private banker.*

This is a useful step. It will reduce the risk of a private client banker being too enthusiastic about getting a new, apparently wealthy client who will presumably be helping him hit his financial targets. It will also reduce the risk of corruption, as a new client wishing to subvert a bank into laundering his funds will not be able to achieve this by bribing just one person. Even so, there is evidence that suggests that a greater number of bankers than one might hope will be willing to engage in illegal activity[1].

1   Ehrenfeld, Rachel *Evil Money*, Harper Business, New York, 1992, pp 44–7. See also *Daily Express*, International Edition, 23 April 1992.

Client acceptance: situations requiring additional diligence/attention

Numbered or alternate name accounts

6.101   *Numbered or alternate name accounts will only be accepted if the bank has established the identity of the client and the beneficial owner.*

High-risk countries

6.102 *The bank will apply heightened scrutiny to clients and beneficial owners resident in and funds sourced from countries identified by credible sources as having inadequate anti-money-laundering standards or representing high-risk for crime and corruption.*

This is a useful step, though it would help if the Principles referred to a source where up-to-date information on this could be obtained from time to time. Perhaps an appendix, updated from time to time, on the Transparency International website, or that of a third party.

Offshore jurisdictions

6.103 *Risks associated with entities organised in offshore jurisdictions are covered by due diligence procedures laid out in these guidelines.*

High-risk activities

6.104 *Clients and beneficial owners whose source of wealth emanates from activities known to be susceptible to money laundering will be subject to heightened scrutiny.*

Public officials

6.105 *Individuals who have or have had positions of public trust such as government officials, senior executives of government corporations, politicians, important political party officials, etc and their families and close associates require heightened scrutiny.*

This is a particularly important addition given the unfortunate tendency of political leaders in certain parts of the world to regard their country's national wealth as a personal piggy bank from which monies can be removed at will. It will also make it more complicated for such people to launder such monies, though there are no shortage of methods that they could adopt to disguise what was going on, for example by utilising fake trading transactions involving state entities.

Updating client files

6.106 *The private banker is responsible for updating the client file on a defined basis and/or when there are major changes. The private banker's supervisor or an independent control person will review relevant portions of client files on a regular basis to ensure consistency and completeness. The frequency of the reviews depends on the size, complexity and risk posed by the relationship.*

Practices when identifying unusual or suspicious activities

Definition of unusual or suspicious activities

6.107 *The bank will have a written policy on the identification of and follow-up on unusual or suspicious activities. This policy will include a definition of what is considered to be suspicious or unusual and give examples thereof. Unusual or suspicious activities may include:*

- *account transactions or other activities which are not consistent with the due diligence file;*
- *cash transactions over a certain amount;*
- *pass-through/in-and-out-transactions[1].*

1   For a discussion of how these may be sued see Haynes *Journal of International Banking Law*, Vol 11, issue 1, pp 29–31.

Identification of unusual or suspicious activities

6.108 *Unusual or suspicious activities can be identified through:*

- monitoring of transactions;
- client contacts (meetings, discussions, in-country visits etc);
- third-party information (eg newspapers, Reuters, internet);
- private banker's/internal knowledge of the client's environment (eg political situation in his/her country).

Follow-up on unusual or suspicious activities

6.109 *The private banker, management and/or control function will carry out an analysis of the background of any unusual or suspicious activity. If there is no plausible explanation a decision will be made involving the control function:*

- to continue the business relationship with increased monitoring;
- to cancel the business relationship;
- to report the business relationship to the authorities;
- the report to the authorities is made by the control function and senior management may need to be notified (eg Senior Compliance Officer, CEO, Chief Auditor, General Counsel). As required by local laws and regulations the assets may be blocked and transactions may be subject to approval by the control function.

These guidelines are very useful. The one troubling element is the suggestion that one of the options is to cancel the business relationship. This will simply warn the client that they have aroused suspicion. Their reaction will be to take their business elsewhere and do a better job of disguising it. If the bank is suspicious it should instead be reporting the matter to the relevant authority and taking their guidance as to whether to continue to act. The regulators will normally want the bank to continue acting, thus giving them the opportunity of watching what is taking place (see para **6.35** above). The only potential outstanding issue that could then arise is where the bank suspected it to be a situation where a true owner might later arrive in pursuit of the funds. This is a distinct possibility where large amounts of funds have been pillaged from a state. The bank's fear will be that they may then be made liable to repay the funds even if they have parted company with them[1]. As discussed above, the best course of action in such circumstances is to seek a closed sitting at the appropriate civil court, seeking an order that, having made a suspicious transaction report, the bank should continue to act.

1   *Agip (Africa) Ltd v Jackson* [1990] BCC 899.

Monitoring

6.110   *A sufficient monitoring programme must be in place. The primary responsibility for monitoring account activities lies with the private banker. The private banker will be familiar with significant transactions and increased activity in the account and will be especially aware of unusual or suspicious activities (see 4.1). The bank will decide to what extent fulfilment of these responsibilities will need to be supported through the use of automated systems or other means.*

Control responsibilities

6.111   *A written control policy will be in place establishing standard control procedures to be undertaken by the various 'control layers' (private banker, independent operations unit, Compliance, Internal Audit). The control policy will cover issues of timing, degree of control, areas to be controlled, responsibilities and follow-up etc.*

Reporting

6.112   *There will be regular management reporting established on money laundering issues (eg number of reports to authorities, monitoring tools, changes in applicable laws and regulations, the number and scope of training sessions provided to employees).*

Education, training and information

6.113   *The bank will establish a training programme on the identification and prevention of money laundering for employees who have client contact and for compliance personnel. Regular training (eg annually) will also include how to identify and follow up on unusual or suspicious activities. In addition, employees* *will be informed about any major changes in anti-money-laundering laws and regulations. All new employees will be provided with guidelines on the anti-money-laundering procedures.*

Record retention requirements

6.114　*The bank will establish record retention requirements for all anti-money-laundering related documents. The documents must be kept for a minimum of five years.*

Exceptions and deviations

6.115　*The bank will establish an exception and deviation procedure that requires risk assessment and approval by an independent unit.*

Anti-money-laundering organisation

6.116　*The bank will establish an adequately staffed and independent department responsible for the prevention of money laundering (eg Compliance, independent control unit, Legal).*

Conclusions

6.117　These Principles represent a bold and imaginative step forward. The practical limitations bankers and other financial institutions will find themselves faced with in the situations concerned are largely unavoidable. However, it is hoped that an increasing number of financial institutions will adopt the Principles and that this will assist in the struggle to stop the world's financial systems being used to launder illegal funds.

6.118　Reinout van Lennep, head of ABN Amro private banking, recently went on record as saying[1]:

'These principles reflect decent and adequate standards; we neither expect nor wish to see the standards being raised higher.'

The experience of banks since statutory requirements were first brought in during the mid 1980s, suggests that this may be optimistic.

1　http://www.moneyunlimited.co.uk

Special compliance obligations: insider dealing, market abuse and other criminal offences

Introduction

7.1   Although there have always been legal obligations imposed on those who handle information and monies on behalf of third parties – the rules of equity, for example – it has only been in relatively recent times that a comprehensive set of laws have attempted to regulate the situation where someone is in possession of private information which offers the opportunity of easy money by trading in the shares of the company to which the information relates. This is currently effected by the Criminal Justice Act 1993[1]. However, this only deals with the activities of those individuals who engage in insider dealing, encourage others to deal or who disclose information outside the proper performance of their duties. There is a separate legal, regulatory and ethical issue which arises where either an employer or employee engages in unacceptable behaviour concerning the abuse of non-public information with regard to qualifying investments on a traded market. The former is dealt with by the laws relating to insider dealing: the latter by the laws relating to market abuse.

1   Which put into effect EC Directive 89/592.

7.2   The similarities between the two are that both criminal offences relate to information that is not available to the public and the achievement of a profit or avoidance of a loss as a result of that information being improperly used. Where they differ is that insider dealing relates to the activities of those working in businesses or who carry out work as a result of their employers or as a consequence of having a contract to perform services for another firm. Market abuse relates to the activities of the firm itself. The key distinction between them is that insider dealing is a crime of commission or intent, whereas market abuse is essentially a crime of effect.

7.3   Also, although both are criminal offences, insider dealing would be investigated as a normal criminal offence by the police or, in practice, the Serious Fraud Office. Market abuse is policed by the FSA and they have the capacity to bring criminal proceedings, even against those who are not authorised persons. In the case of those who are authorised persons, there would be potential regulatory consequences as well in the case of both crimes.

Insider dealing

The nature of the offence

7.4   There are three potential offences:

- *Insider dealing.* This occurs when a party who is able to access information relating to the company concerned deals in securities whilst in possession of such information, which must be unpublished and likely to affect the price of the securities concerned.
- *Encouraging others to deal.* This offence is committed where someone encourages another to deal in securities whose price is likely to be affected by inside information in their possession. The insider will be committing an offence even if the person being encouraged does not know the facts. A transaction need not actually take place. It is sufficient that encouragement takes place.
- *Disclosure.* This consists of disclosing inside information outside the proper performance of the person's duties. For a conviction to succeed it is not necessary for there to be evidence that the party making the disclosure intended it to be acted upon.

Key elements

What is an 'insider'?

7.5   The Criminal Justice Act 1993, s 57 defines this as someone who has inside information from an inside source and knows that this is the case. The person concerned will need to have acquired the information as a result of being:

- an employee;
- a director; or
- a shareholder of an issuer of securities;

though it is not necessary for the crime to relate to shares in that company. However, the access to the information concerned should have arisen as a result of that person's employment, office or protection.

7.6   There are, however, two statutory limitations which stop this catching those who, as a part of their business or professional activities, are rightfully involved in price analysis:

- the Criminal Justice Act, s 58 states that information is not inside information if it can be either readily acquired by those likely to deal in securities or be acquired by those exercising due diligence;
- the possibility of interpreting the description of information being accessed by virtue of the insider's employment to exclude situations where an expert accesses information by virtue of his employment. There is no direct case on the point but either of the two traditional rules of statutory interpretation – the golden rule[1] or the mischief rule[2] would assist. The former adopts the approach that the literal meaning of a statute should be followed unless this leads to an absurd result at which point common sense is applied in interpreting the words at issue. The mischief rule adopts the approach that the fault with the pre-existing law that led to the passing of the statute should be considered where there is one. Any doubts over the interpretation of the statute should be interpreted in the light of that.

1   *Grey v Pearson* (1857) 6 HL Cas 61.
2   *Heydon's Case* (1584) 3 Co Rep 7a.

7.7   Secondary insiders are also caught as are parties they pass the information on to, subject to this not extending to situations where the act of passing on the information has made it public. There is no requirement for the secondary insider to have taken any active steps to acquire the information. It is sufficient that they know that it was inside information and was obtained from an inside source.

What is 'inside information'?

7.8   This is:

- Specific information which relates either to:
  (a) specific securities; or
  (b) a specific issuer of securities.
- If made public it would have a 'significant effect' on the price of any securities. This is not defined but the relevant Stock Exchange Guidance Note states: 'it is not feasible to define any theoretical percentage movement in a share price that will make a piece of information price sensitive'. The Takeover Panel suggested 10% price movement in a day.

7.9   The information concerned need not be precise though. The crucial element is that it must not be publicly available. The Criminal Justice Act 1993, s 58 provides guidance by containing a non-exhaustive list. It covers two categories:

- Those where information must be treated as publicly available:
  (a) where it is published in accordance with the rules of a regulated market to inform investors and their advisers;

(b) where the information is publicly available as a result of being set out in public records, eg Companies House;

(c) the information can already be readily acquired; or

(d) it is derivable from publicly available information.

- Those where information may be treated as publicly available even though:

  (a) it can only be worked out by experts or analysts;

  (b) communication has only been to a section of the public;

  (c) where the information can only be found by observation;

  (d) where money has to be paid to get the information; or

  (e) where the information is published abroad.

7.10 Such information must in any case be price sensitive. This means that the price or value of the securities concerned is likely to be significantly affected – see the Criminal Justice Act 1993, s 56.

7.11 The Stock Exchange Guidance Note on the subject suggests that to avoid falling on the wrong side of the law, appropriate steps to take would be to:

- develop a consistent procedure for determining what is price sensitive information and for releasing that information to the market;
- ensure price sensitive information is kept confidential until the moment of announcement and to consider whether unaudited quarterly statements or announcements updating the market at the end of a financial period are needed;
- brief employees who meet analysts visiting the company's premises as to the extent and nature of information that can be communicated; and
- obtain and record the consent of parties attending a meeting at which price sensitive information is to be given that they will not deal in the company's securities before the information is made public.

Securities

7.12 The securities that the insider dealing laws relate to have a definition which is idiosyncratic to the Criminal Justice Act 1993. Schedule 2 lists them as:

- *Shares*. Shares and stock in the value of a company.
- *Debt securities*. Any instrument creating or acknowledging indebtedness which is issued by a company or public sector body, including, in particular, debentures, debenture stock, loan stock, bonds and certificates of deposit.
- *Warrants*. Any right (whether conferred by warrant or otherwise) to subscribe for shares or debt securities.
- *Depositary receipts*. The rights under any depositary receipt means a

certificate or other record (whether or not in the form of a document) which is issued by or on behalf of any person who holds any relevant securities of a particular issuer, and which acknowledges that another person is entitled to rights in relation to the relevant securities or relevant securities of the same kind. In this context 'relevant securities' means shares, debt securities and warrants.

- *Options.* Any option to acquire or dispose of any security falling within any other paragraph in this Schedule.
- *Futures.* Rights under a contract for the acquisition or disposal of relevant securities under which delivery is to be made at a future date and at a price agreed when the contract is made. The references in the Act to a 'future date' and to 'a price agreed when the contract is made' include references to a date and a price determined in accordance with terms of the contract, and 'relevant securities' means any security falling within any other paragraph of this Schedule.
- *Contracts for differences.* Rights under a contract which does not provide for the delivery of securities but whose purpose or pretended purpose is to secure a profit or avoid a loss by reference to fluctuations in a share index or other similar factor, connected with relevant securities, the price of particular relevant securities; or the interest rate offered on money placed on deposit. In this context 'relevant securities' means any security falling within any other paragraph of this Schedule. The securities concerned must either be listed on an official exchange of a State within the EEA, or be admitted to dealing on, or have their price quoted, on a regulated market.

Dealing

7.13   The Criminal Justice Act 1993, s 55 provides three categories:

- *Acquiring securities.* This may be as principal or agent.
- *Disposing of securities.* This may also be as principal or agent.
- *Procuring another party to acquire or dispose of the securities.* This may be done directly or indirectly.

7.14   *A-G's Reference (No 1 of 1975)*[1] held that 'procure' means 'to produce by endeavour'. In none of these cases need the insider be proven to have benefited from the deal, though in practice this is obviously the normal motive.

1   [1975] QB 773.

Defences

7.15   Once the offence has been shown to have satisfied the elements of their definition (as shown at para **7.4** ff above) the burden of proof shifts to the accused to show that there is a valid defence. The defences fall into two categories – general and specific. General defences apply where the person charged has dealt, disclosed or encouraged another person to deal other than in the proper performance of their employment, office or profession. Specific defences only apply in certain stated situations to individuals who would otherwise be guilty of insider dealing[1].

1   Gil Brazier *Insider Dealing: Law and Regulation*, p 143, Cavendish, London, 1996.

General defences

7.16   These include:

- where the accused did not expect to make a profit or avoid a loss[1];
- where the accused reasonably believed that the information concerned was widely distributed enough to avoid prejudicing the interests of anyone else involved in the deal[2]; and
- where the accused can show that they would have entered into the arrangement in any event[3].

1   The Criminal Justice Act 1993, s 53(6).
2   The Criminal Justice Act 1993, s 53(1)(b) and (2)(b).
3   The Criminal Justice Act 1993, s 53(1)(c) and (2)(c).

7.17   In the event of the accused being charged with disclosing price sensitive information, there are two general defences:

- that the accused did not expect anyone to deal in securities as a result of his disclosure[1]; or
- that the accused did not expect anyone to deal at a profit or avoid a loss as a result of the disclosure[2].

1   The Criminal Justice Act 1993, s 53(3)(a).
2   The Criminal Justice Act, s 53(3)(b).

Specific defences

7.18   These include:

- market makers and dealers can plead that they were acting in good faith in the course of their business[1];
- where the information was market information and it was reasonable of the accused to act as they did[2];
- where the information was market information which the insider acquired as a result of being involved in buying or selling securities[3]; and
- where the insider can show that they acted in line with the FSA's Price Stabilisation Rules[4].

1   The Criminal Justice Act 1993, Sch1, para 1.
2   The Criminal Justice Act 1993, Sch 1, para 2.
3   The Criminal Justice Act 1993, Sch 1, para 3.
4   The Criminal Justice Act 1993, Sch 1, para 5.

Territorial limits

7.19   The territorial limit for the crimes concerned is the UK. Thus, the accused must either:

- have been within the UK when the act concerned was committed; or
- the market concerned must have been situated in the UK; or
- the crime must have involved an intermediary who was situated in the UK; or
- either the disclosure must have been made by the accused when they were situated in the UK or the recipient of the information or of the encouragement to deal was so situated.

Penalties

7.20   On summary conviction, this would be a maximum fine of £5,000 or imprisonment of up to six months, or both[1]. On indictment, this would be an unlimited fine or imprisonment of up to seven years, or both[2].

1   The Criminal Justice Act 1993, s 61(1)(a).
2   The Criminal Justice Act 1993, s 61(1)(b).

7.21   Directors may be disqualified as the crime is one which shows sufficient connection with corporate management – see *R v Goodman*[1].

1   [1994] 1 BCLC 349.

7.22   Any profits may also be seized under the Proceeds of Crime Act 1995. This provides that, where an offender is convicted of a criminal offence and the court believes that the criminal has profited from it, or from another offence of which he was convicted at the same hearing, or another offence taken into consideration, an order may be made ordering the offender to pay that amount[1]. This may be done if the prosecutor gives notice that he thinks it appropriate or the court decides so. The court has the power to decide not to make an order if a victim of one of the types of crime mentioned has indicated that they wish to take civil proceedings in respect of the same. This could be relevant if proceedings on the basis of para **7.31** below were taken.

Dealing in directors' options

7.23   It is also a criminal offence for a director to:

- buy a call option in shares or debentures[1]; or
- buy a put option in shares or debentures[2]; or
- buy the right, at the director's election, to call for or make sale of a specified number of quoted shares or debentures at an agreed price at an agreed date in the future[3].

1   Companies Act 1985, s 323(1)(a).
2   Companies Act 1985, s 323(1)(b).
3   Companies Act 1985, s 323(1)(c).

7.24   This extends to shadow directors, spouses, and infant children unless they can show they did not have reason to know of the directorship.

7.25   It does not extend to unquoted securities, rights to buy shares or the purchase of convertible debentures.

Penalties

7.26   On summary conviction, this can lead to a fine of up to £1,000 or up to six months' imprisonment, or both. On indictment, this can lead to an unlimited fine, or up to two years' imprisonment, or both.

The FSA Principles

7.27   The eleven principles (see **Chapter 5**) have an all pervading effect and some are relevant here:

- *Principle 1.* A firm must conduct its business with integrity.
- *Principle 5.* A firm must observe proper standards of market conduct.
- *Principle 8.* A firm must manage conflicts of interest fairly, both between itself and its customers and between one customer and another.

7.28   The Statements of Principle for Approved Persons could also be relevant. In particular, Principle 1: 'An approved person must act with integrity in carrying out his controlled functions', and Principle 3: 'An approved person must observe proper standards of market conduct in carrying out his controlled function.

7.29   It is not only in the event of a successful prosecution that the FSA could bring disciplinary proceedings against authorised persons under these Principles. Even in the event of a prosecution failing, the FSA Tribunal could determine that a breach of a Principle had occurred.

Civil law issues

7.30   Contracts governing the main offences of insider dealing are specifically stated by the Criminal Justice Act 1993 not to be void or unenforceable[1]. However, other related contracts could be void under the principle in *Mackender v Feldia*[2].

1   Section 62(2).
2   [1967] 2 QB 590.

7.31   Any profit wrongly made by a director will belong to the company of which he is a director. This is a consequence of his owing a fiduciary duty as constructive trustee: see *Boardman v Phipps*[1] and *A-G for Hong Kong v Reid*[2]. This approach was confirmed in the case of *Nanus Asia Co Inc v Standard Chartered Bank*[3] where confidential information obtained in breach of an employee's duty of fidelity gave rise to a constructive trust over profits resulting from its use.

1   [1967] 2 AC 46, HL.
2   [1994] 1 AC 324, PC.
3   [1990] HKLR 396.

7.32   If a third party in receipt of information should realise that the information was given to them in breach of a fiduciary duty then the same principle will apply.

7.33   If the information is given in breach of confidence then an action will lie on that basis. This will extend to employees.

7.34   Directors do not normally have a fiduciary obligation to the company or shareholders, but *Coleman v Myers*[1] suggests that they can acquire one where they are dominant directors in a small company. Directors must also declare secret profits: see *Regal (Hastings) v Gulliver*[2].

1   [1977] 2 NZLR 225, NZCA.
2   [1967] 2 AC 134n.

Relevant Codes

7.35   Rule 2.1 of the City Code on Takeovers and Mergers states that anyone who is in possession of confidential information relating to offers must only make it available when it is necessary. Rule 4.1 goes on to bar dealing in the securities of an offeror or offeree prior to the information relating to the deal becoming publicly available.

7.36   The Model Code for Securities Transactions by Directors of Listed Companies requires the directors to notify an appointed party on his board of directors before so doing. He is debarred from dealing if he is in possession of unpublished price sensitive information.

7.37   Dealing where the criminal law would be broken would clearly be a breach of FSA Principle 1, the Statements of Principle for Approved Person 1 and may be in breach of the Conduct of Business Rules 7.13.2, 7.13.4 and 7.13.6.

Market abuse

Introduction

7.38 Market abuse was introduced as a result of the FSMA 2000, s 118. The aim of the creation of this new crime is to create open, transparent and fair markets for trading by stamping out abusive practices. The crime has two main parts: there must be a breach of one or more of the three statutory conditions plus one or more of the behaviour requirements. The statutory conditions are:

'... behaviour...

(a) which occurs in relation to qualifying investments traded on a market to which this section applies;
(b) which satisfies any one or more of the conditions set out in subsection (2); and
(c) which is likely to be regarded by a regular user of that market who is aware of the behaviour as a failure on the part of the person or persons concerned to observe the standard of behaviour reasonably expected of a person in his or their position in relation to the market.'

7.39 The conditions relating to behaviour are:

'*(a) the behaviour is based on information which is not generally available to those using the market but which, if available to a regular user of the market, would or would be likely to be regarded by him as relevant when deciding the terms on which transactions in investments of the kind in question should be effected;*
(b) the behaviour is likely to give a regular user of the market a false or misleading impression as to the supply of, or demand for, or as to the price or value of, investments of the kind in question;
(c) a regular user of the market would, or would be likely to, regard the behaviour as behaviour which would, or would be likely to, distort the market in investments of the kind in question.'

7.40 This extends to unauthorised as well as authorised persons, ie potentially anyone who trades on the markets. However, the unauthorised person will solely be concerned with the criminal consequences, whereas authorised persons will be concerned with the regulatory consequences as well.

7.41 A qualifying investment is an investment of a kind that has been admitted for trading on a prescribed market. The prescribed markets are: LSE, LIFFE, LME, IPE, OM, Tradepoint and Coredeal.

Behaviour

7.42   The types of behaviour that come within the scope of market abuse are:

- dealing in qualifying investments;
- dealing in commodities or investments that are the subject matter of (or where price is determined by reference to) a qualifying investment;
- acting as an arranger in respect of qualifying investments;
- causing, procuring or advising others to deal;
- disseminating statements or information that are reasonably likely to be regarded as relevant in determining the terms on which transactions in qualifying investments should be entered into;
- corporate finance advice; and
- managing qualifying investments.

7.43   The FSMA 2000, s 118(2) defines behaviour based on the misuse of such information as:

'behaviour based on information which is not generally available to those using the market but which, if available to a regular user of the market, would or would be likely to be regarded by him as relevant when deciding the terms on which transactions in investments of the kind in question should be effected.'

Information

7.44   Information is taken to be generally available if it can be obtained by research or analysis conducted by or on behalf of users of a market. The following would be examples of when information would be regarded by the FSA as generally available:

- when it has been disclosed through an approved channel of communication on a prescribed market;
- when it is obtainable from records that are open to inspection by the public;
- when the information has been made public or is derived from information that has been;
- whether it can be obtained by observation;
- where it has been published overseas;
- when it has been made available to a section of the public; or
- it is available on the payment of a fee.

7.45   In determining whether information can be relevant it is necessary to consider:

- how specific it is;
- how material it is;

- how current it is;
- how reliable it is;
- its relationship to other material already publicly available; and
- the extent to which the information is new.

7.46   The draft code also categorises various types of publishable information most of which is self evident. The only element that is not is that it declares that information does not have to have been released simultaneously to all market users to have been published.

Requiring and encouraging

7.47   The FSMA 2000, s 123 gives the FSA the power to impose penalties on anyone engaging in market abuse. It also enables the FSA to make a declaration that someone's behaviour does or does not amount to market abuse. It may decide not to impose penalties if that person believed on reasonable grounds that what they were doing did not amount to market abuse or that they had taken all reasonable precautions and exercised all due diligence to avoid engaging in market abuse. In theory, other bodies could also bring proceedings[1], namely the DTI, the Serious Fraud Office and the Crown Prosecution Service. However, it is anticipated that the FSA's activity in this area will result in them being the party normally involved.

1   Blair et al *Financial Services and Markets Act 2000*, p 114, Blackstone Press, London, 2001.

7.48   This extends to anyone who requires or encourages another to carry out what would be an act of market abuse if they did it themselves. This will inevitably involve the FSA in having to analyse hypothetical situations. It is also complicated by the fact that the rules of some of the recognised investment exchanges require market members to take some responsibility for customers' orders. Some degree of clarification is going to be needed from the FSA in this area and it is expected in due course.

The Financial Services Authority Code of Practice

7.49   This was issued because the FSMA 2000, s 119 requires that the FSA issues a code on the subject. Amongst other things the code aims to '...bring clarity to the description of market abuse...'. It also gives the FSA the opportunity to describe behaviour that amounts to market abuse, that which does not and factors that will be taken into account in determining it.

7.50   The Code does not set out all the standards of behaviour that are expected. However, it does make clear that the standards expected from a regular user will depend on that user's experience, skill and level of knowledge. A professional market participant, such as an investment bank, will have a more exacting requirement than an infrequent retail investor.

7.51 The Code adds that if behaviour was reasonable at the time, but ceases to seem so with the benefit of hindsight, it may still be safe from being adjudged to be market abuse. In this context it is worth noting that the FSA have said that the regular user standard is the equivalent of the courts' reasonable man test[1].

1   Consultation Paper 59, para 6.6.

7.52 The Code acknowledges that the motivation for the behaviour can be a crucial element. Thus, it will be an offence where the person concerned 'knows…that the principal effect of the transaction…on the market will be…artificially to inflate or depress the apparent supply of, or demand for, or the price or value of, a qualifying investment or relevant product such that a false or misleading impression is likely to be given to a regular user, unless the principal rationale for the transaction in question would amount to what a regular user would consider a legitimate commercial rationale notwithstanding the principle effect of the transaction'. Behaviour that is in line with the Code of Market Conduct will not amount to market abuse[1].

1   FSMA 2000, ss 118(8) and 122.

What does 'distort the market' mean in FSMA 2000, s 118?

7.53 It will certainly cover abusive squeezes. These were described in the Code as occurring where someone:

- has a significant influence over the supply of a product;
- has entered into deals on a prescribed market whereby the counterparty will buy or sell that product or a contract for a basket of deliverables is entered into; and
- he uses the above situation to create an abnormal price.

7.54 It will also cover situations where the contact with the prescribed market is indirect. This could occur by A entering into an OTC contract with B and B then entering into a back-to-back contract on a prescribed exchange. A could use such a situation to create an abusive squeeze.

Safe harbours

7.55 Clearly, a crucial part of the new regime is the extent to which certain activities are made immune from it because there are sensible grounds for so doing. For example, the rules of some of the recognised investment exchanges contain a number of provisions that allow behaviour that might otherwise be seen as market abuse. Therefore, the following are given specific safe harbours:

- reporting a legitimate transaction where this is either permitted or required as a result of the rules of a prescribed market;
- reporting a legitimate transaction in accordance with a legal or regulatory requirement;
- entering into a cross-transaction where the rules of the relevant prescribed market permit or require it; and
- maintaining a quotation at a particular level when the rules of a prescribed market so require.

7.56 It will also cover dealing in order to satisfy a contractual or regulatory obligation that pre-dates the information coming into their possession. It is even sufficient for a safe harbour if it can be shown that the decision to deal on the same terms had been entered into before the information came into your possession. If it can be shown that the information did not influence the decision to deal, a safe harbour is also available.

7.57 A safe harbour exists where the information relates to another person's intention to deal in qualifying investments or relevant products unless this relates to a takeover bid. It is also possible, where a takeover bid is to be launched, to deal in shares in the target company for the purpose of building a stake. However, own account dealing in such shares would normally be market abuse, as would dealing in derivatives to obtain an economic exposure to the movements in the price of the target company's shares.

7.58 There is a specific safe harbour where behaviour has complied with the LME's rules in 'Market Aberrations: the Way Forward', which governs the behaviour of those holding long positions.

7.59 There is, however, no general safe harbour whereby you are safe if you satisfy the various FSA rules. The reason given is that it could create uncertainty and that, in any event, many of the rules are irrelevant in this context. It is probable that acting in accordance with the listing rules will be made a safe harbour.

7.60 There is no general safe harbour where the participant can show that they were obeying the rules of a recognised investment exchange. The reason the FSA have given is that those rules change from time to time and the FSA do not control them. However, being able to show that action was in line with exchange rules is always going to be a material factor in determining whether market abuse has taken place.

7.61 The FSMA 2000, s 120 specifically allows the FSA to provide a safe harbour where the provisions of the Takeover Code are satisfied. The FSA have stated that, in the event that they needed to use their market abuse powers during a takeover bid, they would liaise with the Takeover Panel. This is important as otherwise those trying to frustrate a takeover bid could allege that market abuse was taking place in the trading of their shares and obtain a delay by seeking a referral to the FSA.

7.62 Any safe harbour granted by the FSA requires the Treasury's approval.

Disclosure of information

7.63 The information at issue must relate to matters that a regular user would reasonably expect to be disclosed to other market users on an equal basis. It may be disclosable information that has to be released pursuant to a legal or regulatory requirement, or information that is normally subject to a public announcement, eg corporate credit ratings or the composition of equity indices.

7.64 Commodity derivatives raise specific issues. A party involved with a particular commodity may come into possession of information that suggests that a change in the price of that commodity is highly probable. That party clearly retains the right to take hedging positions to protect its commercial position. However, it may conceivably become market abuse if they were to take further positions in the market to make a profit. The issue of disclosable and announceable information is unlikely to be much of an issue with commodity derivatives. Much of the information that determines the price of contracts is not shared out in the marketplace. In addition, Chinese Wall arrangements should keep traders away from information that should not be influencing their trading.

7.65 A firm may trade ahead of publication of its own research material, subject to the Conduct of Business rules being satisfied. However, there will always be information that some market users have access to but not others. It is not considered that it will inevitably follow that profiting from such information will be market abuse.

The FSA Principles

7.66 The eleven principles (see **Chapter 5**) have an all pervading effect and two are particularly relevant here.

- *Principle 1*. A firm must conduct its business with integrity.
- *Principle 5*. A firm must observe proper standards of market conduct.

7.67   However, it should be borne in mind that the principles are, by nature, much wider in scope than the market abuse law. Behaviour in a relevant context that is in breach of a principle will not necessarily be a breach of the market abuse regulations. Breach of the regulations will, however, always be a breach of Principle 5.

Jurisdiction

7.68   The FSMA 2000, s 118(5) states that:

'Behaviour is to be disregarded ....unless it occurs:

(a) in the United Kingdom; or
(b) in relation to qualifying investments traded on a market to which this section applies which is situated in the United Kingdom or which is accessible electronically in the United Kingdom.'

7.69   Clearly, an international investment bank engaging in international investment may find itself in a position where an activity it is engaging in may be acceptable in one jurisdiction, but not another. This is exacerbated by the fact that the various investment transactions may all be part of one wider investment activity. The only answer is to make sure that a legal view has been taken on what is permissible on each market and that those organising the trading have it made clear to them that they cannot move investment to other exchanges without it being cleared. This is a particular issue with some of the US exchanges. In the event of transgression within their jurisdiction, an aggressive response from the SEC can be expected.

Other criminal offences

7.70   A detailed examination of the criminal law is beyond the remit of this book. However, in any jurisdiction the most likely criminal offences to be committed where wrongful behaviour takes place in the firm are likely to relate to the laws of theft, fraud, obtaining property by deception, conspiracy to defraud and misleading advertisements.

7.71   In the UK the FSMA 2000, s 397 creates the offence of issuing misleading statements. The offence is committed by anyone who[1]:

- makes a statement, promise or forecast which they know to be misleading, false or deceptive in a misleading particular;
- dishonestly conceals any material fact, whether it is in connection with a statement promise or forecast or otherwise;
- recklessly makes a statement, promise or forecast, whether honestly or otherwise, which is misleading, false or deceptive in a material particular.

1   Section 397(1).

7.72 An offence is committed where the person making such a statement, promise, forecast or concealment of facts is made for the purpose of inducing, or is reckless as to whether it induces, another person to[1]:

- enter into or refrain from entering into a 'relevant agreement' (this has a statutory definition[2] but is largely dependent on statutory instruments to clarify some of the terms); or
- exercise or refrain from exercising any rights conferred by a 'relevant investment' (see **Chapter 5**).

1   FSMA 2000, s 397(2).
2   FSMA 2000, s 397(9).

7.73 In addition, it is an offence[1] for a person to engage in a course of conduct which creates a false or misleading impression as to the market in, or the price or value of, any 'relevant investments' (see **Chapter 5**). The act must be done for the purpose of creating that impression and with a view to inducing another person to acquire, dispose of, subscribe for or underwrite the investments concerned, or to refrain from doing so. Breach of the section can be punished with up to six months' imprisonment or a fine on summary conviction or up to seven years' imprisonment or a fine on indictment. There would undoubtedly be regulatory repercussions as well.

1   FSMA 2000, s 397(3).

7.74 Furthermore, communications with the FSA are also protected by the criminal law. The FSMA 2000 states that it is a criminal offence to knowingly or recklessly provide information to them that is false or misleading to a material extent[1]. The criminal penalty is a fine, but the regulatory consequences could be much more serious.

1   Section 397(3).

7.75 It is a defence where the person who is charged under the above shows that:

- they acted in line with price stabilisation rules or the control of information rules. Given that the FSA is now responsible for these, there is unlikely to be cause for any conflict; or
- they reasonably believed that the act or conduct concerned would not create an impression that was false or misleading.

7.76 Pending the existence of any case law on the subsection, it is best to place a restrictive interpretation on 'reasonably believed'.

7.77 A further issue arises with regard to these crimes because the FSMA 2000 goes on to state[1] that, where an offence has been committed by a body corporate with the consent, connivance or negligence of an officer of the company, both can be prosecuted.

1   Section 400.

7.78 There is, in addition, a financial promotion regime governed by the FSMA 2000[1] and the Financial Promotion Order. An examination of the detail of this would, however, be beyond the scope of the book.

1   Section 21.

7.79 Profits made as a result of criminal activity can be seized under the Proceeds of Crime Act 1995[1]. This allows money to be seized where the prosecution have served notice to the effect that they think it would be appropriate, or the court decides for themselves that it is. Such a step would not be taken where the court has reason to believe that a victim of the crime is going to bring civil proceedings against the accused to obtain compensation (see para **7.37** above).

1   Section 1.

CHAPTER 8

Enforcing compliance obligations in multi-level and multi-business enterprises

Introduction

8.1 This chapter concentrates on internal arrangements and mechanisms that a firm should have in place to ensure that its staff comply with regulatory obligations. It will be naïve of any company to assume that merely because it operates in a regulated environment and specific rules and guidance are published to the firm by its regulator, that all members of its staff will comply naturally. There can be a variety of reasons why the compliance standards within a firm break down. It must be remembered that nearly all compliance breaches will be caused by the actions or admissions of a member of staff. The UK regulatory environment and indeed the majority of regulatory environments around the world control entry into the market by granting authorisation to those persons wishing to conduct investment business and removing that authorisation from participants where there have been cases of regulatory breaches. It must, however, be remembered that the majority of participants in the marketplace are corporations and thus the person granted authorisation will not only be a corporation but also is merely a legal fiction. Some of the largest market participants employ tens of thousands of staff and, when a breach of regulatory requirements occurs, it is not the firm itself that has caused the breach, but either an individual person, or department or division.

8.2 This issue has been recognised by regulators for many years, and most regulators have introduced methods of gaining accountability from senior employees of an organisation where their acts or omissions may give rise to a breach of regulatory requirements. Under the FSMA 2000, an approved persons regime has been created. This regime, which will be explored in further detail at para **8.47** ff below, ensures that all members of staff within an organisation that fulfil a controlled function must obtain approval to fulfil that role before it can be commenced. Approval is gained from the FSA, and will only be granted where the authority considers that the applicant for approval is a fit and proper person. Consequently, it is open for the authority to remove approval or impose disciplinary measures where the regulatory breach or misconduct is identified.

8.3   It is not, however, acceptable for a firm to merely rely on the approval regime and the threat of discipline by a regulator to ensure that compliance standards are met within its own organisation. The fact of the matter is that regulator enforcement will only be able to deal with the issues after a rule breach has occurred. The firm must consider methods, and have in place arrangements to promote and maintain good standards of compliance throughout the firm's business operation, and encourage compliance standards to be met. After all, prevention is better than cure.

FSA Principles for Business

8.4   FSA Principle for Business 3 dictates an authorised firm must take reasonable care to organise and control its affairs responsibly and effectively, with adequate risk management systems. It can apply not only to procedures that firms should have in place, but also to the methods they undertake to ensure that their staff comply with those procedures.

8.5   Often, the best method for a firm to convey the necessity for compliance is through the compliance culture that exists within it. A firm's culture can infer either that business must be conducted at all costs and staff are put under pressure to manage their business around regulatory standards. Or that 'good compliance is good business' where compliance with regulatory standards is part of business processes and day-to-day responsibilities of staff members.

8.6   There are two schools of thought as to how compliance can be integrated within the firm's business. The top-down approach to compliance exists where a firm establishes a dictatorial compliance department or senior executive board. As staff conduct their day-to-day responsibilities, the compliance department from time to time undertakes regulatory reviews for the purpose of identifying failings and dealing with those failings through disciplinary measures. This type of approach often creates an atmosphere of threat within an organisation. Members of staff who are attempting to ensure compliance even where they may not be that familiar with the standards which they are attempting to meet, may be afraid to draw to the attention of senior management difficulties they are experiencing through fear of disciplinary action. Perhaps, also, the mentality of the likelihood of non-compliant behaviour being identified is remote, therefore they will take a chance with any rule breaches they cause.

8.7   The second approach is one of the bottom-upwards style. Compliance standards are integrated within the firms' everyday working practices. Staff are fully trained so that they understand both their working practices and, therefore, implicitly the compliance standards that they are required to achieve. The model works on the premise that compliance will happen automatically as a member of staff is not able to distinguish between an abstract business process and a distinct regulatory requirement.

8.8   The firm must identify the best approach to ensuring compliance standards to suit its own type of business. There are certainly occasions when one style of compliance management would be better suited. For example, a firm that is undergoing significant procedural change, either as a result of a change to its business model, or where it is managing its way through a regulated disciplinary action, may find that the top-down approach to compliance is preferable.

8.9   However, in the main, most firms will attempt to adopt a compliance culture that will fall somewhere between each style. For example, an approach where compliance procedures and regulatory standards are built into everyday operational procedures, a compliance department that is involved with routine supervision and monitoring of compliance standards to ensure deficiencies are brought to the attention of the firm, acted upon appropriately, and where significant breaches occur, appropriate enforcement action is taken against the member of staff.

Senior management and compliance responsibility

8.10   An effective compliance culture will no doubt exist in an organisation where all senior management of the firm take responsibility for compliance. It has been the case for some time that regulators do take this view, rather than what was perhaps the original view, that compliance was the preserve of only the compliance department within an organisation. By way of example in paragraph 3 of Appendix 38, the rules of the Securities and Futures Authority (SFA) states 'compliance with Principle 9 is a matter for which senior management is responsible and not simply a matter for compliance officers'. In paragraph 6, the SFA went on to state:

'although the Board and the Senior Executive Officer in particular have the overall responsibility, it is important to stress that all members of staff have a duty of compliance. The Senior Executive Officer should take reasonable steps designed to ensure that staff are aware of this duty and that a commitment to compliance exists within the firm, starting at the top. At all levels, compliance with regulatory requirements and the observance of higher standards of business conduct should become a state of mind, and the accepted discipline, in common with compliance with other codes of practice and ethical standards which are part of everyday business.'

This concept is now repeated by the FSA. For example, FSA Rule 3.2.6 (SYSC) states a firm must take reasonable care to establish and maintain effective systems and controls for compliance with applicable requirements and standards under the regulatory system and for countering the risk that the firm might be used to further financial crime.

Furthermore, Statement of Principle 7 of the Approved persons Code of Practice provides 'An approved person performing a significant influence function must take reasonable steps to ensure that the business of the firm for which he is responsible in his controlled function complies with the relevant requirements and standards of the regulatory system.'

Dissemination problems

8.11   A compliance officer will often experience problems of disseminating information regarding rules, regulations and guidance both up and down the organisation and across business units. Difficulty in communication is a common problem in multilevel and multi-business enterprises and can be solved using a variety of methodologies.

8.12   Written memoranda, notices and newsletters or updates are, of course, a frequently used method. However, the messages contained in such material are likely to be forgotten rapidly (or consigned to the waste bin) unless they are reinforced. Periodic compliance seminars are useful in reconfirming the points made in written compliance notes, particularly when the seminars are interactive. Workshops can be very helpful in prolonging the awareness of various compliance points, although considerable time is required in order to script a workshop that is applicable to both the organisation and the audience.

8.13   Technology is now also employed frequently to communicate compliance points to the widespread business. Short focused interactive sessions with an optional or mandatory question section at the end can be used effectively to raise compliance awareness and this can be achieved at times that are convenient for the participants. If a reporting section is incorporated in the programme it can provide valuable feedback to the compliance department as to the areas needing further work to ensure a suitable level of competence.

Written acknowledgments

8.14   Keeping track of which departments and businesses have been updated can be difficult unless the updates are made using technology. In this case, it should be sufficient to keep a note of the mailing list. If further confirmation is required, several e-mail programs allow the sender to record the receipt of a document (and sometimes the opening of a document by the recipient).

8.15 When written compliance notices are sent out or compliance seminars held it is an important record for the participants. Formal written acknowledgments that a significant new piece of compliance regulation or guidance will be complied with are helpful in ensuring that the target audience understands its obligations. However, frequent use of such acknowledgments runs the risk of debasing the authority of the compliance unit through the perception of a bureaucratic tendency.

8.16 In a large organisation the administration required for the above can be significant but it is important for both management and regulatory purposes to have a record of compliance communications to the organisation. This can be useful in helping to demonstrate training and competence within a firm, in assisting in developing the knowledge base of a member of staff and, potentially, for disciplinary matters.

Geographically dispersed businesses

8.17 The problems mentioned at para **8.11** ff above can be multiplied by a business that has a wide geographic spread. It is vital to ensure that businesses operating in different regulatory environments comply both with home and host regulations. Whilst the need to comply with the host country's regulations is obvious, the firm will frequently find (at a group level) that the home country regulator expects compliance with all its regulations even when technically they do not apply. Although there can be much philosophical debate surrounding this point, it is a practicality that a group compliance officer must recognise and action. In order to ensure compliance with a set of regulations that may not even be culturally familiar at a group level, it is advisable for the local subsidiary (or branch) to use either a local firm of lawyers or employ a compliance officer with local regulatory knowledge (if the subsidiary or branch is large enough).

Head office versus business versus local

General

8.18 Although compliance staff working in the business or for a local subsidiary are very much at the cutting edge of compliance decisions, it is the head office compliance staff who must ensure that all businesses, subsidiaries and branches conform to a minimum acceptable level of compliance. There is a potential clash of needs as worldwide minimum compliance requirements are interpreted at a local level, frequently in cultures where head office strictures make only marginal sense. For a large organisation, there is a significant administrative overhead in ensuring that local business needs are met whilst maintaining an ethical standard that is acceptable to the organisation worldwide and, in particular, to the head office. Additionally, there is sometimes a perception that certain businesses carry different risk profiles and therefore require more (or less) compliance intervention.

Head office responsibility

8.19   The group or head office compliance team should be responsible for providing an overall compliance vision, guiding principles, an organisational structure for compliance and a compliance strategy. Also, head office should provide liaison and co-ordination to ensure minimum standards and should act as recipients for periodic compliance reports from the businesses and local and regional compliance functions.

Business compliance team

8.20   The business compliance team will, by contrast, be very involved in day-to-day compliance decisions relating to transactions and clients. Whilst many of these decisions will be made with reference to group compliance policies, it is inevitable that many decisions will also be made which are at the boundaries of (or beyond) the group's compliance policies. It is in this area that the overall compliance vision and guiding principles from head office will provide valuable insight as to the direction in which decisions should be made.

Local compliance staff

8.21   Local compliance staff face the formidable task of ensuring compliance with head office requirements as well as local regulatory needs in the context of day-to-day business requirements relating to transactions and clients. The local and regional staff may be in very different time zones from head office and there may therefore be very little practical support that can be given during the local subsidiary's business day.

Local (host) regulators

8.22   There may be significant differences in the regulatory approaches of the host and home regulators. Some regulators are driven through cultural or local needs to be very prescriptive and detailed in their approach whilst others, through the same needs, may be apparently light in their approach. The perception of an apparent lightness in a regulatory approach should be tested through reference to local expertise as it may well be that general regulations are significantly added to through interpretive notices which may be known about by only a subset of the regulated entities. Additionally, some regulators may focus on the form of compliance (or letter of the law) whereas others may look at the substance (or spirit of the law).

Changing regulatory cultures

8.23   As in all matters in the financial services industry, past performance is no guide to the future, ie regulators can and do change their minds as to what was acceptable and will be acceptable in the future. Compliance officers must recognise that regulators are often driven by political needs as well as by their own agendas and that changing cultures over time lead to changing regulatory perceptions of what is acceptable and unacceptable. It is also possible that the home regulator may not understand the culture of the country in which the subsidiary or branch operates. Additionally, the culture of the host regulator may also be different, either in concept as to what is acceptable or in detail as to the form and substance of supervision and enforcement. It was only relatively recently that most regulators finally agreed that insider trading was unacceptable.

The predominant compliance culture

8.24   It is also of some concern that the influence of the Anglo-Saxon culture is gaining in all areas of the world in that the world's cultural diversity is rapidly being eroded through a move to the economic values of a single predominant culture. Local compliance staff also face the problem that compliance with the most strict regulations in the world (which is the easiest and obvious route to take) often produces difficulties for doing business where certain strict cultural taboos are not recognised or, even worse, are ridiculed.

Hybrid products

8.25   Another area of challenge for the compliance officer in the multi-business enterprise is the crossover of products between businesses. It is, of course, one of the objectives of senior management of a major organisation to ensure that each business can leverage off the other businesses as much as possible. This is a well-recognised management technique for increasing profitability and is frequently the objective behind a merger or acquisition. For the group or head office compliance officer, the creation of hybrid products reinforces the concerns around ensuring a minimum standard of compliance in all areas of business whilst allowing the flow of knowledge that is vital to the creation of products which provide superior profitability through the unorthodox combining of different areas of expertise.

8.26   The solution to this concern is in good training within the compliance department itself as well as across the businesses of the firm. Training (and reinforcing the message) within the compliance department of a large organisation is one of the fundamental necessities for keeping the minimum standards of compliance at an acceptable level. It will also enable the communication of different standards expected by different industry regulators and by different country regulators. The awareness of these different standards within the compliance department can do much to ensure that the organisation has consistent standards itself across all products as well as regions. Periodic meetings of senior compliance officers from around the firm, in addition to the encouragement of less formal networking opportunities, enables the sharing of information on new products as well as new regulatory standards.

8.27   There is also often a lack of understanding of the impact of one business on another. A common problem is the inadvertent sharing of inside information with another business. It may be that the holder of inside information requires a derivative product in order to create the hybrid product. However, a derivatives trader frequently requires a significant amount of information in order to properly price a product. Great care must be taken by the holder of inside information in communicating sufficient information to the derivatives trader to enable accurate pricing whilst ensuring that the actual inside information is not passed until it is absolutely necessary. In order to do this successfully, significant training time must be invested in departments such as corporate finance. It is also necessary to train to high standards the receiving departments such as derivatives trading. All traders should be aware of the dangers of the accidental transfer of inside information and the consequences on the trading activities when such a transfer takes place.

Inside information

8.28   There is clearly a need to keep the information within the corporate finance department separate from the rest of the business. This need has been well-documented and there have been a number of regulatory and legal cases on this point. Given the ability to physically separate departments through the use of swipe cards, the major concern now is probably to avoid careless conversations being overheard in lifts, restaurants, etc. The use of a log recording the inside information held by the corporate finance department (or any other department within the firm) and those who have been brought inside the Chinese wall is vital in both ensuring that the minimum standards are kept and in providing potential defence for the firm in the event of action against it.

Understanding of compliance culture

8.29   Delivery of compliance focused training is an important tool in assisting staff understanding of their compliance obligations through the organisation. Regulatory requirement for the maintenance of a training and competence scheme and the regulatory definition of competence supports the idea that compliance understanding is a competency required of all staff. The compliance department should consider becoming involved, where appropriate, in the delivery of training to ensure that a good compliance message is delivered.

8.30 Training should be considered at a variety of stages throughout the career of an individual. Possibly the most critical time of any employee's career is that period when they are a new starter. Induction courses are operated in many organisations and, if they are not, serious consideration should be given to running an induction course, which includes reference to compliance obligations. Basic information can be delivered during the training, including identification of the company's registered compliance officer and compliance department. Key obligations that staff will have, such as those relating to personal account trading, insider trading, complaints handling, anti-money laundering procedures and the handling of customers' money and assets should be dealt with. Reference should also be considered to the compliance culture operated within the firm, particularly where compliance operates an open-door policy for the purpose of prevention of compliance problems. Finally, it may be appropriate to deliver and explain the availability of the company's Compliance Procedures Manual.

8.31 The training should be continued throughout an employee's career. Further training should also be considered in relation to compliance-related matters. These should be considered in the light of the need to maintain employees' competence and training can also be considered as a way of ensuring that the knowledge of compliance culture given to an employee during any induction training is not lost. Many firms choose to deliver by way of continued education training of matters such as trading and market ethics, with updates on regulatory developments that may affect an individual's role within an organisation. For example, during the consultation and implementation phase for the implementation of the FSMA 2000 many firms delivered training to staff on changes that would affect them.

8.32 A significant aspect of compliance understanding relates to the firm's compliance procedures manual. Training should be given in relation to the procedures that affect members of staff and staff should also be provided with a copy of the procedures, or should have access to them. It is often a useful practice to place a copy of the manual on an internal website, thus ensuring that staff access is available at all times. It also allows for the compliance department's updating of the manual to be made available instantly.

8.33 It is important that any updates to the firm's procedures manual are communicated and distributed promptly. On occasion, members of staff may dispute that they have received the manual. Particularly where the compliance department has identified rule breaches caused by members of staff, it is good practice to have members of staff sign a receipt for compliance manuals and any updating pages. That receipt can also include a statement from the employee confirming that they have read and understood the material contained within the manual.

8.34   On many occasions, the compliance department will be required to give guidance on either their own written procedures or in relation to regulators' application of the rules.

8.35   It aids enforcement if the compliance department can issue this guidance in writing to the employees of the firm. A variety of methods can be applied. Consideration can be given to the department issuing regular compliance newsletters in which fundamental compliance messages can be explained. More urgent messages can be provided by way of simple compliance bulletins or alerts. These should all be published in writing. It would certainly aid communication if an available Intranet site within the firm could retain copies. Once again, it can assist enforcement of compliance procedures if affected members of staff can confirm receipt and their understanding of information contained within such bulletins or alerts.

Role of the compliance department

8.36   Firms will want to arrange their compliance function in a manner that best suits their business. However, it is often the case that a compliance department will be involved in both establishing the firm's compliance policy and monitoring its effectiveness. Also, the department may conduct investigations where rule breaches have been identified or are suspected. This broad spectrum of responsibilities can be best described as:

- *Prevention.* Preventing compliance problems from occurring within a firm through good quality rules analysis, procedure drafting, communication of procedures, compliance guidance, training and the provision of compliance advice in relation to individual transactions or business developments.
- *Detection.* Detection of any compliance problems through both a monitoring programme designed to keep under regular review all areas of the firm that give rise to a regulatory risk. Where breaches have been identified, a specific investigation into that matter will be conducted. In relation to both monitoring and investigations, this will mean feeding back to management the conclusions so that adjustments to the company's business procedures may be made.
- *Resolution.* Resolving any specific compliance breaches identified during monitoring and investigations may require actions relating to individual customers or transactions, or a firm wide response. This could include

additional training of staff to ensure that repeat breaches do not occur. Adjustment to product materials, procedures relating to the transactions of those products through to more strict measures such as the removal of individual staff.

Notification to regulators

8.37   Once any compliance breach has been identified the firm should give serious considerations to whether the breach should be notified to its regulator. Most regulators require notification of breaches and consider such a notification requirement to be an essential tool in the way in which they supervise authorised firms. For example, FSA Principle for Business 11 states that 'a firm must deal with its regulators in an open and co-operative way and must disclose to the FSA appropriately anything relating to the firm of which the FSA would reasonably expect notice.' The question of whether or not to report a matter to a regulator presents many firms and compliance departments with a dilemma. The manner in which notification can be managed is dealt with more specifically in Chapter 10 below.

8.38   Firms must be aware, however, of the obligations placed upon them to make an appropriate disclosure. When enforcement issues are identified within a firm it is not merely a question of addressing the matter internally. Consideration must then be given to how notification should be provided to the regulator and consequences of providing that notification. It must also be remembered that any action that the regulator may take, whether against the firm or any individuals within the firm, will be viewed in light of such notification and the manner in which the firm has dealt with the rule breach in question. Should the regulator determine to take its own enforcement action it should be remembered that such action will be taken as a result of the rule breach itself and not the decision by the firm to notify. This should be balanced against the likelihood that, if the rule breach in question is serious, and is identified by a regulator during a routine supervision visit, any enforcement action taken will be more severe if they conclude that the matter should have been reported but was not.

Internal disciplinary procedures

8.39   It can be an important tool within a firm if formalised internal disciplinary procedures are maintained. The maintenance of a disciplinary system will not only ensure compliance with applicable employment protection legislation but can also be a powerful vehicle for communicating the seriousness with which the firm approaches good standards of compliance.

8.40 Disciplinary systems must at all times, however, be fair and provide ample opportunity for any disciplinary case against an individual to be properly investigated, responded to by the employee, considered by a senior person within the firm, and allow an appropriate response to be provided. Certainly firms involved in complex areas of business should consider establishing a formalised internal disciplinary system and having rules or procedures setting out how such systems will operate. A very simple and standardised approach could mirror the process followed by an employment tribunal. This will include the establishment of a disciplinary panel. The panel could contain a senior member of the compliance department to act as chairperson and other members of the panel to provide expert advice on how compliance procedures are generally recognised or implemented within the firm.

8.41 An investigating prosecuting officer within the compliance department should be responsible for the preparation of the investigation reported to the matter. This should be thoroughly written up and contain all references to allegations of rule breaches and supporting materials. A copy of the report should be provided to the employee sufficiently in advance of the hearing so that they may provide an adequate and thorough response in advance. The report should be presented to the disciplinary panel. The panel may take the opportunity to ask relevant questions. The employee to which allegations are made should be entitled to present a written document containing their response to each of the allegations made. They should have an opportunity during the hearing to respond verbally and make submissions. The company's internal procedures may also allow for the accused employee to be supported at the hearing by a friend or colleague.

8.42 Consideration should be given to recording the hearing so that any need to refer back to what was discussed during the hearing can be easily accommodated. Finally, the decision of the panel should be fully articulated and set out in writing.

8.43 It may be the case that employment law will require an internal appeals process to be offered to the employee should he wish to challenge the decision of the hearing.

8.44 It should be noted that, despite the thoroughness of any internal disciplinary system, it may be open to the employee to commence some form of employment proceedings against the company should they be dismissed. The thoroughness with which the employing company had prepared the disciplinary case and the fairness in which the case has been dealt with will assist the company is defending such action.

8.45 Following the outcome of the hearing, the firm and the compliance department may wish to publish the outcome of the matter. This can be a useful way of ensuring that employees of the organisation are aware of the type of rule breaches that can happen and the manner in which the company deals with them. It does, however, serve little purpose to use this method of communication as a form of retribution against the employee who has caused the rule breach and serious consideration should be given to avoiding naming any specific members of staff. However, a communication setting out in detail the events leading up to the breach, the rules in question that have been breached, the reasons why the breaches occurred and the action that the firm has taken can help to improve the staff's understanding of compliance obligations. Moreover, such communication will help to ensure that employees have a clear statement of the seriousness the firm attaches to compliance obligations.

Employment issues

Introduction

8.46   Employment arises as a key issue in relation to compliance. There are two reasons for this. Firstly, the approved persons' regime means that anyone connected with financial services is going to have to be approved as well as the firm. Secondly, the firm must deal with its employees in a manner that both satisfies the requirements of the FSA and is within the parameters allowed by employment law and the Human Rights Act 1998. Each of these will be considered in turn.

Approved persons

8.47   The FSA have determined[1] that controlled functions fall into seven categories of job function.

1   Consultation Paper 53, Chapter 5.

Significant influence functions

Governing body functions

8.48   These consist of being:

- a director of either a company or a holding company;
- a non-executive director of a company;
- a chief executive officer. This is widely interpreted and covers joint chief executives operating under the immediate control of the board where there is more than one. In the case of a UK branch of a non-EEA insurer, the role includes the principal UK executive;
- partners and limited partners (where appropriate) are all regarded as carrying on controlled functions where the firm is primarily carrying on

regulated investment business. Limited partners whose role is that of an investor are excluded. If a partnership's primary business does not relate to specified investments but a separate part of the business does then, provided a distinct partner or set of partners deal with that aspect of the business, only they need be approved;

- directors of unincorporated associations;
- those directing or regulating the specified activities of a small friendly society; and
- sole traders.

Required controlled functions

8.49 There are four of these:

- the director or other senior member responsible for apportionment and oversight;
- the director or senior manager responsible for investment business compliance;
- the money laundering reporting officer; and
- in the case of insurance companies, the appointed actuary.

Management functions

8.50 These consist of the members of senior management reporting to the governing body in relation to the following activities:

- the financial affairs of the firm;
- setting and controlling risk exposure; and
- internal audit.

Significant management functions in relation to business and control

8.51 The functions set out at para **8.53** below are added to cover those situations where the firm concerned has senior managers whose functions are equivalent to that of a member of the firm's governing body. They do not apply if the activity is a specified activity as this would automatically be an approved persons' role. They fall into five categories of senior management:

- those operating in relation to investment services, such as the head of equities. This will often be a controlled function in any event;
- those operating in relation to other areas of the firm's business than specified investment activity, eg head of personal lending or corporate lending, head of credit card issues etc;
- those responsible for carrying out insurance underwriting other than in relation to contractually-based investments, eg head of aviation underwriting;
- those responsible for making decisions concerning the firm's own finances, eg chief corporate treasurer; and
- those responsible for back office functions.

Temporary and emergency circumstances

8.52 Should the function of undertaking such a role continue for more than eight weeks in a 12-month period, then the person primarily responsible will need to be an approved person.

Dealing with customer functions

8.53 There are seven main functions within this category:

- life and pensions advisers;
- life and pensions advisers when acting under supervision;
- pension transfer advisers: such people can also give ancillary advice in relation to packaged products;
- investment advisers, including those advising in relation to packaged products, but not life and pensions advice;
- investment advisers acting under supervision;
- corporate finance advisers; and
- advisers to underwriting members of Lloyd's in relation to becoming a syndicate member.

Dealing with customers' property

8.54 This covers two main types of activity:

- those individuals who deal or arrange deals on behalf of customers. It does not extend to execution only business and feeding orders into automatic execution systems; and
- discretionary fund management.

Appointed representatives

8.55 The FSMA 2000, s 19 states:

'No person may carry on a regulated activity in the United Kingdom, or purport to do so, unless he is–

(a) an authorised person; or

(b) an exempt person.'

8.56 There is a continuation of the exception that existed under the previous regime whereby the FSMA 2000, s 39 exempts appointed representatives. An 'appointed representative' is defined by the section as being: someone who is

'(a) a party to a contract with an unauthorised person (his principal) which–

     (i) permits or requires him to carry on business of a prescribed
description, and

     (ii) complies with such requirements as may be prescribed, and

  (b) is someone for whose activities in carrying on the whole or part of
that business his principal has accepted responsibility in writing.'

8.57 Anyone satisfying this description is exempt from the general
prohibition in relation to any regulated activity when they are acting within
the remit of the area of business for which their principal has accepted
responsibility. Thus, the principal will be responsible for the appointed
representative's acts[1] and will therefore need to be an authorised person.
There is some protection for the principal, though, as the FSMA, s 39(6)
states that 'nothing…is to cause the knowledge or intentions of an appointed
representative to be attributed to his principal for the purpose of determining
whether the principal has committed an offence, unless in all the
circumstances it is reasonable for them to be attributed to him'.

1   FSMA 2000, s 39(4).

8.58 Under the FSMA 2000, s 40 applications to carry on regulated
activities can be made by individuals as well as corporate entities,
partnerships and unincorporated associations.

CHAPTER 9

Ensuring international and national co-ordination

Introduction

9.1   Recent years have seen the increasing internationalisation of banking, insurance and other financial services businesses. Coupled with this has been a breaking down of the barriers that traditionally existed between the various parts of the financial services industry. This is against a background of an ever increasing proportion of the world's wealth being reflected in capital flows, some related to international trade but the majority by way of investment. The proportion of capital flows in developing markets that is accounted for by the private sector has also increased rapidly. In 1989 it accounted for less than 50%; by 1999 it was over 80%[1]. As a consequence, the regulation of financial services has become a task requiring a far wider range of activities than used to be the case. This is a primary reason for the creation of the FSA in the UK. In addition, it is necessary, in an increasingly inter-linked world, for there to be an agreed set of international standards by which financial institutions should be regulated. This does not require total commonality, but a large degree of equivalence is certainly highly desirable to facilitate economic stability and sustained economic growth. There is also evidence from the recent economic crisis in Asia that a failure to create high quality economic regulation can both facilitate a financial crisis and aggravate it when it arises. In addition, the extent to which world capital markets have become integrated has limited the ability of national regulators to monitor firms effectively without a considerable degree of international co-operation[2].

1   International Standards and Codes to Strengthen Financial Systems, Financial Stability Forum, April 2001.
2   Little, Parry and Taylor *Bond Markets: Law and regulation*, p 221, Sweet & Maxwell, London, 1999.

9.2   The proposals considered below which help develop a set of international financial regulations articulate five key features[1]. It represents a reform of the nexus of international financial regulation; a bringing together of a group of limited codes and standards; international collaboration between a disparate set of linked codes and standards; international collaboration between a disparate set of states, markets, financial regulators and financial institutions. It engages both international and domestic compliance assessments and there is a clear acceptance that there is a direct relationship between adopting such regulations and codes, and maintaining financial stability.

1   Y V Reddy *Issues in Implementing International Financial Standards and Codes*, Centre for Banking Studies at the Central Bank of Sri Lanka, Colombo, 28 June 2001.

9.3   The motivation is also clear. In the words of a G7 Communiqué[1]:

'Close international co-operation in the regulation and supervision of financial institutions and markets is essential to the continued safeguarding of the financial system and to prevent erosion of necessary prudential standards.'

1   Background Document, *Review of International Financial Institutions*, pp 9–10, Halifax summit, 15–17 June 1995.

9.4   At a national level co-operation is much less of a problem. Home state regulators have long since had agreements in place to deal with the issues of co-operation. In the UK the width and extent of the SFA's powers reduce the scale of the problem. It can carry out most of the regulatory steps itself. In instances where it cannot do so, there are provisions in place to facilitate them. The real issues arise in the context of international and pan European regulation.

Organisations

9.5   A number of bodies stand out as being key players in this process. In alphabetical order they are:

- *The Basel Committee on Banking Supervision*. This provides a meeting place for the central banks of the G10 countries and facilitates co-operation on the regulation of banking.
- *Committee on Payment and Settlement Systems*. Also created by the G10 central banks this, as its name suggests, provides a meeting place for those central banks on matters arising in relation to payment and settlement systems. Their concern is not limited to domestic considerations but extends to cross-border operations and netting. Much of their work concerns supervisory standards and recommendations of best practice.
- *Financial Action Task Force*. Created by the G7, its role is to ascertain the threat to financial institutions from money laundering and to recommend steps that can be taken to counter this. There are now 29

member states and a key function of the Task Force is to monitor the extent to which these countries are taking appropriate steps to deal with the problem.

- *Financial Stability Forum.* Following a meeting of the Finance Ministers and Central Bank Governors of the G7 countries, Hans Tietmeyer, the then President of the Bundesbank, was commissioned to draft a report considering what new structures might be appropriate to improve co-operation between the existing national and international regulatory bodies. The aim was to facilitate increased stability in the regulation of world finance and financial services. As a consequence of the report he produced, the Forum was created.
- *International Accounting Standards Board.* The aim of this institution is to bring about the convergence of accounting standards. This is of importance, partly in increasing the financial safety by having high common standards, and also in reducing the risk of financial failure or loss to investors due to accounts not representing a true and fair view in the generally understood meaning of the words.
- *International Association of Insurance Supervisors.* Its purpose is to develop a set of generally accepted standards in this area to increase the effectiveness of insurance regulation. Over 100 states have become members.
- *International Federation of Accountants.* This is made up of the national accountancy bodies that represent accountants involved in the public sector, large organisations and commerce and industry. Its primary aim is to increase the quality of the accounting regulations and increase their international equivalence.
- *International Monetary Fund.* This is the body that sets international standards in relation to overseeing the world's monetary system. It has created a range of standards in relation to monetary and fiscal policy and has assisted in creating methods of assessment for the standards used for the supervision of banking and insurance.
- *International Organisation of Securities Commissions.* As its name implies, this is an organisation made up of the securities and derivatives regulators of the member countries. Its main purpose is to create high standards to govern the regulation of the securities markets.
- *Organisation for Economic Co-operation and Development.* The aim of this body is to promote world economic growth and to this end it promotes the development of financial markets regulation to a high common standard.
- *The World Bank.* This aims to reduce poverty in the world by facilitating private investment in the regions concerned.

Key standards

9.6 In its role as a facilitator of increased international co-operation the Financial Stability Forum has issued a set of 12 standards which it believes are a pre-requisite to creating a system of stable, well regulated financial systems. These are as follows:

Subject Area	Key Standard	Issuing Body
Macroeconomic Policy and Data Transparency		
Monetary and financial policy transparency	Code of Good Practices on Transparency in Monetary and Financial Policies	IMF
Fiscal policy transparency	Code of Good Practices on Fiscal Transparency	IMF
Data dissemination	Special Data Dissemination Standard (SDDS) General Data Dissemination System (GDDS)	IMF
Institutional and Market Infrastructure		
Insolvency	Principles and Guidelines on Effective Insolvency and Creditor Rights Systems	World Bank
Corporate governance	Principles of Corporate Governance	OECD
Accounting	International Accounting Standards (IAS)	IASB
Auditing	International Standards on Auditing (ISA)	IFAC
Payment and settlement	Core Principles for Systemically Important Payment Systems	CPSS
Market integrity	The Forty Recommendations of the Financial Action Task Force on Money Laundering	FATF
Financial Regulation and Supervision		
Banking supervision	Core Principles for Effective Banking Supervision	BCBS
Securities regulation	Objectives and Principles of Securities Regulation	IOSCO
Insurance supervision	Insurance Core Principles	IAIS

9.7   The 12 standards are dealt with in turn.

Code of Good Practices on Transparency in Monetary and Financial Policies

9.8   The essence of this is that it highlights the approaches that create the appropriate level of transparency to enable the public to assess what is happening and thus facilitate accountability. The Code specifically highlights four key areas:

- roles, responsibility and objectives should be clearly stated;
- policy decisions should have clearly defined processes determining how they are reached and reported;
- policies and information pertinent to them should be publicly available; and
- accountable systems should exist to guarantee integrity.

Code of Good Practices on Fiscal Transparency

9.9   The role of transparency is critical in that it makes the regulatory authorities more accountable. To facilitate this the Code provides four principles:

- that the roles and responsibilities of those involved should be clear;
- there should be access to the information by the public;
- that key financial steps such as budgets, accounts and financial reports should be publicly available; and
- integrity should be underpinned by independent means.

Data dissemination

9.10   There are two key agreements in this area. The first is the Special Data Dissemination Standard issued by the IMF. This was produced to resolve the problem of instability induced, if only in part, by insufficient information being available in the marketplace. Those countries who subscribe (and the significant economies already do) agree to satisfy this function in four key regards and to do so in standard form:

- that data, particularly regarding reserves and foreign currency holdings should be made publicly available, promptly and at appropriate periods;
- that the public should be informed of the dates on which such data will be available;
- clear laws determining both the above and proposed changes in the same, coupled with government access to data and comment being released by the relevant government officials; and

- the making available to the public of information to articulate how the data should be formulated and of any other material against which it can be assessed.

9.11   The second is the General Data Dissemination System, also issued by the IMF. This is more severe in its demands than the Special Data Dissemination Standard and the developed economies are expected to apply it. It requires that detailed, high quality information relating to financial, economic and social issues be made publicly available on a timely basis. It adopts the same four-stage structure as the Special Data Dissemination Standard.

Principles and Guidelines on Effective Insolvency and Creditor Rights Systems

9.12   The existence of a clear, fair set of rights for creditors is a key ingredient for a stable economy. It also assists commercial lenders in determining the degree of risk they are taking on. This has been primarily driven by the World Bank, the United Nations Commission of International Trade Law, the IMF and INSOL.

Principles of Corporate Governance

9.13   This is a system of corporate regulation which applies to a company when it determines its objectives, seeks to achieve them and in assessing its performance. It is crucial to have such regulation to create a high quality corporate environment to attract international capital. Key issues to be found within corporate governance regulations are:

- shareholder rights;
- stakeholder rights (this is a contentious area in terms of its future development);
- disclosure of information; and
- Board responsibility.

International Accounting Standards

9.14   A succession of international accounting standards have been issued to determine the extent of the detail, range, relevance and reliability of the information to be included in the accounts. To represent a true and fair view accounts must be regulated by clear and detailed regulation. There are specific types of accounts, those relating to banks, securities houses and insurance companies for example, which give rise to specific issues when determining what should be included.

International Standards on Auditing

9.15   If there are to be accepted standards of accountancy then it follows that there must also be internationally accepted standards of auditing to maintain it. The standards on auditing that have been issued cover:

- audit responsibilities;
- audit planning;
- internal controls;
- evidence;
- practice statements relating to international auditing;
- external auditing; and
- audit characteristics and considerations.

Core Principles for Systemically Important Payment Systems

9.16   To function in a stable way financial markets require stable, effective settlement systems. The aim of the Core Principles is to facilitate this by requiring a degree of safety and efficiency in these systems. The Principles themselves require that domestic and international payment systems satisfy criteria relating to design and operation. Guidance is also provided on interpreting the Principles.

The Forty Recommendations of the Financial Action Task Force on Money Laundering

9.17   These were intended to provide a set of recommendations which, if followed, would optimise the response of banking and financial bodies that were being used to launder illegal money. They cover areas such as:

- criminal justice systems;
- law enforcement;
- the banking and financial systems;
- banking and financial regulation; and
- international co-operation.

9.18   All member states are subject to periodic mutual analysis to determine whether they are satisfying the recommendations. They must also carry out an annual self assessment exercise to the same end.

Core Principles for Effective Banking Supervision

9.19   To assist in stabilising the world's banking system the Basel Committee on Banking Supervision have published a set of 25 Core

Principles and additional criteria for banking supervision. These cover issues such as:

- the preconditions for effective banking supervision;
- licensing requirements;
- ongoing banking supervision;
- powers of supervisors; and
- cross-border banking.

Objectives and Principles of Securities Regulation

9.20 IOSCO have published a set of objectives and principles to help bring about a system of sound regulation of the securities markets. The key objectives are:

- protecting investors;
- making sure the markets function in a fair, efficient and transparent manner; and
- reducing the risk of systemic failure.

9.21 There are also 30 Principles relating to securities regulation.

Insurance Core Principles

9.22 As their name implies, these were produced to facilitate that the regulatory supervision of the insurance industry is taking place at a suitably proficient and effective manner. The Principles themselves cover key areas such as:

- the role of supervisors;
- licensing of insurance companies;
- corporate governance of insurance companies;
- prudential controls;
- market conduct;
- monitoring by the regulator; and
- sanctions for failure to satisfy the regulations.

Monitoring regulatory observance

9.23 Clearly, it is insufficient to create a series of desirable standards without some system for ascertaining whether they are being subscribed to in practice. States themselves will sometimes carry out research into the state of affairs within their own jurisdiction. In addition, the IMF and the World Bank both produce reports on the extent to which the standards and codes discussed above are being met. The IMF has produced them in relation to the distribution of data and fiscal transparency. The World Bank has done so in relation to accounting, auditing, corporate governance, insolvency and creditors' rights. How well standards in the financial sector are carried out and what the priorities need to be to rectify any shortcomings are dealt with under the auspices of the joint IMF and World Bank 'Financial Sector Assessment Programme'.

Facilitating regulatory observance

9.24   The Financial Stability Forum has suggested[1] that member states could take a number of key steps to facilitate awareness and observance of regulatory standards:

- an ongoing campaign should be run to raise the level of awareness in their financial centres as to the requirements of the standards;
- the bodies creating the standards in the first place should themselves facilitate and encourage this process of education;
- the bodies creating the standards and the national regulators should help explain how satisfying the requirements of the standards will help avoid certain types of risk. In this context explaining how past market problems have led to the standards will assist;
- external assessments of the application of standards should be undertaken by the bodies setting the standards;
- peer discussions should be encouraged to facilitate the implementation of standards; and
- technical advice and training should be provided by the more developed states to the others.

1   Report of the Follow-up Group on Incentives to Foster Implementation of Standards, 7/8 September 2000.

9.25   There are a number of reasons why this is thought necessary. The importance of the standards is primarily in that they facilitate a sound financial system. To this end it is important that not only the authorities, but also relevant private bodies, should put them into effect.

Key issues other than regulatory observance

9.26   Turning to the regulated financial institutions themselves, there are factors other than the quality of regulation that will determine whether institutions will proceed with a financial arrangement[1]. A suitable legal system and framework are vital. Key elements are efficiency, transparency and a predictable outcome in the sense that it should be determined by clearly stated laws rather than other factors. In some states it can prove difficult to successfully pursue certain parties through their courts due to corruption. Political risk and economic fundamentals also need to be within acceptable levels. If not, there will be no point pursuing a financial arrangement further. Parties do not always fully understand how the regulations relate to the risks they were created to try and manage.

1   Information provided to the Financial Stability Forum by market participants.

9.27   Some firms are by their very nature less concerned with regulatory issues. The international investment portfolios managed by those such as hedge funds, pension funds and insurance companies are more concerned with market analysis that relates to capitalisation.

9.28   Rating agencies are a key source of information and their role in providing assessments will involve an analysis of supervisory and regulatory issues as well as financial and market issues.

Consequences of regulatory failure

9.29   There are instances of countries having lax regulatory controls and surviving for some time with no serious problems. However, the absence of a system of decent controls both increases the risk of a crisis arising and of it becoming systemic, leading to a larger scale problem when it does. The Asian financial crisis of 1998 has been generally regarded as having been partly caused by lax regulation[1]. In addition, the crisis was able to develop to a greater extent before it became apparent that it was occurring than should have been the case because of poor corporate governance and a lack of transparency. This was exacerbated by the high proportion of businesses in the area that were owned and managed by the same people which, coupled with traditional business practices, resulted in weak corporate governance. Then, as the crisis accelerated, those outside the countries concerned were unable to draw a distinction between those institutions in the states concerned that were a real risk and those that were not. This resulted in a flight of matured short-term debt and a refusal by those outside the jurisdictions to hold debt and equity securities denominated in those states' currencies due to fear of devaluation[2].

1   68th Annual Report, Bank for International Settlements, 8 June 1998.
2   See 'Causes, Effects and Regulatory Implications of Financial and Economic Turbulence in Emerging Markets', Emerging Markets Committee, The International Organisation of Securities Commissions, September 1998.

9.30   The key steps deemed necessary to reduce the risk of such a crisis in the future were[1]:

• increasing transparency;
• enhancing the free flow of capital;

- strengthening states' financial systems;
- leaving the responsibility and risk associated with lending with the private institutions responsible; and
- increasing the involvement of international financial institutions.

1   'Strengthening the Architecture of the Global Financial System', G7, 1998.

9.31   It has been suggested that[1] the larger credit rating agencies have an important role to play in this context.

1   Robert Chote 'Crystal Balls in Washington' and Gerard Baker 'Tea Leaves in Jakarta' in *Financial Times*, 17 April 1998.

Memoranda of understanding

9.32   The main way in which international co-operation has been put in place is through memoranda of understanding. Originally these tended to be bi-lateral but, more recently, a multi-lateral approach seems to have gained ground. A considerable amount of work has gone into key issues such as the exchange of information between regulators to arrive at the best design for such memoranda[1]. These agreements do not impose legally binding obligations on the signatories. Nor can they override domestic laws and regulations. What they can do, however, is give rise to a much freer flow of information between regulators than would otherwise be the case. This facilitates the national regulators building a more accurate picture of the financial scene of which they are regulating one part. It is important to bear in mind that a memorandum of understanding is not always a pre-requisite to co-operation being provided. For example, the US Exchange Act specifically allows the SEC to utilise its powers to assist foreign regulators if there is no memorandum of understanding in place. They are also mandated to try and develop reciprocal arrangements with states that are not in a position to sign them. Nonetheless, they represent the most effective and comprehensive way of proceeding.

1   Working Party on Enforcement and Exchange of Information, IOSCO, 1990.

9.33   The Principles that the IOSCO Report of 1990 suggested as giving rise to an optimal memorandum of understanding are that the memoranda should provide for assistance to an investigation from an overseas state requesting information even if the behaviour under investigation would not be a breach of the laws or regulations of the country from which it is requested. If that is not possible because of the laws of a state signing a memorandum then they should request a change in their domestic law to permit it. This principle overrides what has been a long-standing principle of extradition type laws, namely that someone can only be extradited if the offence concerned is one in both the requesting state and the requested. This has to be overridden in the context of financial regulation as otherwise it would be impossible to police international financial organisations effectively. A decision could be made in a part of a financial organisation in one country to do something that was a breach of financial regulation in another. If the regulator in the state where the offence occurred were to find out there would be little they could do to proceed against the parties responsible without a memorandum drafted on the basis of this principle. They could otherwise only take steps against the branch or subsidiary in their own jurisdiction which may be insufficient.

9.34 This has been a particular issue for the US. US law does not require that, when a non-US regulator seeks assistance, the events concerned must also be an offence in the US. This is important as US securities laws generally tend to be wider than the securities laws of other countries[1]. However, reciprocity arises in another way in that the Exchange Act requires the SEC to consider whether the overseas regulator would reciprocate were the SEC to request assistance from them. If not then assistance should be refused.

1   Berman *A Practical Guide to SEC Regulation outside the United States*, p 246, City & Financial Publishing, 2000.

9.35 That a memorandum should provide that information received by a regulator should be treated 'with the highest possible level of confidentiality'[1]. This is stated to mean that the information should be treated with the same degree of confidentiality as domestically acquired information. The memorandum should also give the authority that is asked for information the opportunity to say what degree of confidentiality should be attached to the information provided.

1   Principles of Memoranda of Understanding. Report of Working Party No 4, IOSCO p 1.

9.36 The memorandum should also set out the procedures to be followed in requesting information and in responding to such requests. This is a fundamental issue to be agreed and, in most cases, one that should not be too difficult for the parties to agree on.

9.37 The memorandum should state that, when an investigation is going on in one state as a result of a request from a regulator in a second state, it should not impact on the rights that a person has in the first state. This is necessary because otherwise the memorandum will find itself inoperable in the first state. In many nations the rights concerned will be constitutional ones, and so the matter is not negotiable.

9.38 The memorandum should contain an agreement that the signatories will consult with each other during the period of operation of the memorandum. The need for this could become apparent when there is a difference of view as to whether assistance should be provided in a particular case. It is also hoped that the facility for consultation will give rise to a relaxed relationship between the regulators concerned. Highlighted by IOSCO are three situations where consultation is likely to be particularly important: namely where unforeseen circumstances arise, where there is an overlap of jurisdiction and where one country's laws or regulations change.

9.39   As a matter of political and legal reality, it is accepted that there must be a public policy exclusion. This permits a regulator to refuse to provide assistance to a request where to do so would violate the public policy of its state. The IOSCO Report defines public policy in this context as being 'issues affecting sovereignty, national security or other essential interests[1]'. This may prove a narrower definition than that which some state's judges may give it.

1   IOSCO, p 3.

9.40   The memorandum should provide that the signatories take all reasonable steps to utilise fully their powers when faced with a request for information. This should include obtaining documents and, where appropriate, testimony from witnesses, giving access to any relevant non-public files they may have and carrying out inspections of the regulated entity concerned in the investigation. This is a particularly important principle given that there have been instances of regulators refusing to provide information that it can obtain from the regulated firm on a voluntary basis because of an unwillingness to enforce requests for information against the firm. In some cases this has occurred for legal reasons.

9.41   There should be an agreement allowing an authority requesting assistance to take part directly in its execution. This can be useful in cases where the investigating authority is the one with most of the background information on the issue concerned. In addition, it may be the case when the investigation proceeds further that the requesting authority starts to find information that it would not have been able to request in the first place because it could not have known of its existence.

9.42   Finally, the memorandum should allow the regulator being requested to provide assistance to share the costs with the regulator requesting it. This would be important in cases where an investigation were likely to prove expensive, especially where the regulator being requested to provide assistance has limited resources. It could also prove relevant if, over a period of time, one regulator finds itself requesting more information from another than is requested in return. It is useful to have a mechanism for dealing with this.

9.43   In addition, FESCOPOL has published a suggested multilateral memorandum of understanding. FESCOPOL is made up of the senior officials of the bodies responsible for overseeing securities activity in their own states in the EEA. Its aim is to bring about the sharing of information between its members. The multilateral memorandum has five aims[1]:

- investigating, enforcing and monitoring laws and regulations relating to insider dealing, market manipulation and other types of fraudulent or manipulative behaviour in relation to securities;
- investigating, enforcing and monitoring compliance with laws and regulations relating to dealing in, advising on, managing, administering and safekeeping securities;
- making sure that authorisation and licensing requirements are satisfied;
- supervising the financial markets and, in particular, clearing, settlement and OTC securities transactions;
- monitoring and enforcing compliance with laws and regulations relating to the issuing of securities.

The multilateral memorandum of understanding is reproduced below as an appendix to this chapter.

1   http://www.europefesco.org/ul/pFescopol.htm

Appendix: Multilateral memorandum of understanding on the exchange of information and surveillance of securities activities

9.44   The members of the Forum of European Securities Commissions (FESCO).

Considering the provisions of European Directives in the financial field stating that the closest co-operation should take place between the competent authorities of the Member States for the purpose of carrying out their duties;

Considering the increasing internationalisation, harmonisation and interdependence of European Financial Markets due eg to the use of modern technology, closer co-operation between European exchanges and the completion of Internal Market for financial services;

Considering that broader objectives have been set by the members of FESCO as competent Authorities of the Contracting States of the European Economic Area (EFA) in order to achieve a successful oversight of the European financial markets;

Considering the means stated in the FESCO Charter to achieve these objectives, in particular those relating to the provision of the broadest possible mutual assistance, and the strengthening of cross-border co-operation in order to enhance investor protection to promote the integrity of financial markets and more generally to facilitate performance of the supervisory functions and the effective enforcement of the laws and regulations governing the markets;

Considering that such approach entails the sharing of different types of information given the various duties vested in the Authorities;

Considering that the most expedient way to achieve a necessary consensus is a Memorandum of Understanding;

The FESCO Members have thus reached the following understanding:

Article 1 – Principles

Without prejudice to the provisions set forth by the EU legislation, the purpose of this Multilateral Memorandum of Understanding is to establish a general framework for co-operation and consultation between the Authorities referred to hereinafter in order to facilitate the fulfilling of their supervisory responsibilities.

Article 2 – Definitions

1. 'Authority' means any member of FESCO as listed in Annex A (not reproduced).
2. 'Requested Authority' means the Authority to whom a request is made under this Multilateral Memorandum of Understanding.
3. 'Requesting Authority' means the Authority making a request under this Multilateral Memorandum of Understanding.
4. 'Laws or regulations' means any laws or regulations in force in the respective states of the Authorities.
5. 'Person' means any natural or legal person.
6. 'Securities' means shares, bonds and other forms of securitised debts, futures and derivative products including commodity derivatives units of undertakings in collective investment schemes and other financial products traded in the respective states of the Authorities.
7. 'Financial markets' means EEA regulated markets as defined in the Council Directive 93/22/EEC of 10 May 1993 on investment services in the securities field (Investment Services Directive, ISD) and any other securities and derivatives market supervised by a competent authority.
8. 'Intermediary' means any investment firm, bank, collective investment scheme and any other person acting within the scope of competence of the Authorities.
9. 'Issuer' means a person making an offer to the public or seeking listing of a security.

Article 3 – Scope of assistance

1. The Authorities shall provide each other with the fullest mutual assistance in any matters falling within the competence of the Authorities including, in particular, the following areas:

   a. investigations and enforcement in connection with applicable laws or regulations relating to insider dealing, market manipulation and other fraudulent or manipulative practices in the securities field;
   b. investigation and enforcement of, and monitoring compliance with applicable laws and regulations relating to dealing in, advising on and the management, administration and safekeeping of securities;
   c. checking that the conditions for the taking up of (or continuing in) business as an intermediary are met (including eg the enforcement of requirements to be authorised);
   d. enforcing and monitoring compliance with applicable laws and regulations relating to the disclosure of interests in securities, takeover bids or the acquisition of influence over financial intermediaries;
   e. the supervision of the Financial Markets, including the clearing and settlement, the monitoring and surveillance of OTC-transactions in securities listed on EEA regulated markets as defined in the ISD;
   f. enforcing or monitoring compliance with applicable laws relating to the duties of issuers and offerors of securities in relation to the disclosure of information.

2. In cases where the information requested may be maintained by or available to, another authority within the country of the Requested Authority, the Authorities will endeavour to provide full assistance in obtaining the information requested to the extent permitted by law. If necessary the Requested Authority shall provide the Requesting Authority with sufficient information to establish direct contact between the Requesting Authority and the other authority.

3. If the request for assistance is made on the basis of regulations under European law it must be in line with these regulations. In other cases the Requested Authority may only refuse to act on a request for assistance where communication of the information might adversely affect the sovereignty, security or public policy of the State of the Requested Authority or where judicial proceedings for the imposition of criminal penalties have already been initiated in the jurisdiction of the Requested Authority in respect of the same actions and against the same persons or, on the grounds that the provision of assistance might re-stilt in a judicial or administrative sanction being imposed where a non appealable judicial or administrative sanction has already been imposed, in the jurisdiction of the Requested Authority in respect of the same actions, and against the same persons.

4. To the extent permitted by their respective national law and procedures and without prior request each Authority should provide any other

Authority with any relevant factual information available to it and which it believes to be helpful to the other Authority for the discharge of its functions and for the purposes which may specify in the communication (unsolicited information).

Article 4 – Requests for assistance

1. Requests for assistance shall be made in writing and addressed to the contact person of the Requested Authority listed in Annex B (not reproduced).
2. In case of emergency, requests for information and replies to such requests may be transmitted orally provided that these requests are confirmed in the manner required in this Article unless the Requested Authority agrees to waive such requirements.
3. To the extent available to the Requesting Authority and in order to facilitate the Requested Authority's work the Request should specify the following:

   a. a description of the subject matter of the request and the purpose for which the information is sought and the reasons why this information will be of assistance;

   b. a description of the specific information requested by the Requesting Authority: in case of discharging their responsibilities pursuant to European directives or regulations the Requesting Authority shall also name these directives and regulations;

   c. in so far as the request results from investigations of violations of any laws or regulations a short description of the relevant provisions that may have been violated and if known to the Requesting Authority a list of the persons or institutions believed by the Requesting Authority to possess the information sought or the places where such information may he obtained:

   d. in so far as the request concerns information relating to transactions in specific securities.

      • a description of the securities in question as precise as possible (including eg the securities code),
      • the names of those firms with whose dealings in the securities the Requesting Authority is concerned,
      • the dates between which transactions in the securities are considered relevant for the purposes of the request,
      • the names of any persons on whose behalf relevant transactions in the securities are believed or suspected to have been entered into;

   e. in so far as the request relates to information concerning the business or activities of any person such precise information as the Requesting Authority is able to provide so as to enable such persons to be identified;

   f. an indication of the sensitivity of the information contained in the request and whether the Requesting Authority is content for the fact that it has made the request to be disclosed to persons whom the Requested Authority may need to approach for information;

   g. whether the Requesting Authority is or has been in contact with any other authority or law enforcement agency in the State of the Requested Authority in relation to the subject matter or the request;

   h. any other Authority whom the Requesting Authority is aware has an active interest in the subject matter of the request:

   i. an indication of the urgency of the request, or the desired time period for the reply.

Article 5 – Execution of requests for assistance

1. To the extent permitted by law the Requested Authority shall make all reasonable steps to obtain and provide the information sought.
2. The Requested Authority shall use the relevant means at its disposal for the execution of the request. The Authorities shall consult and agree on the types of enquiry that may be necessary for the execution of a request.

To the extent permitted by law the Requesting Authority shall provide the Requested Authority with such further assistance as may reasonably be required for the efficient execution of the request including the provision of further information as to the circumstances surrounding the request staff or other resources.

Without prejudice to the provisions set forth by the EU legislation relating to the inspection of branches, the Authorities will consider (to the extent permitted by law) conducting joint investigations in cases where the request for assistance concerns violations of laws or regulations where it would assist in the effective investigation of the alleged violations. The Authorities should consult to define the procedures to be adopted for conducting any joint investigation, the sharing of work and responsibilities and the follow up actions to such investigations.

Article 6 – Permissible uses of the information exchanged and confidentiality

1. If the information is exchanged pursuant to the provisions of any of the Relevant European Directives, the Requesting Authority shall observe the requirements of the Directives.
2. If the information is not exchanged pursuant to the provisions of any of the relevant European Directives, the Authorities shall use the information exchanged solely for the purposes of:

   a. securing compliance with or enforcement of the domestic laws or regulations specified in the Request:

b. initiating, conducting or assisting in criminal administrative, civil or disciplinary proceedings resulting from the violation of the laws or regulations specified in the Request;

c. any of the particular purposes specified in Act 3(1)a–f to the extent that they are administered by the Requesting Authority.

The Authorities to which unsolicited information is supplied will use this information solely for the purposes stated in the transmission letter or for the purposes of criminal or administrative proceedings or for the discharge of the obligation to report to judicial authorities.

3. To the extent permitted by law each Authority will keep confidential any request for assistance made under this Multilateral Memorandum of Understanding the contents of such requests and the information received under this Multilateral Memorandum of Understanding as well as the matter arising in the course of its operation, in particular consultations between Authorities.

4. If an Authority intends to use or disclose information furnished under this Memorandum for any purpose other than those stated in this Article and in the request, it must obtain the prior consent of the Authority which provided the information. If the Requested Authority consents to the use of the information for purposes other than those stated, it may subject it to certain conditions.

5. Nothing in paragraphs 2 and 3 of this Article shall prevent an Authority from using or disclosing information in circumstances where such use or disclosure is required in order to comply with the obligations under European Directives.

6. If an Authority decides to make public an administrative or a disciplinary sanction within the course of its duties it may, with the consent of the Authority providing the information, indicate that the successful outcome of the case has been achieved with the aid of the international co-operation mechanisms provided for in this Multilateral Memorandum of Understanding.

Article 7 – Consultations

The Authorities will review the implementation of this Multilateral Memorandum of Understanding regularly and conduct consultations in order to improve its operation and to resolve possible difficulties.

Article 8 – FESCO Exchange of Information and Surveillance Co-ordination Group

Senior officials of each Authority who are responsible for the surveillance of securities activities and the exchange of information should meet regularly, in particular in order to clarify issues of co-operation. FESCO shall specify the particulars regarding the frequency and the organisation of such meetings. Senior officials of Authorities pursuing enquiries in the same or related matters may meet to co-ordinate their activities where appropriate.

The Authorities may where appropriate invite senior officials from other competent authorities of Member States of the European Union or of the Contracting States of the European Economic Area, which are responsible for the surveillance or securities activities and the exchange of information, also to take part in such meetings.

Article 9 – List of regulated markets and directory of competent authorities

1. The Authorities will submit any changes to the list of regulated markets as referred to in this Multilateral Memorandum of Understanding in Article 2(7) and enclosed as Annex C (not reproduced) to this Multilateral Memorandum of Understanding and make available the relevant rules of procedures and operation of these regulated markets upon request. The Authorities might consider making available the list of regulated markets under their respective jurisdiction on their Internet homepages.
2. The Authorities will provide each other with a directory of competent authorities within their jurisdictions, setting out the responsibilities of each body. In case of any changes thereto the respective Authority will provide the other Authorities with an updated version of the directory.

Article 10 – Amendments to the multilateral memorandum of understanding

The Authorities may by common consent make amendments and add further Annexes to the Multilateral Memorandum of Understanding they consider necessary.

Article 11 – Additional parties

The Authorities which are members of FESCO shall by common consent agree that further authorities of the Member States of the European Union or of the Contracting States of be European Economic Area become party to this Multilateral Memorandum of Understanding by execution of the Joinder Agreement appended hereto as Annex D (not reproduced).

Article 12 – Publication

The Authorities agree to publish this Multilateral Memorandum of Understanding.

Article 13 – Relations between this multilateral memorandum of understanding and the other bilateral memoranda signed by FESCO authorities

This Multilateral Memorandum of Understanding replaces any conflicting provision which is more restrictive to co-operation contained in bilateral Memoranda of Understanding signed prior to the date of its entry into effect.

Article 14 – Entry into effect and termination

1. This Multilateral Memorandum of Understanding shall be effective as to the undersigned at the date set out below this Article. It shall be effective as to additional parties at the date set out in the Joinder Agreement (Annex D – not reproduced).
2. This Multilateral Memorandum of Understanding shall be concluded for an unlimited period of time and may be denounced by any of the Authorities at any time by giving at least thirty days prior written notice to each other Authority. If the Requested Authority undertakes to denounce the Multilateral Memorandum of Understanding, requests for information communicated before the effective date of denunciation will still be processed under this Multilateral Memorandum of Understanding.

Article 15 – Annual report

FESCO shall prepare an Annual Report setting forth the result achieved in using and complying with the present Memorandum. The report shall be published within the first quarter of each year starting in the year 2000.

CHAPTER 10

Dealing with regulators and law enforcement

Managing the relationship with your regulator

Introduction

10.1 This chapter considers methods that may be utilised to best manage a firm's relationship with its regulators. The first part of this chapter considers a general approach to managing regulator relations, including methods to develop a working relationship, report rule breaches, manage regulator supervision visits and any potential regulator investigations. The second part considers the more contentious area of managing enforcement actions that may be taken against a firm by a regulatory authority, the effect that such actions may have on a firm and whether firms should, as part of general risk management, have in place an action plan to deal with potential enforcement issues.

Managing regulator relations

10.2 Historically, UK financial services regulators' focus on firms has been between desk-based paper supervision, such annual returns that compile details of the firm's business levels, numbers of registered individuals and capital requirements, and periodic supervision visits. Such supervision visits have been undertaken within timescales that only expose an authorised firm to a visit perhaps once every three years. Regulators that have applied this approach will have attempted, during such a visit, to review every aspect of the firm's business. This necessitates the regulator's staff in undertaking a very broad review of a firm, attempting to understand the firm's entire approach to the conduct of its business in a very limited period of time. Under the FSA's revised approach to supervision, it is considered that such a broad and infrequent approach to supervision is inapplicable. It considers it more appropriate to keep regular contact with member firms that pose a higher risk to the investment market, meeting with the member firm and senior staff regularly, and getting to understand the firm's approach to business. It will leave lower-risk firms to desk-based supervision and potential for supervision visits relating to regulatory themes.

10.3   Notwithstanding this revised approach to supervision, there is a great deal of merit for member firms to develop and maintain a good working relationship with their regulator. Compliance departments and senior management of a firm will benefit greatly from maintaining regular contact with a regulator's supervision staff and senior personnel at their regulatory agency.

10.4   An authorised firm should consider establishing a programme of regular contact with its regulator's supervision staff. The contact should be conducted with a view to ensuring that the firm's business model and approach to regulatory obligations are explained and understood by the regulatory agency. It should be acknowledged that such a programme of events can only provide comfort to the regulator and cannot be used as a method of allowing the regulator to test the firm's approach to compliance. Nonetheless, a well thought out and conducted programme of contact can significantly contribute to the development of a regulator's confidence in an authorised firm.

10.5   A firm should consider introducing a regulator to the following areas:

- its business model;
- the types of business it conducts;
- its general approach to the conduct of business;
- the organisational structure within the firm;
- the role of the compliance department;
- activities performed by the compliance department;
- a brief overview of how compliance activities are conducted;
- the experience of senior compliance staff;
- methods used by the compliance department to communicate compliance procedures and policy;
- an open and honest approach to areas of risk within the firm and how the compliance department and senior management of the firm deal with those matters.

10.6   The firm should consider the frequency with which it intends to have direct contact with the regulator's staff. For more complex firms, a contact frequency of once a quarter may be sufficient. With less complex firms, an attempt to make contact once every six months may be appropriate.

10.7   At the beginning of a firm's relationship with its regulator, whether that follows granting of authorisation or, alternatively, a change in business permission or authorised activity or even the transfer of a firm from one regulator supervision team to another, steps should be taken to explain the fundamentals of the firm's business, its regulatory history and its organisational arrangements. Thereafter, the firm should attempt to keep the regulator staff up to date with any business issues arising at the firm. Matters such as changes to senior staff or management, launch of new products or investment offerings, or changes in business direction could all be explained.

10.8 The key objectives in maintaining a programme of dialogue and communication is to ensure that the regulator has a firm understanding of the firm's business and is confident that the firm is able to deal with any regulatory issues or breaches that occur. Methods of managing potential enforcement actions brought against the firm are explored at para **10.30** ff below. However, it is fair to say that the regulator is more inclined to avoid serious enforcement action where it is confident that an authorised firm is able to deal with any rule breaches in a sound, organised and controlled manner. Whereas if the regulator holds the view that rule breaches have been caused by the firm's lack of controls and that such identified rule breaches will not be managed adequately then enforcement action is likely.

10.9 FSA Principle for Business 11 requires firms to notify the regulator of any matter which the FSA would reasonably be expected to want to be notified of. FSA Principle for Business 11 states:

> 'a firm must deal with its regulators in an open and co-operative way and must disclose to the FSA appropriately anything relating to the firm of which the FSA would reasonably expect notice.'

10.10 Firms will often be concerned about notifying the regulator of rule breaches through fear that enforcement action will occur. It should be noted, however, that it is not the notification that causes any such enforcement action but the rule breach itself. Although regulatory outcomes can never be guaranteed, the firm should consider that any enforcement action is less likely where the regulator has developed trust in a firm's ability to manage its regulatory affairs in a controlled and structured manner. The key message for all firms is that regulator staff do not like surprises. Where a regulator identifies rule breaches through its supervision activities, which they have not had prior notification of, then the investigation they may conduct is likely to be more thorough and wide ranging. Whereas, if the firm has proactively reported details of any rule breaches in a logical and controlled manner within a culture of trust between the regulator and the firm, then enforcement action is less likely.

Managing rule breach reporting

10.11 The question of whether or not to report regulatory issues or rule breaches to the regulatory agency is a difficult one for a firm and its

181

compliance staff. It is certainly the case that not all rule breaches should be reported, but a firm must be able to demonstrate that any rule breaches that have been identified have been managed internally in an appropriate manner. It may be difficult for senior management of the firm to predict whether an isolated incident or more widespread rule breach should be reported. In determining whether a report is necessary the following questions may be asked:

- Is the matter sufficiently material that the regulator will want to be notified of the matter? Materiality can be defined as something of great importance or consequence.
- Is the issue widespread within the organisation? For example, if during the firm's compliance monitoring programme it is identified that the firm has failed to meet its regulatory obligation either universally or for a statistically significant number of customers, then the firm should consider reporting this matter. However, if the incident is related to no more than one or a few customers then it may be sufficient not to report.
- Where there is a clear obligation to the regulator to make a report, such as in the requirement under the approved persons regime to make a statement in relation to the reasons for the dismissal by the firm of an approved person.

10.12   When making any report to the regulator it is essential to ensure that the manner in which the report is made is clearly composed and includes the following:

- the extent of the problem;
- the background to the problem;
- the extent of the rules breach;
- any actions taken by the organisation to identify the extent of the breach;
- the actions taken to ensure that the breach does not recur;
- actions taken to identify any liability that has been caused for customers;
- the calculated compensation due; and
- any procedural changes that have become necessary within the organisation.

10.13   It is an important element of reporting to convey a clear impression of the control the organisation has over the reported matter and corrective action it proposes to put in place to deal with the rule breaches. If the regulator concludes that there is little merit in it becoming involved in the matter it will leave the resolution of the problem to the firm. However, if the regulator feels uncomfortable with the firm's methodology in identifying the extent of the problem and eliminating any potential recurrence of the problem then it is possible that the regulator may wish to intervene on either a formal or informal footing. A report of rule breaches presented to the regulator should be clear and in writing, containing as much support material as necessary to justify the methodology applied in identifying the breach, the investigation the firm is conducting to identify the extent of the breaches and any corrective work either undertaken or proposed to eliminate the risk of further recurrence. The report should also contain, where necessary, a clear timescale over which corrective action will be completed. It may be that there needs to be milestone dates at which certain actions are to be taken and this may very well include further contact with the regulatory authority. In the case of systemic breaches within the firm, the compliance department or senior management may also wish to retain a firm of external advisers or reporting accountants to review periodically the corrective work it will undertake to ensure that it is carried out to the standard deemed acceptable by the regulatory authority. Moreover, the firm may wish to offer external adviser reports to the regulatory authority as a way of providing further comfort.

10.14 Preparation of rule breach reports should be carefully considered. Particular care should be given to the planning of any corrective work that is proposed and the timescales over which corrective work should be completed. Whilst it is important to ensure that the response of the firm to any identified rule breaches will be acceptable to the regulatory authority, it is also vital to ensure the firm does not fall into the trap of over committing itself to corrective work. Such over commitment can take place through the extent of the work proposed and the timescales over which the work is to be completed It is vital for a firm not to try and impress the regulatory authority with its commitment to dealing with the matter by an over elaborate and unrealistic commitment. It undoubtedly will be the case that the regulatory authority will be more impressed with a realistic approach to corrective work. It will no doubt be distressed by any failing by the firm to complete any corrective work which with hindsight is proven to be an over commitment by the firm.

10.15 Finally, dependent upon the nature of the breaches identified and reported upon, it may be necessary for the firm to negotiate and agree with the regulatory authority the extent of any corrective work. whether this approach is correct is very much based on the judgement of the firm's management and compliance staff and any advice received from external advisers. It would certainly be prudent for the firm to suggest the type of corrective work it considers appropriate, followed by an invitation to its regulator to discuss whether its proposals are suitable.

10.16 In conclusion, whenever a firm is placed in a position where it must make a rule breaches report it is important that the firm's response and written report clearly conveys its commitment to resolving the problem in a controlled and structured manner. It should not only eliminate or reduce further regulatory risk, but should also set out a methodology which the firm can retain control over, as opposed to allowing the regulator to take significant involvement in addressing the matter with the firm.

10.17   Needless to say, for some firms the extent or nature of rule breaches reported will be sufficiently serious for regulators to want to exercise greater scrutiny over the matter and perhaps deal with the breaches as an enforcement issue. The possibility of this and the methods of approach were explored in detail at para **10.30** below.

Managing regulator visits

10.18   From time to time, all authorised firms will be subject to detailed and thorough supervision visits from their regulatory agency. These visits may take the form of a general wide ranging visit that will attempt to consider all the areas of the firm's business or a themed visit which will focus on specific areas of the firm's business and concentrate on the regulatory issues impacting on those areas. It may be considered appropriate during a visit or investigation to focus on a specific area of the firm's business activities for the purpose of identifying whether or not rule breaches have occurred. The firm should always consider it appropriate to attempt to manage any regulator visit as professionally as possible. Of course, such an approach should not be confused with attempting to control the visit, disguise materials or misrepresent information requested during a visit. A professionally controlled visit will convey a good impression that the firm is in control of its regulatory responsibilities and will help to portray the firm in a good light.

10.19   An imperative for any firm is always be prepared. It may be that the regulatory agency has requested information from the firm in advance of the visit that will assist the regulator's supervision staff to conduct the visit more productively. Where material has been requested in advance, the firm should always ensure that it is complied with diligently and made available to the regulator's staff on time, whether that is in advance of the visit or at a time requested during the visit. It is, of course, diligent practice for the firm to ensure that it understands the information that it is presenting to the regulator and, if the information reveals any particular risks or potential rule breaches, that it is in a position to respond to any questions.

10.20   It may also be appropriate, depending upon the type of visit being conducted, for the firm to agree a visit schedule with the regulator. Such schedules may identify certain staff that need to be made available for interview or meeting with the regulator, the extent to which those staff will be interviewed and the areas of business they may be interviewed on. The schedule may also identify which areas of the firm's business will be reviewed and the manner in which the review will take place. Once again, this will allow the firm to ensure that all relevant and appropriate materials are made available to the regulatory authority promptly and in a manner which is meaningful to the visit being conducted.

10.21   It is certainly the case that any staff that will be potentially exposed to regulators' interviews should appreciate the responsibility they have when being interviewed and the skills that they should apply during the interview. The compliance department should consider providing a staff briefing in advance of any visit to clarify any areas of business likely to be reviewed, the types of questions that may be raised and also to settle any concerns a member of staff may have about being interviewed. It may often be the case that members of staff exposed to regulator interviews for the very first time will be unnerved by the prospect. Without guidance on how visits are conducted, they may, as a result of nervousness, misdescibe the organisation's procedures or, through nerves, portray the organisation in a poor light.

10.22   During a visit, compliance staff should also be prepared to accompany regulators' staff . This can serve a number of purposes:

- to ensure that any interviews or visits remain focused;
- to provide comfort to the member of staff being interviewed;
- to allow the compliance staff to explain any misunderstood items that may be addressed during an interview; and
- to ensure that other compliance staff and management of the firm are kept up to date with the progress of the visit.

Regulator feedback meetings

10.23   Once the regulator's visit is concluded, a short feedback meeting may take place during which an explanation will be provided of any findings from the visit. Any informal or verbal feedback meetings must always be accepted for what they are. That is 'informal feedback', which may alter once the regulator's staff have returned to their office and compiled their visit report.

10.24   Feedback meetings can, however, be a valuable opportunity to discuss any immediate findings from the audit and will provide strong indications to the firm as to the likely items that will be reported upon by the regulator.

10.25   Ultimately, following a visit, it is likely the regulator will formally report its findings in writing and will expect written responses to any corrective actions required. Some corrective actions may be specific whereas others may require a response from the firm setting out actions it is prepared to take to deal with a particular item that has been identified.

10.26   Any written reports required from the firm should be carefully considered and, once again, it is important for the firm not to over commit itself to corrective work or time required to complete actions. It is certainly the case that most regulators will not object to a further discussion about the proposed corrective action or if a firm considers that an alternative approach or timescale may be more appropriate. In this instance, it is always sensible for dialogue to take place and an agreement reached between the firm and the regulator's supervision staff.

10.27   When responding to visit reports, the firm should ensure that the response it provides is articulated in a clear and unambiguous manner and, of course, that any corrective work required is in fact conducted.

10.28   It is a useful discipline for a firm, when completing more complex corrective work, to have that work independently audited whether by the internal audit department or an external audit firm. This can be a useful mechanism to ensure that corrective work will be completed to the satisfaction of the regulatory authority prior to any attempt by the regulatory agency to view the completion of the corrective work.

10.29   It should always be remembered that any corrective work will be the subject of further review by the regulatory agency. It will undoubtedly be the case that, if the agency considers that corrective work has not been completed seriously or in accordance with specifications set, it may very well treat this failure as a regulatory breach and escalate it to an enforcement issue.

Managing enforcement proceedings

General

10.30   The effect of formal disciplinary proceedings on an authorised person's business activities can be enormous. Indirect costs, such as the disruption of working practices, the diversion of management time and the collective loss of face, together with the direct costs of rectifying non-compliant procedures and compensating the victims of non-compliance, can vastly exceed any financial penalty arising from the disciplinary action itself. Each of these issues can create an enormous burden for the disciplined firm. Furthermore, the firm will often experience a sense of regulatory overload during the progress of any disciplinary case. The practical implications of being involved in regulators' disciplinary proceedings, the future of disciplinary actions under the FSMA 2000 and how an authorised firm may best manage its response to any action it becomes involved in are now considered.

Recent developments and public perception

10.31   Regulator enforcement is viewed as an effective method of ensuring satisfactory standards of compliance. Since July 1997 there have also been some significant disciplinary cases. By way of example, the life assurance industry came under significant pressure to make progress in its review of non-compliant pension transfers and opt-outs business and the Personal Investment Authority (PIA) levied its two largest disciplinary fines against members that have failed to make satisfactory progress with the review. Also, on 1 September 1997, DBS Financial Management plc, an independent intermediary network, was fined £425,000 and, on 30 September 1997, Friends Provident (one of the country's largest life assurance companies) was fined £450,000.

10.32   Since these cases PIA has publicly disciplined further firms and, between January and September 2001, the Authority had taken disciplinary action against 57 firms, resulting in fines totalling £2,062,000. A total of £46 million had been set aside by PIA authorised firms for compensation.

10.33   A recent PIA disciplinary action, announced on 24 July 2001, related to the Royal London Mutual Insurance Society. In its disciplinary press release PIA reported that Royal London was expected to provide £15 million in compensation, to approximately 65,000 customers, and has been fined £400,000 for breaches of rules relating to the sale of investment products to customers. In its press release PIA made clear the rationale for disciplinary action by stating:

> 'Customers place their trust in the advice that firms give them. Where we find that the advice is not backed by adequate compliance and sales procedures, we will ensure that those sales are reviewed and customers receive the proper redress where appropriate.'

10.34   These PIA actions, however, seem minor when compared with IMRO's action against two Deutsche Morgan Grenfell companies, publicised in April 1997. Collectively, the two companies were fined £2m by IMRO's disciplinary tribunal and ordered to pay another £1m to cover IMRO's costs of investigating and conducting the case. Commenting on the case, IMRO's then Chief Executive said:

> 'The mismanagement of these funds has caused unnecessary concern to a number of investors. The firm has paid dearly as a consequence of inadequate control. The affair plainly illustrates the dangers of ignoring clear and repeated warnings.'

10.35   Despite the enormity of the Morgan Grenfell fine, which surpassed IMRO's previous highest fine of £750,000, the press was critical of the regulator's handling of the affair and of the outcome of the disciplinary action. The day after the fine was publicised, there was a suggestion that the size of the fine was not proportionate to the investors' losses caused by Morgan Grenfells' IMRO rule breaches. For example, the *Independent* stated:

'...As to the quantum of the fine, £2m is neither here nor there to Deutsche Bank, Morgan's parent...a fine of less than 1 per cent of the black hole left by Mr Young's dealings means the punishment hardly fits the crime...[IMRO] might for instance have stripped Morgan Grenfell Asset Management of its licence... '

10.36 Historically, the media and the public have had high expectations of regulator disciplinary proceedings. The *Independent* newspaper's comments suggest that the public view a regulator's disciplinary process and ability to fine as in some way akin to criminal law sanctions and that a delinquent firm's punishment should be in direct proportion to the rule breach. If such a perception is in future translated to the FSA's application of its disciplinary system, firms will have to pay greater heed to the manner in which proceedings against them are controlled and disposed of.

What of disciplinary actions under the FSMA 2000?

10.37 Schedule 1 provides that the FSA must maintain arrangements for enforcing the provisions of, or made under, this Act (see Sch 1, para 6(3)). The FSA's Enforcement Manual describes the policies and procedures for the exercise of the enforcement powers granted to the FSA.

10.38 At para 1.2.1 of the Enforcement Manual the FSA state, inter alia:

'The FSA's effective and proportionate use of its enforcement powers to enforce the requirements of the Act, the rules, the Statements of Principle and other relevant legislation (for example, the Criminal Justice Act 1993, and the Money Laundering Regulations 1993) play an important role in the pursuit of its regulatory objectives. For example:

(1) in relation to the market confidence objective, the FSA's powers to bring criminal prosecutions for insider dealing and misleading statements and practices offences, and to impose financial penalties for market abuse, help to maintain confidence in the financial system;
(2) in relation to the public awareness objective, the imposition of disciplinary measures such as public censures and public statements of misconduct show that regulatory standards are being upheld;
(3) in relation to the protection of consumers' objectives, the imposition of disciplinary measures helps to deter future contraventions, ensure high standards of regulatory conduct and protect consumers...'

10.39   The enforcement manual goes on to state that:

'Disciplinary measures are one of the regulatory tools available to the FSA. They are not the only tool, and it may be appropriate to address many instances of non-compliance without recourse to disciplinary action. However, the effective and proportionate use of the FSA's powers to enforce the requirements of the Act, the rules and the Statements of Principle will play an important role in buttressing the FSA's pursuit of its regulatory objectives. The imposition of disciplinary measures (ie financial penalties, public censures and public statements) shows that regulatory standards are being upheld and helps to maintain market confidence, promote public awareness of regulatory standards and deter financial crime. An increased public awareness of regulatory standards also contributes to the protection of consumers.'

Responding to discipline

10.40   Clearly all authorised persons should avoid serious compliance failings and exposure to discipline by investing sufficient time, resources and expertise into the company. However, for a variety of reasons, compliance breaches may occur and serious breaches of rules, even if identified by the company's own compliance function, can result in regulator disciplinary proceedings.

10.41   When faced with the prospect of discipline or enforcement actions, few firms are prepared for the many difficulties that will inevitably confront them. Valuable time and energy is often wasted in deciding how to manage the company's response to the disciplinary action and identifying how the regulator's disciplinary system operates. In addition, it is often the case during an enforcement action, that the working relationship between the company's managers can become very strained, as individual managers come to terms with the fact that the company is being accused of significant rule breaches that are considered deserving of discipline. Many firms, having been disciplined, often complain that they had no idea of the pitfalls they would encounter at the start of the process.

A disciplinary risk management plan

10.42   A company that develops a disciplinary risk management plan is able to make provision for a structured management response to any enforcement action. It can create policy mechanisms with a view to safeguarding its future business conduct and ensuring that the regulator receives a response to allegations that are in the interest of effective regulation and not to the complete disadvantage of the company's existing customers or the company itself. The latter can certainly happen in a company's hasty attempt to demonstrate that it is keen to co-operate with its regulators.

10.43 Whilst some may consider that prior planning for a potential but unknown disciplinary action is a cynical manoeuvre, it can make business sense. It should be viewed no differently from other areas of risk management or disaster recovery. Who would ever suggest that a company's back-up systems for dealing with computer system failure, lapse of health and safety standards or the involvement of the company in high profile litigation, have a cynical motive behind them? A contingency plan will save time, energy and unnecessary expense should the worst happen.

10.44 Many companies have developed written risk management strategies. Viewed simply, these often predict and identify the areas of risk or catastrophe that may arise. They envisage procedural responses to those risks and allocate responsibilities for dealing with those risks to certain staff or departments. Fundamentally, a disciplinary risk management plan is no different. At a fundamental level, certain issues can be specified in a disciplinary risk management plan. These could include:

- establishing a management steering committee to oversee the company's regulatory, public and internal response to the allegations;
- ensuring management separation of the handling or defence of the disciplinary proceedings, regulator corrective work and ongoing compliance responsibility, so as to avoid regulatory overload;
- eliminating from the management steering committee and day-to-day disciplinary case management any personnel who may have a conflict of interest in the company's defence or response;
- ensuring that the company responds to the allegations swiftly, intelligently and openly so as to avoid or limit the possibility of regulator intervention proceedings;
- the objective analysis of the regulator's allegations and whether the action should be defended or settled;
- the immediate need to start communicating with the regulator; and
- how best to protect the company's business reputation.

The separation of disciplinary action management from continuing compliance

10.45 Experience suggests that compliance departments and senior compliance personnel often bear the brunt of dealing with and responding to the disciplinary proceedings a company may face. Their task will often include:

- co-ordinating corrective work with the regulator;
- developing methods of revised compliance;
- briefing and co-ordinating any external advisors instructed to act for the firm during the disciplinary proceedings;
- dealing with any internal corporate changes that come about as a result of the matter;
- trying to develop a better relationship with the regulator; and
- preparing the company for any follow-up or verification visit from the regulator which will be checking to see whether the corrective work has been completed.

10.46   Compliance officers faced with these many tasks often experience regulatory overload. They are expected to deal with many competing areas of the company's business. Each of these areas often requires detailed and urgent attention and, inevitably, the compliance officer or compliance department will cease to function effectively. It can be self-defeating for a company to operate in this manner and therefore makes sound sense for the management of any disciplinary proceedings and resulting corrective work to be managed by a person or department separate from the person or department that has day-to-day compliance responsibility.

Avoiding conflicts of interest

10.47   When allocating responsibility for the management of the company's disciplinary proceedings to any person, a company must eliminate (in so far as it is possible) any conflicts of interest. When a regulator accuses a firm of regulatory misconduct, its accusation invariably involves some direct or indirect criticism of the company's staff or officers. It is absolutely essential that managers or other persons who are subject to such criticism are not involved in the management of the disciplinary case. Companies often make this mistake and soon discover that these people then embark on a campaign to protect their own reputation, to pursue self-serving avenues of enquiry or to defend the indefensible as an indirect way of defending their own position or involvement in the alleged breaches.

Limiting disciplinary action and intervention

10.48   Depending on the circumstances which have given rise to the disciplinary action, companies may find it possible to mitigate or eliminate some of the more exacting enforcement remedies available to the regulators if they act quickly. If, despite its misconduct, the company is able to act effectively and responsibly in correcting the compliance failures in question, its responsible behaviour may persuade the regulator not to exercise powers of intervention. In turn such response may even assist the firm in mitigating the outcome of the disciplinary action, although it is unlikely that it will act to prevent or withdraw the disciplinary action completely.

10.49   The company's responses will of course have to be commensurate with the misconduct in question and may, in severe circumstances, restrict its ability to take on new business for a time. It is, however, far better if the company is seen to be in control of its rule breach rectification than if its regulatory body is 'setting the pace' instead.

10.50   Companies can only respond promptly if the circumstances giving rise to the proceedings come to its attention quickly. If the company has identified the problem itself but is obliged to tell the regulator, it ought to accompany the notification with a full statement of how it proposes to respond. If, however, the company only becomes aware of misconduct when it receives formal notification about the conduct from the regulator, that notification may take the form of an intervention order. In that case, the company ought to provide the regulator with a speedy description of how it can respond to the misconduct and manage any corrective work that may be necessary.

Admit or defend?

10.51   Many regulators' disciplinary systems are designed to bring disciplinary actions to a speedy end through a process of admission and negotiated settlement. The extent to which a regulated firm is prepared to accept a disciplinary settlement is undoubtedly dependent on the punishment which the regulator is seeking to impose. Those regulated firms facing expulsion or exceptionally large fines may be more inclined to contest the allegations, but there are many advantages for a firm which settles disciplinary proceedings as promptly as possible.

10.52   The experience of securities firms in the US indicates that those facing discipline generally consent to the settlement of the proceedings rather than litigate. The reasons for this are often determined by the circumstances of the individual action or the type of defendant. For example, settlement may be necessary because the SEC has a strong case, because the litigation costs will be high or because normal operations will be severely disrupted and management time wasted. In fact about 90% of SEC enforcement actions are settled pursuant to a process available where the defendant neither admits nor denies the commission's allegations.

10.53   For most regulated firms, it is soon apparent whether the regulator has a strong case. If it has, little is to be gained from contesting the allegations. Those acting for the regulated firm should decide how strong the allegations are and should quickly begin a dialogue, with the regulator's enforcement staff, seeking to identify the disciplinary sanctions the regulator is seeking.

10.54 This approach is best in the majority of disciplinary actions. Negotiations at least allow the disciplined firm some involvement in the outcome of its own case. They also ensure that the firm has some control over the content of any resulting press release. Many regulated firms find that the conclusion of disciplinary proceedings is something of a release; it relieves tension that can often build up within the company, it ends speculation amongst the media and competitors and it allows management effort to be rechanelled into managing improvements to compliance procedures and repairing the damage to the company's reputation.

Identifying the objectives of the regulator

10.55 Those responsible for the management of a firm's response to disciplinary proceedings should always aim to identify the regulator's overall objective in commencing the disciplinary proceedings. An understanding of the objective of the case will allow them to understand:

- how receptive the regulator will be to the company's own proposals for corrective work;
- whether there is scope for a negotiated settlement; and
- how to plan a public relations exercise to protect the company's reputation.

10.56 In understanding these, firms should look at any statement the regulator has published about its approach discipline. By way of example, the FSA has a developed set of criteria that can be used to calculate how seriously it may treat disciplinary cases. In introducing these criteria the FSA state:

'In determining whether to take disciplinary action in respect of conduct appearing to the FSA to be a breach, the FSA will consider the full circumstances of each case. A number of factors may be relevant for this purpose. The following list is not exhaustive: not all of these factors may be relevant in a particular case, and there may be other factors that are relevant.'

10.57 Although each regulated firm's case has to be treated on its own merits, the FSA will use these criteria to ensure that their own disciplinary actions are conducted consistently and that an individual sanction can be justified against pre-determined standards.

10.58 The FSA's statement should not, however, be treated as exhaustive, but it is a useful tool for firms to judge the seriousness with which the regulator will view the firm's misconduct and the likely outcome of the action.

10.59 The following list of criteria are set out in Section 11 of the FSA's Enforcement Manual:

'(1) *The nature and seriousness of the suspected breach*

(a) whether the breach was deliberate or reckless;

(b) the duration and frequency of the breach (including, in relation to a firm, when the breach was identified by those exercising significant influence functions in the firm);

(c) the amount of any benefit gained or loss avoided as a result of the breach;

(d) whether the breach reveals serious or systemic weaknesses of the management systems or internal controls relating to all or part of a firm's business;

(e) the impact of the breach on the orderliness of financial markets, including whether public confidence in those markets has been damaged;

(f) the loss or risk of loss caused to consumers or other market users;

(g) the nature and extent of any financial crime facilitated, occasioned or otherwise attributable to the breach; and

(h) whether there are a number of smaller issues, which individually may not justify disciplinary action, but which do so when taken collectively.

(2) *The conduct of the firm or the approved person after the breach*

(a) how quickly, effectively and completely the firm or approved person brought the breach to the attention of the FSA or another relevant regulatory authority;

(b) the degree of co-operation the firm or approved person showed during the investigation of the breach;

(c) any remedial steps the firm or approved person has taken since the breach was identified, including: identifying whether consumers have suffered loss and compensating them; taking disciplinary action against staff involved (where appropriate); addressing any systemic failures; and taking action designed to ensure that similar problems do not arise in future; and

(d) the likelihood that the same type of contravention (whether on the part of the firm or approved person concerned or others) will recur if no disciplinary action is taken.

(3) *The previous regulatory record of the firm or approved person*

(a) whether the FSA (or any previous regulator) has taken any previous disciplinary action resulting in adverse findings against the firm or approved person;

(b) whether the firm or approved person has previously given any undertakings to the FSA (or any previous regulator) not to do a particular act or engage in particular behaviour;

(c) whether the FSA (or any previous regulator) has previously taken protective action in respect of a firm, using its own-initiative powers, by means of a variation of a Part IV permission (see ENF 3) or otherwise, or has previously requested the firm to take remedial action, and the extent to which such action has been taken; and

(d) the general compliance history of the firm or approved person, such as previous private warnings or the type of correspondence referred to in ENF11.3.9G.

(4) *Guidance given by the FSA*

The FSA will take into account whether any guidance has been issued relating to the behaviour in question and if so the extent to which the firm or approved person has sought to follow that guidance – see the Reader's Guide part of the Handbook .

(5) *Action taken by the FSA in previous similar cases*

The FSA will take account of action which it has taken previously in cases where the breach has been the same or similar.

(6) *Action taken by other regulatory authorities*

Where other regulatory authorities propose to take action in respect of the breach which is under consideration by the FSA , or one similar to it, the FSA will consider whether their action would be adequate to address the FSA's concerns, or whether it would be appropriate for the FSA to take its own action' (see ENF 11.8).

Early communication with the regulator

10.60   A meaningful, 'without prejudice' dialogue should begin with the regulator as soon as practically possible. Early dialogue should assist the firm in identifying the regulator's concerns about the alleged misconduct, the acceptability of any proposed corrective work, the likely outcome of the disciplinary action and the prospect of an early settlement.

10.61   Regulated firms embarking upon such dialogue should, however, treat any early views given by the regulator's staff with an element of caution as many regulatory disciplinary procedures specify that decisions about the commencement of proceedings, the suitability of corrective action and settlement negotiations must be taken by a disciplinary/enforcement committee. While such committees are guided by the judgement of the regulator's staff, they do not always follow it.

Protecting the firm's reputation

10.62   Publicity and comment about the outcome of disciplinary action will obviously cause some damage to the reputation of the company. The extent of the damage is determined by the scale of the regulatory misconduct, the penalty involved, the notoriety of the company and the immediate political atmosphere. Other matters may also play their part. Issues such as the time of year, other items of news at the time and the actions of other investment companies which are involved in disciplinary actions will all contribute to the attention the media give to a company's case.

10.63   News of the disciplinary action may come to the attention of the media – often through 'leaks' – months before formal conclusion of the action is expected. The most logical solution to this is for regulated firms to enlist and brief an experienced public relations companies. However, this is an expensive luxury which all but the largest of financial institutions can ill afford.

Conclusion

10.64   During the foreseeable future, regulators will place ever-increasing demands on the financial services industry. The severity of punishment will inevitably climb to hitherto-unseen levels. Already, the costs associated with corrective work following a disciplinary action can run into millions of pounds. Because of these and other direct or hidden costs it is essential that the case should be properly managed. All companies should have enough foresight to devise risk-management systems for the purpose of ensuring that, should the worst happen, they are able to respond immediately and save valuable management time and energy.

CHAPTER 11

Authorisation, permissions and approved persons

11.1 One basic concept, consistent throughout the financial services regulatory systems in developed countries, is that of authorisation. Entry and participation in the financial services market through a system of authorisation ensures that only persons considered by the regulatory laws of the county to be suitable to conduct financial services business are allowed to participate in the market. In addition, a process to approve key personnel involved in the management and operation of the companies goes some way to ensure that companies will be managed in accordance with regulatory standards.

11.2 Whilst an analysis of the systems of authorisation through different countries is outside the scope of this chapter, an analysis of the approach to authorisation under the FSMA 2000 will give some insight to requirements for authorisation and the approach taken by the FSA.

11.3 In this chapter consideration will be given to the need for authorisation for any person wishing to conduct investment business, the process that is to be followed when applying for authorisation, provisions in place to ensure that key members of an authorised person's management are approved, involved in management of the company and, lastly, the approach that is taken when it becomes necessary to vary the authorisation granted by the FSA.

The requirement for authorisation

11.4 The FSMA 2000 controls entry and participation in the market through the general provision in s 19. Section 19(1) states that no person may carry on a regulated activity in the UK or be thought to be doing so unless he is:

- an authorised person; or
- an exempt person.

11.5   Regulated activities are described in FSMA 2000, s 22 and Sch 2 as being activities of a specified kind carried on by way of business and relating to a specified kind of investment. The test, therefore, as to whether a person needs to be authorised to carry on a particular activity requires an analysis of three issues:

- Does the person's activity relate to a specified type of investment?
- Is the person's activity specified under the Act?
- Is the person's activity in relation to the investment carried on by way of business?

11.6   The FSMA 2000 specifies those activities which are treated as regulated investments and regulated activities and these are explored in more detail in **Chapter 5**.

Investments

11.7   FSMA 2000, s 31 specifies the manner in which a person may be authorised. Certain authorisation is granted to qualifying firms. Section 31(1)(a) specifies that a person who has a Part IV permission to carry on one or more regulated activities is an authorised person for the purpose of the Act. The method of obtaining permission is considered below.

11.8   FSMA 2000, ss 38 and 39 set out certain exemptions from the requirement to obtain authorisation. In particular, an appointed representative is an exempted person. An appointed representative is defined as 'a party to a contract with an authorised person, which permits or requires them to carry on investment business ... and whose activities in carrying on that business are the accepted responsibility of the authorised person.'

11.9   Under Pt IV, provision is made for the application for obtaining permission from the FSA. Under s 40, sub-s 1, permission may be granted to an individual, a body corporate, a partnership or an unincorporated association. Paragraph 41(1) specified that, in order to obtain permission, the FSA must ensure that the person will satisfy and continue to satisfy certain threshold conditions[1].

1   Refer to FSMA 2000, Sch 6.

Threshold conditions

11.10   The threshold conditions required to be satisfied are as follows:

- *Legal status.* Specific legal status is required for those seeking permission to carry insurance business. The person either must be a body corporate, registered friendly society or a member of Lloyd's. Moreover, the person seeking permission to carry on business of deposit taking must be either a body corporate or a partnership.

- *Location of offices.* It is a requirement that a body corporate constituted under any part of the UK must have its head office and registered office in the UK. Furthermore, where a person has a head office in the UK but is not a body corporate, he must carry on business in the UK.
- *Close links.* Close links are specified in FSMA 2000, para 3(2). These will include, for example, where another person is a parent or subsidiary undertaking of the person seeking permission, where the third party owns or controls 20% or more of the voting rights, or capital of the person seeking permission. Or where the person seeking permission owns or controls 20% or more of the voting rights or capital of the third party. In the event that a close link exists, the FSA has to be satisfied that the links are not likely to prevent effective supervision of the person seeking permission[1].
- *Adequate resources.* The person seeking permission must have resources which, in the opinion of the FSA are adequate in relation to the regulated activities they seek to carry on. In reaching the opinion, the FSA may take into account the person's membership of any group[2].

The FSA is required to ensure that a firm has adequate resources in relation to the   specific regulated activity or regulated activities which it seeks to carry on, or carries on. The FSA interprets the term 'adequate' as meaning sufficient in terms of quantity, quality and availability, and 'resources' to include all financial resources, non-financial resources and means of managing its resources, for example capital, provisions against liabilities, holdings of or access to cash and other liquid assets, human resources and effective means by which to manage risks[3].

In its assessment of adequate resources, the FSA may have regard to any person appearing to it to be, or likely to be, in a relevant relationship with the firm, in accordance with s 49, for example a firm's controllers, directors or partners, other persons with close links to the firm and other persons that exert influence on the firm which might pose a risk to the firm's satisfaction of the threshold conditions.

The FSA's Handbook on Threshold Conditions sets out, at 2.4.4(2)G, some useful guidance on those matters the FSA will have regard to when considering resources. Relevant matters may include, but are not limited to:

(a) whether there are any indications that the firm may have difficulties if the application is granted, at the time of the grant or in the future, in complying with any of the FSA's prudential rules;

(b) whether there are any indications that the firm will not be able to meet its debts as they fall due;

(c) whether there are any implications for the adequacy of the firm's resources arising from the history of the firm, for example whether the firm has:

— been adjudged bankrupt, or

— entered into liquidation, or

— been the subject of a receiving or administration order, or

— had a bankruptcy or winding-up petition served on it, or

— had its estate sequestrated, or

— entered into a deed of arrangement or an individual voluntary agreement (or in Scotland, a trust deed) or other composition in favour of its creditors, or is doing so, or

— within the last ten years, failed to satisfy a judgment debt under a court order, whether in the United Kingdom or elsewhere,

(d) whether the firm has taken reasonable steps to identify and measure any risks of regulatory concern that it may encounter in conducting its business (see COND 2.4.6G) and has installed appropriate systems and controls and appointed appropriate human resources to measure them prudently at all times: see SYSC 3.1 (systems and controls) and SYSC 3.2 (areas covered by systems and controls); and

(e) whether the firm has conducted enquiries into the financial services sector in which it intends to conduct business (see COND 2.4.6G) that are sufficient to satisfy itself that:

— it has access to adequate capital, by reference to the FSA's prudential requirements, to support the business including any losses which may be expected during its start-up period, and

— client money, deposits, custody assets and policyholders' rights will not be placed at risk if the business fails.

The FSA will expect firms to plan business appropriately so that the likely risks of regulatory concern can be identified, measured and managed . The FSA observes that any newly-formed firm can be susceptible to early difficulties. Such difficulties could arise from a lack of relevant expertise and judgement, or from ill-constructed and insufficiently tested business strategies. It is also recognised that a firm may be susceptible to difficulties where it substantially changes its business activities. As a result, the FSA would expect a firm which is applying for a Part IV permission, or a substantial variation of that permission, to take adequate steps to satisfy itself and, if relevant, the FSA that:

(a) it has a well-constructed business or strategy plan for its product or service which demonstrates that it is ready, willing and organised to comply with the relevant requirements in IPRU and SYSC that apply to the regulated activity it is seeking to carry on;

(b) its business or strategy plan has been sufficiently tested; and

(c) the financial and other resources of the firm are commensurate with the likely risks it will face.

- *Suitability*. When determining whether the firm will satisfy and continue to satisfy threshold condition 5, the FSA will have regard to all relevant matters, whether arising in the UK or elsewhere. Relevant matters include, but are not limited to, whether a firm:

(a) conducts, or will conduct, its business with integrity and in compliance with   proper standards;

(b) has, or will have, a competent and prudent management; and

(c) can demonstrate that it conducts, or will conduct, its affairs with the exercise of due skill, care and diligence.

The authority has to be satisfied that the person seeking permission is a fit and proper person, which will include an analysis of any connection the person may have with any other individual, the nature of the regulated activity to be carried on, and the need to ensure that the person's affairs are conducted soundly.

As to suitability, the firm is required to satisfy the FSA that it is 'fit and proper' to have a Part IV permission having regard to all the circumstances, including its connections with other persons, the range and nature of its proposed (or current) regulated activities and the overall need to be satisfied that its affairs are and will be conducted soundly and prudently (see also PRIN and SYSC)[5].

The FSA will also take into consideration anything that could influence a firm's continuing ability to satisfy this threshold condition. Examples include the firm's position within a UK or international group, information provided by overseas regulators about the firm, and the firm's plans to seek to vary its Part IV permission to carry on additional regulated activities once it has been granted that permission by the FSA.

The FSA make it clear, at 2.5.3 G, that the emphasis of the threshold condition of suitability is on the suitability of the firm itself. It states that, generally, the suitability of each person who performs a controlled function will be assessed by the FSA under the approved persons regime. It further states that, in certain circumstances, however, the FSA may consider that the firm is not suitable because of doubts over the individual or collective suitability of persons connected with the firm.

1   FSMA 2000, Sch 6, Pt I, para 3.
2   FSMA 2000, Sch 6, Pt I, para 4.
3   2.4.3G.
4   SYSC 3.2.17G.
5   2.5.2G.

Conducting business with integrity and in compliance with proper standards

11.11   The FSA also consider the question of a person's ability to conduct its business with integrity and in compliance with proper standards. In determining whether a firm will satisfy, and continue to satisfy, threshold condition 5 in respect of its conduct of business the following issues will be considered:

- whether the firm has been open and co-operative in all its dealings with the FSA and any other regulatory body and is ready, willing and organised to comply with the requirements and standards under the regulatory system and other legal, regulatory and professional obligations; the relevant requirements and standards will depend on the circumstances of each case, including the regulated activities which the firm has permission, or is seeking permission, to carry on;
- whether the firm has been convicted, or is connected with a person who has been convicted, of any unspent offence involving fraud, corruption, perjury, theft, false accounting or other dishonesty, money laundering, market abuse or insider dealing, offences under legislation relating to insurance, banking or other financial services, companies, insolvency, consumer credit or consumer protection or any significant tax offence; where relevant, any spent convictions excepted for this purpose under the Rehabilitation of Offenders Act 1974 will be taken into consideration;
- whether the firm has been the subject of, or connected to the subject of, any existing or previous investigation or enforcement proceedings by the FSA, the Society of Lloyd's or by other regulatory authorities (including the FSA's predecessors), clearing houses or exchanges, professional bodies or government bodies or agencies; the FSA will, however, take both the nature of the firm's involvement in, and the outcome of, any investigation or enforcement proceedings into account in determining whether it is a relevant matter;
- whether the firm has contravened, or is connected with a person who has contravened, any provisions of the FSMA 2000 or any preceding financial services legislation, the regulatory system or the rules, regulations, statements of principles or codes of practice (for example the Society of Lloyd's Codes) of other regulatory authorities (including the FSA's predecessors), clearing houses or exchanges, professional bodies, or government bodies or agencies or relevant industry standards (such as the Non-Investment Products Code); the FSA will, however, take into account both the status of codes of practice or relevant industry standards and the nature of the contravention (for example, whether a firm has flouted or ignored a particular code);
- whether the firm, or a person connected with the firm, has been refused registration, authorisation, membership or licence to carry out a trade, business or profession or has had such registration, authorisation,

membership or licence revoked, withdrawn or terminated, or has been expelled by a regulatory or government body; whether the FSA considers such a refusal relevant will depend on the circumstances;

- whether the firm has taken reasonable care to establish and maintain effective systems and controls for compliance with applicable requirements and standards under the regulatory system that apply to the firm and the regulated activities for which it has, or will have, permission;
- whether the firm has put in place procedures which are reasonably designed to:

  (a) ensure that it has made its employees aware of, and compliant with, those requirements and standards under the regulatory system that apply to the firm and the regulated activities for which it has, or will have permission,

  (b) ensure that its approved persons (whether or not employed by the firm) are aware of those requirements and standards under the regulatory system applicable to them,

  (c) determine that its employees are acting in way compatible with the firm adhering to those requirements and standards, and

  (d) determine that its approved persons are adhering to those requirements and standards;

- whether the firm or a person connected with the firm has been dismissed from employment or a position of trust, fiduciary relationship or similar or has ever been asked to resign from employment in such a position; whether the FSA considers a resignation to be relevant will depend on the circumstances, for example if a person is asked to resign in circumstances that cast doubt over his honesty or integrity; and
- whether the firm or a person connected with the firm has ever been disqualified from acting as a director.

Competent and prudent management and exercise of due skill, care and diligence

11.12 The FSA also consider the question of the whether the applicant will exercise competent and prudent management and due skill, care and diligence. The following issues will be considered[1]:

- the governing body of the firm is made up of individuals with an appropriate range of skills and experience to understand, operate and manage the firm's regulated activities;
- if appropriate, the governing body of the firm includes non-executive representation, at a level which is appropriate for the control of the regulated activities proposed, for example, as members of an audit committee (see SYSC 3.2.15G (audit committee));
- the governing body of the firm is organised in a way that enables it to address and control the regulated activities of the firm, including those

carried on by managers to whom particular functions have been delegated (see SYSC 2.1 (apportionment of responsibilities) and SYSC 3.2 (areas covered by systems and controls));

- those persons who perform controlled functions under certain arrangements entered into by the firm or its contractors (including appointed representatives) act with due skill, care and diligence in carrying out their controlled function (see APER 4.2 (Statement of Principle 2) or managing the business for which they are responsible (see APER 4.7 (Statement of Principle 7));
- the firm has made arrangements to put in place an adequate system of internal control to comply with the requirements and standards under the regulatory system (see SYSC 3.1 (systems and controls));
- the firm has approached the control of financial and other risk in a prudent manner (for example, by not assuming risks without taking due account of the possible consequences) and has taken reasonable care to ensure that robust information and reporting systems have been developed, tested and properly installed (see SYSC 3.2.10 (risk assessment));
- the firm, or a person connected with the firm, has been a director, partner or otherwise concerned in the management of a company, partnership or other organisation or business that has gone into insolvency, liquidation or administration while having been connected with that organisation or within one year of such a connection;
- the firm has developed human resources policies and procedures that are reasonably designed to ensure that it employs only individuals who are honest and committed to high standards of integrity in the conduct of their activities (see, for example, SYSC 3.2.13G (employees and agents));
- the firm has conducted enquiries (for example, through market research or the previous activities of the firm) that are sufficient to give it reasonable assurance that it will not be posing unacceptable risks to consumers or the financial system;
- the firm has in place the appropriate money laundering prevention systems and training, including identification, record-keeping and internal reporting procedures (see ML); and
- where appropriate, the firm has appointed auditors and actuaries, who have sufficient experience in the areas of business to be conducted (see SUP 3.4 (auditors' qualifications)

1   2.5.7G.

The granting of permission

11.13   If the authority gives permission to the applicant to carry on the regulated activity or activities, the authority may incorporate in the description of the regulated activities either:

- such limitation as it considers appropriate;
- a narrower or wider description of the regulated activities than that applied for; and
- permission for carrying on of regulated activities which are not included within the application[1].

1   FSMA 2000, s 42(6) and 42(7).

11.14 Furthermore, the FSA may impose requirements on the condition, which could include the requirement that the person seeking permission takes specified action or refrains from taking specified action. This could include an action by reference to the person's relationship with other members of a same group of companies, or activities which are not themselves regulated activities.

Procedure for making an application

11.15 The FSA's authorisation manual sets out guidance and procedures to be followed by the authority when dealing with an application for authorisation and permission. At Annex 1G a flowchart sets out a useful process for helping a person establish whether authorisation may be required.

11.16 At paragraph 1.6.9 the FSA also sets out useful general guidance for persons considering applying for authorisation. It states:

'Among other things, the applicant will need to:

(1) determine the precise scope of the permission it wishes to apply for; this should include the regulated activities (the specified activities and the specified investments in respect of which the activities are carried on: see AUTH 2 Ann 2G) and any limitations and requirements the applicant wishes to apply for to refine the scope of the regulated activities; an example includes a limitation on the types of client it wishes to carry on business with or a requirement not to hold or control client money;

(2) determine whether it needs to apply to the Society of Lloyd's for admission to the register of underwriting agents or to any other bodies; the timing of these applications should be included in the applicant's plans;

(3) determine which prudential category (and, if relevant, sub-category) will apply, and therefore its minimum regulatory financial requirements;

(4) determine the rules in the Handbook which will apply to the activities it proposes to carry on, and take all reasonable steps to ensure that it is ready, willing and organised to comply with those rules;

(5) determine the systems and controls necessary both to support its activities and to comply with the relevant rules, and have plans to implement and test these systems before the FSA determines its application;

(6) prepare a business plan setting out the planned activities (and related risks), budget and resources (human, systems and capital);

(7) determine which persons will fall under the FSA's approved persons regime and apply for the necessary approval; and

(8) obtain any auditors' or reporting accountants' reports that are required to support its application or have been requested by the FSA; the auditors or other professionals should be involved early in the process to ensure that the planned work on the application will be sufficient to enable them to provide any opinions required.'

11.17 A person, when making an application for permission, must complete an application which should include the following[1]:

'(a) A business plan which describes the regulated activities and any unregulated activities which the applicant proposes to carry on, the management and organisational structure of the applicant and details of any proposed outsourcing arrangements. The level of detail required in the business plan will be appropriate to the risks to consumers arising from the proposed regulated and unregulated activities. For an applicant seeking to carry on insurance business, the business plan should include a scheme of operations in accordance with SUP App 2 (Insurer and friendly societies: schemes of operation).

(b) Appropriately analysed financial budget and projections which demonstrate that the applicant expects to comply with the relevant financial resources requirements appropriate to the applicant's prudential category (and in some cases sub-category).

(c) Details of systems to be used (which do not have to be in place at the time of initial application), compliance procedures and documentation.

(d) Details of the individuals to be involved in running the proposed business (such as directors, partners and members of the governing body, all of whom will be performing controlled functions) and any connected persons.'

1   FSA authorisation manual at 3.9.9(G).

11.18   The FSA would expect the level of detail in a firm's business plan or strategy plan to be appropriate to the complexity of the firm's proposed regulated activities and unregulated activities and the risks of regulatory concern it is likely to face (see SYSC 3.2.11G (management information).

General guidance on the contents of a business plan is given in the business plan section of the application pack for a Part IV permission.

11.19   The application pack should be accompanied by such other information as the applicant reasonably considers the FSA should be aware of for the purposes of determining the application. Any relevant supporting documentation should also be enclosed. The guidance notes to the application pack give further details about information to be provided by applicants, to enable them to answer the questions.

11.20   Applicants should be aware that there may be a delay in processing applications if the information given to the FSA is inaccurate or incomplete; for example, if the business plan for an applicant does not describe in adequate detail the regulated activities for which the applicant seeks Part IV permission. Applicants should discuss any problems with the corporate authorisation department before submitting the application or, if necessary, consider seeking appropriate professional advice.

11.21   At any time after receiving an application and before determining it, the FSA may give notice to the applicant to require it to provide additional information or documents. The circumstances of each application will determine what additional information or procedures are appropriate.

11.22   While applicants will often wish to discuss applications with the corporate authorisation department during the application process, similarly, the FSA will often need to discuss and clarify information that has been submitted within the application pack. The exchange of information during the application process is viewed as important by the FSA, since the final decision about an application needs to be based on as complete a picture of the application as possible.

11.23   In addition, in considering the application, the FSA may:

- carry out any enquiries which it considers appropriate, for example discussions with other regulators or exchanges;
- ask the applicant, or any specified representative of the applicant, to attend meetings at the FSA to give further information and explain any matter the FSA considers relevant to the application;
- require any information given by the applicant to be verified in such a way as the FSA may specify (for example, see AUTH 3.9.16G);
- take into account any information which it considers appropriate in relation to the application, for example any unregulated activities which the applicant carries on or proposes to carry on; and
- visit the premises which the applicant intends to use as its place of business.

11.24 Under FSMA 2000, s 51(6), the FSA may require the applicant to verify information provided in such a way as the FSA directs. Thus, as part of the application, the FSA may require the applicant to provide, at its own expense, a report by an auditor, reporting accountant, actuary or other qualified person approved by the FSA . The report may be on such aspects of the information provided, or to be provided, by the applicant as the FSA may specify.

11.25 Under FSMA 2000, s 49 the FSA will, when considering an application for permission, have regard to any person who appears to be, or is likely to be in a relationship with the applicant which is considered relevant.

11.26 When granting an application for permission, the FSA will confirm the permission in a written notice. The notice will state the date from which permission has effect[1].

1   FSMA 2000, s 52.

Granting of permissions with conditions

11.27 Where the authority is to grant permission but impose conditions or requirements, then it will provide the applicant with a warning notice. Furthermore, where the authority is minded to refuse an application for permission, once again a warning notice will be provided.

11.28 Generally, an application for permission has to be determined by the authority within a six-month period from the date that it first receives the completed application.

11.29 Finally, any person who is aggrieved by the manner in which an application for permission is determined, may refer the matter to the Financial Services and Market Tribunal.

Approved persons

11.30 As part of the application for approval, the authorised person must take reasonable care to ensure that no person performs a controlled function in relation to its carrying on of regulated activity, unless the FSA has approved that person to perform in a controlled function. All controlled functions are listed in the table to Rule 10.4.5. The purpose of a firm to undertake to ensure persons to be employed in control functions are fit and proper is explored at para **11.45** below.

Significant influence functions

Governing body functions

11.31   These consist of:

- a director of either a company or a holding company;
- a non-executive director of a company;
- a chief executive officer. This is widely interpreted and covers joint chief executives operating under the immediate control of the board where there is more than one. In the case of a UK branch of a non-EEA insurer the role includes the principal UK executive;
- partners and limited partners (where appropriate) are all regarded as carrying on controlled functions where the firm is primarily carrying on regulated investment business. Limited partners whose role is that of an investor are excluded. If a partnership's primary business does not relate to specified investments but a separate part of the business does then, provided a distinct partner or set of partners deal with that aspect of the business only they need be approved;
- directors of unincorporated associations;
- those directing or regulating the specified activities of a small friendly society; and
- sole traders.

Required controlled functions

11.32   There are four of these:

- the director or other senior member responsible for apportionment and oversight;
- the director or senior manager responsible for investment business compliance;
- the money laundering reporting officer; and
- in the case of insurance companies, the appointed actuary.

Management functions

11.33   These consist of the members of senior management reporting to the governing body in relation to the following activities:

- the financial affairs of the firm;
- setting and controlling risk exposure; and
- internal audit.

Significant management functions in relation to business and control

11.34   The functions set out below are added to cover those situations where the firm concerned has senior managers whose function is equivalent to that of a member of the firm's governing body. They do not apply if the activity is a specified activity as this would automatically then be an approved persons' role. They fall into five categories of senior management:

- those operating in relation to investment services, such as the head of equities. This will often be a controlled function in any event;
- those operating in relation to other areas of the firm's business than specified investment activity, eg head of personal lending or corporate lending, head of credit card issues etc;
- those responsible for carrying out insurance underwriting other than in relation to contractually-based investments, eg head of aviation underwriting;
- those responsible for making decisions concerning the firm's own finances, eg chief corporate treasurer; and
- those responsible for back-office functions.

Temporary and emergency circumstances

11.35   Should the function of undertaking such a role continue for more than eight weeks in a 12-month period then the person primarily responsible will need to be an approved person.

Dealing with customer functions

11.36   There are seven main functions within this category:

- life and pensions advisers;
- life and pensions advisers when acting under supervision;
- pension transfer advisers: such people can also give ancillary advice in relation to packaged products;
- investment advisers, including those advising in relation to packaged products, but not life and pensions advice;
- investment advisers acting under supervision;
- corporate finance advisers; and
- advisers to underwriting members of Lloyd's in relation to becoming a syndicate member.

Dealing with customers' property

11.37   This covers two main types of activity:

- those individuals who deal or arrange deals on behalf of customers. It does not extend to execution only business and feeding orders into automatic execution systems; and
- discretionary fund management.

11.38   The process that is to be undertaken in making an application for approval to perform a controlled function is specified in FSMA 2000, s 60 and will be considered in further detail below[1].

1   Section 59.

Contravention of the requirement to be authorised

11.39   The general prohibition in FSMA 2000, preventing a person from conducting regulated activities without being authorised is enforced by criminal sanction. Section 23 specifies that a person conducting regulated activity without authorisation is guilty of an offence and liable either (a) on summary conviction to a term of imprisonment not exceeding six months, or a fine not exceeding the statutory maximum or both or (b) on conviction on indictment to imprisonment for a term not exceeding two years or a fine or both.

Authorised person acting without permission

11.40   Whilst it is not an offence for an authorised person to conduct a regulated activity for which they have not gained a permission under FSMA 2000, Pt IV, the authorised person will be considered to have acted in contravention of a requirement imposed on him by the FSA under the Act. This will subject the authorised person to enforcement proceedings by the FSA[1]. Section 20(2) makes it clear that such a contravention does not give rise to a criminal offence or to void or unenforceable transactions.

1   FSMA 2000, s 20.

Enforceability of agreements

11.41   A further consequence of conducting a regulated activity without authorisation is that the agreement entered into by the person is unenforceable against any other party[1]. Persons are entitled to recover from unauthorised persons any money or property they have paid or transferred, and obtain compensation for loss sustained as a result of having parted with it.

1   FSMA 2000, s 26.

11.42   FSMA 2000, s 28 specifies the amount of compensation that may be recoverable to such amount as agreed to by the parties or on an application to court, the amount determined by the court.

11.43   A further provision in FSMA 2000, s 27 effectively imposes an obligation on authorised persons to ensure that they only accept business in consequence of something said or done by another person, where that person is themselves an authorised person. This would relate, for example, where a financial adviser has recommended that a consumer purchase a package product with a life assurance company. Where that person is himself not an authorised person, then the investment contract is unenforceable against the provider. This will entitle the investor to recover any money or properties paid and obtain compensation for losses sustained. Providers should, therefore, always ensure that business introduced to them is introduced by an authorised person.

Fitness of approved persons

11.44   A person authorised to conduct regulated activities should take reasonable care not to allow persons to exercise controlled functions without the approval of the FSA[1]. The restriction is imposed in relation to both natural and corporate persons and where the person to perform the controlled function is employed or engaged under an arrangement entered into by a contract of the authorised person.

1   FSMA 2000, s 29(1).

11.45   Those functions performed within an organisation that have been designated as controlled functions have been set out in Chapter 10 of the FSA Supervision Manual. In determining the current controlled functions, the FSA has sought to establish and mark the boundaries of the approved persons regime. They specify those functions, which it sees as key to the performance of regulated activities[1].

1   Supervision Manual, Chapter 10.

11.46   The FSA sets out each of the identified and control functions in the table to rule 10.4.5. Each of the functions is then ordered by the type of functions to be performed. These are listed in paras **11.32–11.38** above, but include governing functions, required functions, systems and controlled functions, significant management functions and customer functions. Furthermore, the FSA has identified that the governing functions, required functions, systems and controlled functions and significant functions are ones which are likely to result in the person responsible for the performance exercising a significant influence on the conduct of its regulated activities.

11.47   Whilst an analysis of each of the controlled functions is beyond the scale of this work, authorised firms and those seeking authorisation should consider the manner in which they identify whether a control function exists within their authorisation and the process that they should follow in ensuring a person who performs that function obtains approval from the FSA.

Appointed representatives

11.48 FSMA 2000, s 19 states that:

'No person may carry on a regulated activity in the United Kingdom, or purport to do so, unless he is:

(a) an authorised person; or
(b) an exempt person.'

11.49 This continuation of the exemption that existed under the previous regime whereby FSMA 2000, s 39 exempts appointed representatives. An 'appointed representative' is defined by the section as being someone who is

' (a) a party to a contract with an unauthorised person (his principal) which:

  (i) permits or requires him to carry on business of a prescribed description, and
  (ii) complies with such requirements as may be prescribed, and

(b) is someone for whose activities in carrying on the whole or part of that business his principal has accepted responsibility in writing.'

11.50 Anyone satisfying this description is exempt from the general prohibition in relation to any regulated activity when they are acting within the remit of the area of business for which their principal has accepted responsibility. Thus, the principal will be responsible for the appointed representative's acts[1] and the principal will therefore need to be an authorised person. There is some protection for the principal though, s 39(6) states that 'nothing…is to cause the knowledge or intentions of an appointed representative to be attributed to his principal for the purpose of determining whether the principal has committed an offence, unless in all the circumstances it is reasonable for them to be attributed to him'.

1 FSMA 2000, s 39(4).

11.51 Under FSMA 2000, s 40 applications to carry on regulated activities can be made by individuals as well as corporate entities, partnerships and unincorporated associations.

Undertaking a review of business structure

11.52 Firstly, it should be noted that a number of the controlled functions are required to exist within relevant organisations. Where appropriate, persons should perform the functions of: (a) apportionment and oversight; (b) EEA investment business oversight function; (c) compliance oversight function; (d) money laundering reporting function and (e) appointed actuary function.

11.53   Firms should complete an organisational chart reflecting the manner in which their business functions are organised, the reporting lines that exist within the organisation and the functional senior management positions that exist. When completing such an organisational chart for the first time, it would also be essential to ensure that all appropriate required functions are included.

11.54   Responsibility statements or job descriptions should also be compiled for each of the controlled functions that exist in an organisation. This will not only satisfy regulatory requirements but also ensure that each person performing a controlled function understands and appreciates the extent of their responsibilities within the organisation. This will also help them to appreciate the extent of the responsibility under the approved persons regime.

Fit and proper status

11.55   Authorised firms have a general obligation not to appoint any member of staff without ensuring the appointee is a fit and proper person. This obligation for firms exists also in respect of those persons to be appointed to a controlled function.

11.56   Firms should establish an internal process by which they screen the applicant's background for certain matters prior to offering that person employment. In addition, they must ensure that prior to the person taking up employment an application under the approved persons regime is also submitted to the FSA. It should be noted that it is a requirement under the approved persons regime that no one may perform a controlled function without receiving prior approval from the FSA to do so.

11.57   A firm's own process in screening an applicant to ensure they are a fit and proper person can be time consuming. Firms must take into account the time required to properly screen when considering the appropriate time to make an offer of employment and the candidate's desired start date. Firms may consider that the following should be screened or verified before an offer of employment is made:

Past employment history

11.58   Firms should consider the importance of verifying the past employment record of an applicant. The dates between which a person has been employed by an organisation and the actual employment should be verified. In addition, any gaps in between employers may also be verified to ensure that the applicant has not attempted to avoid reference to a period of their employment which has caused problems.

Written references

11.59   In addition to verification of employment, it will, in many cases, also be appropriate to obtain from past employers written comment about the applicant's standard of employment. In many cases now most employers will not be prepared to supply verbal references. It is therefore necessary to obtain written references containing comments about the conduct of a person's work, their general performance, the reason for them leaving and inviting any other general comments can be a useful insight into determining whether a person is fit and proper.

11.60   In both verification and written referencing firms should determine the period of time over which they wish to screen the applicant. The FSA provide no specification for the period of time over which background screening should be conducted. It is merely a question of firms determining what is reasonable in all the circumstances. Some firms may choose to verify and reference the employment for the past ten years of an applicant's employment background. Whereas others choose to go back no further than three or four years.

Credit checking

11.61   It is now almost standard practice for firms to undertake, with a credit checking agency, a credit reference on applicants. Such practice should continue to be applied to all persons to be employed in a controlled function. Firms should ensure that they utilise a reliable credit checking agency and respond to all the information that is reported to them. It may be that the agency is not able to identify the applicant from their address and, therefore, return a negative report. In this instance, the applicant should always be asked to provide more reliable information to confirm their address and any prior addresses should also be used to screen the applicant. Where credit referencing identifies particular credit problems, these should be followed through by the firm and a reasonable decision should always be taken as to whether a firm considers it appropriate to appoint a person into a controlled function where they have an adverse credit history.

Academic and professional qualifications

11.62   There are numerous instances of firms identifying, some time after employment, that an employee has overstated their professional or academic qualifications. Certain controlled functions have minimum educational requirements. The firm has a general obligation to ensure that all staff are competent to perform the role they are employed for. Where a firm is relying on the applicant's qualifications, they should ensure they obtain independent verification that the examinations have been passed and are held. Where professional qualifications are held, firms should obtain a reference from the applicant's professional body to identify whether there are any existing or outstanding disciplinary actions against the applicant.

Criminal background

11.63 Firms should consider whether it is appropriate to screen an applicant's background for any past or outstanding criminal convictions. The firm may consider that some criminal convictions are not relevant to an individual's employment. These may very well include minor road traffic offences. However, offences involving fraud, dishonesty or even violence will often be considered unacceptable for somebody wishing to be employed in the financial services industry.

Access to criminal records

The Rehabilitation of Offenders Act 1974 (ROA)

Background

11.64 The Rehabilitation of Offenders Act 1974 (ROA 1974) provides that convictions for certain offences may be considered 'spent' after a specified period (which varies with the nature of the sentenced imposed). Generally, an employer or vetting body cannot take spent convictions into account when assessing a rehabilitated person's suitability for a position, although convictions carrying a custodial sentence of more than two and a half years never become spent and always have to be declared, if required to do so.

11.65 The financial services industry has been one of the few sectors where there have, for some years, been exceptions allowing access to spent convictions in relation to certain posts and offences. These exceptions allow the industry to require disclosure of, and to take account of, information about 'spent convictions' in certain circumstances (eg for posts such as directors, managers, controllers for relevant offences such as insider dealing, fraud or other dishonesty and offences under financial services legislation). The problem to date has been that there have been no arrangements, other than the use of the enforced subject access process, for the industry to obtain this information from the Police.

The New Criminal Records Bureau

11.66   This is due to change in late 2001. The Criminal Records Bureau (CRB) has been set up by the Home Office to improve access to criminal records, with one of its primary sources of information being the Police National Computer. Once the CRB is in action enforced subject access will no longer be permitted.

Three levels of disclosure

11.67   The CRB will provide three levels of disclosure:

- *Basic.* The basic disclosure will be issued to individuals on request, subject to confirmation of identity. It will show all convictions held at national level which are not 'spent' under the ROA 1974. Any employer will be able to request a successful candidate for a position to apply for a basic disclosure.
- *Standard.* The standard disclosure will be available for posts or purposes, which are expected under the ROA 1974 (eg the financial services industry). This disclosure will include details of all convictions on record, including 'spent' convictions under the ROA, and cautions, reprimands and warnings held at national level.
- *Enhanced.* The enhanced disclosure will not be relevant for the financial services industry.

11.68   It should be noted that checking an applicant for possible criminal convictions is not a substitute for making the normal thorough check into an individual's identity and background. Nevertheless, it will be a useful additional check on a person a firm is proposing to appoint to any post covered by the exceptions order.

The CRB process

11.69   Registration began in 2001, with standard disclosures available to SFA authorised firms in the autumn. Basic disclosures will be available in 2002. Firms will have to pay £12 for each check they carry out. In order to take advantage of this new service, firms will need to be registered. Firms that expect to make a large number of requests to the CRB per year are likely to want to be registered in their own right. Smaller firms may want to group together and form or use an umbrella organisation to register on their behalf[1].

1   SFA Board Notice 596.

Matters of concern to the FSA

11.70   As part of an employee's screening consideration should also be given to those matters which are considered by the authority as impacting upon a person's fitness and properness. When making an application for approval a standard FSA application form is completed. This sets out a series of questions relating to the proposed controlled functions' employee's background, including the involvement they have had with previous financial service companies that may have run into difficulties. It is sensible practice for an employing firm to address each of these matters with an applicant in advance of an offer of employment. It would cause difficulties for an employer to have made an offer of employment only to find that the FSA either declines an application or imposes requirements based on answers to the questions in the approved person application form.

Applications for approval by the FSA

11.71   All persons wishing to perform a controlled function and seeking approval to do so from the FSA must submit a standard application. Application forms are available from the FSA and are set out at Annex 4 of the FSA Handbook at reference SUB 10.

11.72   The FSA will only grant an application for approval it is satisfied that the applicant is a fit and proper person. The FSA has a period of three months from the date it receives the application to determined whether to grant the application or provide to the applicant a warning notice that it proposes to refuse the application. All applications, which are granted, are confirmed to the applicant on written notice. A copy of that notice is also provided to all interested parties.

11.73   Where the authority is minded to refuse an application, it must provide a warning of its proposal to refuse. The applicant and each interested party may then refer the matter to the Financial Services and Markets Tribunal[1].

1   FSMA 2000, s 62(4).

Whistleblowing and employment law

Introduction

11.74   As has been seen in **Chapter 6** there are strict legal requirements relating to the reporting of suspicious transactions. In the case of the firm carrying on 'relevant financial business' (for a definition of this see **Chapter 6**) the requirement is to report it to the NCIS. In the case of an individual employed in such a firm the obligation will normally be to report the matter internally to the money laundering reporting officer. However, there may be instances where this will be inappropriate. It may be that the employee has reasons to suspect that the money laundering reporting officer is in some way involved in the arrangement the employee wishes to report or that for some other reason they reasonably believe that the normal reporting lines will be a waste of time[1]. This issue may also extend to accountants who do not wish to sign off the accounts as representing a true and fair view[2] or those who do not wish to sign off financial returns to the FSA as they believe that they misrepresent the firm as meeting the required financial resources requirement. In all these instances, the firm should have a suitable management structure in place so that the person concerned can take their concerns to an appropriate, senior member of the firm.

1   A Haynes 'The Struggle Against Corruption – a Comparative Analysis', *Journal of Financial Crime*, vol 8, no 2 at p 130.
2   A Haynes 'Reporting Suspicions and Blowing the Whistle', *Anti Money Laundering Guide*, CCH , Rider and Nakajima, London, 1999.

Public disclosure

11.75   The Public Interest Disclosure Act 1998 was passed to assist in the reporting of criminal acts, breach of regulations and legal obligations[1]. This Act makes amendments to the Employment Rights Act 1996 to protect employees in the type of situation described above. Section 47B of the amended Employment Rights Act states that it is a criminal offence to subject an employee to disadvantageous treatment for making a 'protected disclosure'. This is a disclosure made to an acceptable person in the situation described at para **11.74** above. Acceptable people include:

- employers;
- the person in the firm who is responsible for the issue causing concern;
- anyone who is named as being the correct person under the firm's whistleblowing procedure;
- the firm's legal advisers;
- in cases where the government may be involved, a government minister; and
- a person stated to be appropriate in a statutory instrument issued pursuant to the Act.

1   Camp 'Openness and accountability in the workplace', *New Law Journal*, vol 149, no 6871, 15 January 1999.

11.76   External protected reports concerning the matter causing concern can also be made provided the matter has already been raised internally or the party concerned reasonably believes they will suffer adverse consequences if it is released internally. In addition, the report must not be released for personal gain, it must be made in good faith and the person making it must believe that it is substantially true[1].

1   Public Interest Disclosure Act 1998, sub-s 43G and H.

Internal management

11.77   Clearly, a well run firm will take steps to ensure that the management structure they have in place should be effective it avoiding external disclosures or reports ever being necessary. Indeed, FSA Principle 3 – 'A firm must take reasonable care to organise and control its affairs responsibly and effectively, with adequate risk management systems', and Statements of Principle for Approved Persons 5 and 6 would seem to require this. These state:

> '5. An Approved Person performing a significant influence function must take reasonable steps to ensure that the business of the firm for which he is responsible in his controlled function is organised so that it can be controlled effectively.
> 6. An Approved Person performing a significant influence function must exercise due skill, care and diligence in managing the business of the firm for which he is responsible in his controlled function.'

11.78   Thus, the firm and its senior executives could face FSA disciplinary measures if they fail to maintain management systems to avoid, as far as possible, the need for external disclosures or reports being made. In some instances, this could be done by having a second reporting line that could be used if the normal one was inappropriate. To some extent, these already exist in firms carrying on relevant financial business by the existence of a money laundering reporting officer and in all FSA regulated firms as there will be a compliance officer and, in larger firms, a compliance department.

Contracts of employment

11.79   The Public Interest Disclosure Act 1998 also renders void any term in a contract of employment that seeks to prevent an employee from making a protected disclosure[1]. It is unlikely that any firm in the financial services, banking or insurance industries would have such a term. However, there may be a danger that some widely drafted confidentiality provisions may effectively debar protected disclosures. It is therefore a good idea to check such documentation to see if any redrafting is necessary.

1   Section 43C.

Confidentiality and professional privilege

11.80   Bankers and others involved in financial service businesses owe a duty of confidentiality to their clients. This, together with the exceptions to it was set out in the case of *Tournier v National and Union Bank of England*[1]. Essentially, this said that a bank must maintain client confidentiality unless one of four exceptions occurred. These were:

- compulsion by law;
- where there is a duty to the public to disclose;
- where the interests of the bank require disclosure; and
- the express or implied consent of the customer.

1   [1924] 1 KB 461.

11.81   The crucial exception in the context under consideration is 'where a duty is imposed by law' as it covers, inter alia, the statutory rules relating to reporting suspicions of money laundering. It will also cover requirements to make returns to the FSA under the Conduct of Business and other FSA rules. The requirement of confidentiality is therefore not an issue that should normally arise as a problem in this context.

11.82   Solicitors have a relationship of professional privilege with their clients and this is far stricter than a duty of confidentiality. It is not overridden by requirements to report suspicious transactions[1] though, of course, if a firm of solicitors believed that they were being used to assist in committing an offence or to handle the proceeds of one, they should refuse to so act. Otherwise, in the former instance, they may be aiding and abetting a criminal offence or, in the latter, be an accessory after the fact. There are also a number of offences in relation to laundering the proceeds of crime that they could be committing in the latter instance (see **Chapter 6**).

1   This will be changed by a forthcoming EU Directive.

Treatment of employees when they act in breach of FSA requirements

Introduction

11.83   There will be occasions when an employee fails to behave in the manner required by the FSA Principles, the Statements of Principles for Approved Persons or the FSA rules. In such instances, the appropriate response will depend on the nature of the breach. Where trivial, it may be sufficient for the fault to be pointed out but, in more serious cases, disciplinary steps will be appropriate. Clearly, an approved person is in breach of their contract of employment if they are in breach of the FSA's requirements. Disciplinary steps by the FSA against the individual, others in the firm and the firm itself are all possibilities. A detailed analysis of employment law is beyond the remit of this book. However, there are certain issues that need to be examined.

Human rights

11.84 The Human Rights Act 1998 potentially impacts here in two respects on how a firm may treat its employees. This Act incorporates the Convention on Human Rights into English law. Article 6 is applicable to the civil rights and obligations applying in circumstances of employment[1], though not to every dispute that may arise. It will only apply where the dispute could determine whether or not the person can continue to work or faces suspension[2], dismissal[3], loss of income[4] or being struck off as a practitioner[5]. The first three of these could arise as a result of steps taken by the employer. The last could only be carried out by the FSA but conclusions reached by an employer could influence that decision.

1   *Obermeier v Austria* (1990) 13 EHRR 290.
2   *Obermeier v Austria* (1990) 13 EHRR 290.
3   *Prince v United Kingdom* (1984) 6 EHRR 583.
4   *Lombardo v Italy* (1992) 21 EHRR 188.
5   *Albert and Le Compte v Belgium* (1982) 5 EHRR 533.

11.85 Article 6(1) of the Convention states that individuals have a right to a fair trial in the process of proceedings that affect their civil rights and obligations. These include a right to:

- an independent and impartial tribunal;
- disclosure of evidence;
- an adversarial hearing;
- having reasons provided for decisions; and
- having decisions made within a reasonable period.

11.86 There is also a right to privacy in the workplace. In one case[1] it was held that an employee's right to privacy had been broken when their telephone calls from work were tapped. Article 8(1) states that 'Everyone has the right to respect for...his correspondence'. However, it was added that a crucial factor was that the employee had never been warned that this might be done. This is important as many financial services firms tape employee calls and, indeed, in some instances are required to by FSA rules. Provided the employee is informed prior to any tapping or recording taking place, the employer will be acting within the Convention. It will normally have been done when they are appointed to that job.

1   *Halford v United Kingdom* (1997) 24 EHRR 523.

11.87 The treatment of approved persons by the FSA is also at issue. Here, art 6(1) will apply as the three pre-requisites will normally be present. They are:

- the issues must be civil in nature;
- the rights concerned must have a basis in domestic law[1]; and
- such rights must be determined by the hearing.

1   *H v Belgium* (1987) 10 EHRR 339.

11.88   The proceedings must also be decisive in relation to a person's private rights[1]. There is no shortage of case law stating that the removal of a licence to practise fits within this description[2]. Therefore, proceedings by the FSA must respect the rights stated above. Issues have also arisen with regard to the impartiality of the FSA Tribunal and the FSA Appeal Tribunal as art 6(1) requires that a tribunal must be 'independent and impartial'. The Government's view is that the bodies concerned are independent. This appears to require[3] that the appointment of the Tribunal's members must be independent from the executive and the FSA, that there are guarantees against outside pressure and that the body must appear to be independent.

1   *Ringeisen v Austria* (1971) 1 EHRR 455.
2   *Ginikanwa v United Kingdom* 55 DR 251 (1988); *Guchez v Belgium* 40 DR 100 (1984) .
3   *Langborger v Sweden* (1989) 12 EHRR 416.

11.89   There have also been claims that, because the FSA has quasi-criminal powers in terms of the steps that it can take against regulated firms and approved persons, the provisions of the Convention relating to criminal proceedings should apply. The UK Government has taken advice and come to the conclusion that this is not the case[1].

1   House of Commons Research Paper 66/98.

Index

All references in this index are to paragraph numbers

Access to criminal records, 11.63, 11.64–9
Accounting standards, 9.14
Acknowledgement,
complaints procedures, 4.32, 4.33–4
enforcement, 8.14–16
Action plans, risk and control framework, 2.52–5
Administering assets, 5.82–3
Admissions, 10.51–4
Advising on investments, 5.87–8
Agent, dealing in investments as, 5.76–7
Agreeing to carry on activities, 5.96
Agreements,
on dissemination, 9.10–11
enforceability, of 11.41–3
Alternate name accounts, 6.101
Appointed representatives, 8.55–8, 11.48–51
Approvals, 3.34
Approved Persons Regime, 3.35, 5.9, 5.12–14, 5.15, 8.2, 8.47–54, 11.30–8, 11.44–7
Arranging deals in investments, 5.78–9
Asian financial crisis, 9.29
Auditors,
external auditors, 1.13
international standards, 9.15
see also INTERNAL AUDIT DEPARTMENT
Authorisation, 11.1–3
access to criminal records, 11.63, 11.64–9
acting without permission, 11.40
applications for approval, 11.71–3
appointed representatives, 8.55–8, 11.48–51
Approved Persons Regime, 3.35, 5.9, 5.12–14, 5.15, 8.2, 8.47–54, 11.30–8, 11.44–7
contravention of requirement to be authorised, 11.39
enforceability of agreements, 11.41–3

Authorisation—*contd*
fit and proper status, 11.55–63
granting of permission, 11.13–14
with conditions, 11.27–9
matters of concern to FSA, 11.70
procedure for application, 11.15–26
requirement for, 11.4–9
review of business structure, 11.52–4
threshold conditions, 11.10–12

Back–stop detect controls, 2.46
Bank of England, 5.16–17
Banks,
confidentiality and, 11.80
supervision, 9.19
Basel Committee on Banking Supervision, 9.5, 9.19
Board of Directors,
assurance for, 1.34
responsibility of, 3.16
Breaches,
logs, 2.23
management of rule breach reporting, 10.11–17
responsibility for, 1.35
Business compliance team, 8.20
Business structure, review of, 11.52–4

Call options, 5.59
Central Gilts Office, 5.17, 5.19
Certificates representing securities, 5.53–4
Change,
management, of 3.5
risk analysis and surveying and, 2.8, 2.69–70
Chief executive officers (CEOs), 1.17
responsibility of, 3.16
Chinese walls, 8.28

Civil law issues,
insider dealing, 7.30–4
money laundering, 6.37–58
grounds for constructive trusteeship, 6.38,
6.42–7
holding property to the order of another,
6.53–6
knowing receipt, 6.48–52
suspicious transaction reports and civil
liability, 6.57–8
Clients, 1.13
checking identification, 6.25–30, 6.67–9,
6.90–8
dealing with property of, 11.37–8
general guidelines on money laundering
and, 6.89–100
situations requiring additional
diligence/attention, 6.101–5
updating of files, 6.106
Codes of practice,
Code on Inter-Professional Conduct (IPC),
5.33–40
fiscal transparency, 9.9
insider dealing, 7.35–7
market abuse, 7.49–52
transparency in monetary and financial
policies, 9.8
Collective investment schemes, 5.55–6,
5.85
**Committee on Payment and Settlement
Systems,** 9.5
Common language, 3.3
Communication,
compliance newsletters, 8.35
compliance systems policy, 3.20–1
problems with, 8.11–13
with regulator, 10.60–1
Complaints procedures, 4.1–72
complex complaints, 4.35–6
compliance officer and, 4.42–4
compulsory scheme, 4.10
consistent approach to complaints, 4.28
disclosure, 4.23–5
internal, 4.15–22, 4.24
investigations, 4.29–31
acknowledgements, 4.32, 4.33–4
analysis of documents, 4.54–6
balancing evidence, 4.59–61
conclusion, 4.62
interviews, 4.49–53
obtaining expertise, 4.57–8
scope of, 4.45–8
time limits, 4.32, 4.34, 4.35–6
offers of redress, 4.38–41
enforcement, 4.41
Ombudsman schemes, 4.3, 4.13–14, 4.23,
4.36–7, 4.39–40
post-investigation matters, 4.63
professional indemnity insurance and,
4.69–70
staff knowledge of, 4.26
staff training/education and, 4.26, 4.66–8

Complaints procedures—*contd*
statutory requirements, 4.7–14
trends, 4.27, 4.64–8
voluntary scheme, 4.11
Compliance culture, 8.24, 8.29–35
Compliance department, 3.34
access to higher management, 1.19
attendance at meetings, 1.30
complaints procedures and, 4.42–4
compliance framework, 1.29
compliance policy drift, 1.22
conflicts of interest, 1.20
decision-making, 1.27
documentation, 1.27
enforcement and, 8.21, 8.36
independence of, 1.18
independent assurance for Board, 1.34
local compliance staff, 8.18, 8.21
need for risk-based compliance, 1.3–4
relationships with others, 1.5–17
requirements and risks, 1.18–36
responsibility for breaches, 1.35
restrictions on compliance staff, 1.21
role of, 1.1–36
secure area, 1.32
systems *see* COMPLIANCE SYSTEMS
taping telephone calls, 1.33
training of staff, 1.28
views of risk, 1.31
Compliance risk *see* RISK
Compliance systems, 3.1–36
change management, 3.5
common language, 3.3
compliance department, 3.34
consolidated procedures, 3.29
documentation, 3.26
cross-reference documents, 3.31–2
understanding of, 3.27
framework, 3.1
monitoring procedures, 3.30
oversight structure, 3.4
procedures manual, 3.30, 3.33, 8.33
relationships and lines of communication,
3.20–1
reporting lines, 3.25
reporting requirements, 3.24
risks covered, 3.8–15
rule review, 3.28
staffing requirements, 3.23
statement/overview, 3.19
timescales, 3.22
training of staff, 3.27, 3.35–6
vision, 3.2
who is responsible, 3.16–18
Confidentiality, 11.80–1
Conflicts of interest, 1.20
avoiding, 10.47
Conflicts room, 1.32
Consequences of regulatory failure,
9.29–31
Consolidated procedures, 3.29
Constructive trusteeship, 6.38, 6.42–7

Consumers Association, 4.2
Contesting disciplinary actions, 10.51–4
Contracts,
for differences, 5.62–4, 5.97, 5.100, 7.12
forex contracts, 5.101
funeral plan contracts, 5.67
gaming contracts, 5.97–101
of insurance, 5.44, 5.73
mortgages, 5.68, 5.94–5
swap contracts, 5.63, 5.97
Control room, 1.32
Co-ordination, 9.1–44
consequences of regulatory failure, 9.29–31
facilitating regulatory observance, 9.24–5
key standards and issues, 9.6–22, 9.26–8
memoranda of understanding, 9.32–44
monitoring regulatory observance, 9.23
organisations, 9.5
Corporate finance department, 1.12
Corporate governance, 9.13
Costs, risk and control framework, 2.47–8
Court proceedings, 4.1–2
Credit checking of staff, 11.61
Credit department, 1.9
Credit swap contracts, 5.63
Creditors' rights, 9.12
Criminal offences, 7.70–9
insider dealing, 7.1–3, 7.4–37
civil law issues, 7.30–4
codes of practice, 7.35–7
dealing in directors' options, 7.23–6
defences, 7.15–19
FSA principles, 7.27–9
key elements, 7.5–14
nature of offence, 7.4
penalties, 7.20–2, 7.26
market abuse, 7.1–3, 7.38–69
behaviour, 7.42–3
code of practice, 7.49–52
distortion of market, 7.53
FSA and, 7.47–8, 7.49–52, 7.66–7
information and, 7.44–6, 7.63–5
jurisdiction, 7.68–9
requiring and encouraging, 7.47–8
safe harbours, 7.55–62
money laundering, 6.9–17
acquisition, possession or utilisation of proceeds, 6.13
assisting another to retain the benefit, 6.10
concealing or transferring proceeds of drug trafficking, 6.9
disclosure, 6.11–12
failure to disclose suspicion, 6.14–15
penalties, 6.17
relevant parties, 6.21–4
terrorism and, 6.7, 6.18–20
tipping off, 6.16
Criminal records, access to, 11.63, 11.64–9
Criminal Records Bureau (CRB), 11.66–9
Cross-reference documents, 3.31–2

Culture,
compliance culture, 8.24, 8.29–35
regulatory culture, 8.23
Currency swap contracts, 5.63

Dealing in investments,
as agent, 5.76–7
arranging deals, 5.78–9
insider, *see* INSIDER DEALING
as principal, 5.74–5
Debentures, 5.49–50, 7.12
Decisions, speed of decision-making, 1.27
Defences,
disciplinary actions, 10.51–4
insider dealing, 7.15–19
Dematerialised instructions, 5.84
Deposits, 5.43, 5.71–2, 7.12
Derivatives,
exchanges, 5.26–9
as gaming contracts, 5.97–101
Differences, contracts for, 5.62–4, 5.97, 5.100, 7.12
Directors' options, insider dealing, 7.23–6
Disciplinary procedures, 10.37–9
contesting, 10.51–4
internal, 8.39–45
limiting, 10 48 50
responding to, 10.40–1
risk management plan, 10.42–4
Disclosure,
complaints procedures, 4.23–5
inside information, 7.4
market abuse, 7.63–5
money laundering, 6.11–12
failure to disclose suspicion, 6.14–15
public disclosure, 11.75–6
Dispersed businesses, enforcement and, 8.17
Dispute resolution, *see* COMPLAINTS PROCEDURES
Dissemination,
agreements on, 9.10–11
problems, 8.11–13
Documentation, 1.27
analysis of documents in investigation of complaints, 4.54–6
compliance systems, 3.26
cross-reference documents, 3.31–2
understanding of, 3.27
Drug trafficking, money laundering and 6.7, 6.9

Employment, *see* STAFF
Enforceability of agreements, 11.41–3
Enforcement, 3.34, 8.1–58
business compliance team, 8.20
compliance culture, 8.24, 8.29–35
dissemination problems, 8.11–13
employment issues, 8.46–58
FSA Principles for Business, 8.4–9
geographically dispersed businesses, 8.17
head office responsibility, 8.18, 8.19

Enforcement—*contd*
hybrid products, 8.25–7
inside information, 8.28
internal disciplinary procedures, 8.39–45
local compliance staff, 8.18, 8.21
local regulators, 8.22
management of enforcement proceedings,
   10.30–63
notification to regulators, 8.37–8
offers of redress, 4.41
regulatory culture, 8.23
role of compliance department, 8.36
senior management and compliance
   responsibility, 8.10–45
written acknowledgements, 8.14–16
Escalation triggers, 2.21–2
Ethical creep, 1.22
European Economic Area (EEA)
   authorities, 5.32
Evidence, complaints investigations,
   4.59–61
Expertise, obtaining expertise in
   investigation of complaints, 4.57–8
External auditors, 1.13
External risk data, 2.56–8

Feedback meetings, 10.23–9
Financial Action Task Force, 9.5, 9.17
Financial Ombudsman schemes, 4.3,
   4.13–14, 4.23, 4.36–7, 4.39–40
Financial promotion, 7.78
Financial resources, 11.10
Financial Services Authority (FSA), 1.1,
   5.3–8, 9.4
   Approved Persons Regime, 3.35, 5.9,
      5.12–14, 5.15, 8.2, 8.47–54, 11.30–8,
      11.44–7
   authorisation by, *see* AUTHORISATION
   enforcement manual, 10.38–9, 10.59
   insider dealing and, 7.27–9
   market abuse and, 7.47–8, 7.49–52, 7.66–7
   money laundering and, 6.59–84
   objectives of, 10.56–9
   principles for business, 5.10–11, 8.4–9,
      10.9
Financial Stability Forum, 9.5, 9.6, 9.24
Forex contracts, 5.101
Forum of European Securities
   Commissions (FESCO), 9.43, 9.44
Front-line prevent controls, 2.43
Funeral plan contracts, 5.67, 5.92
Futures, 5.60–1, 5.97, 7.12

Gaming contracts, 5.97–101
Geographically dispersed businesses,
   enforcement and, 8.17
Government securities, 5.51

Head office responsibility for
   enforcement, 8.18, 8.19
Human rights issues, 11.84–9
Hybrid products, enforcement and, 8.25–7

IMRO, 10.34–5
Indebtedness, instruments creating of
   acknowledging, 5.49–50, 7.12
Information,
   compliance newsletters, 8.35
   dissemination,
      agreements on, 9.10–11
      problems, 8.11–13
   market abuse and, 7.44–6, 7.63–5
   see also INSIDER DEADLING
Information technology, risk and control
   framework, 2.49–51
Insider dealing, 7.1–3, 7.4–37
   civil law issues, 7.30–4
   codes of practice, 7.35–7
   dealing in directors' options, 7.23–6
   defences, 7.15–19
   FSA principles, 7.27–9
   key elements, 7.5–14
   nature of offence, 7.4
   penalties, 7.20–2, 7.26
   separation of departments to prevent, 8.28
Insolvency, 9.12
Insurance,
   complaints procedures and professional
      indemnity insurance, 4.69–70
   contracts of, 5.44, 5.73
   core principles, 9.22
Integrity, 11.11
Interest rate swap contracts, 5.63
Interests in investments, 5.69
Internal audit department, 1.6, 3.34
   reports, 2.24
   risk maps and process flows, 2.15–17
Internal disciplinary procedures, 8.39–45
International accounting standards, 9.14
International Accounting Standards
   Board, 9.5
International Association of Insurance
   Supervisors, 9.5
International Association of Securities
   Commissions, 9.5
International Commodities Clearing
   House (ICCH), 5.19
International Federation of Accountants,
   9.5
International Monetary Fund, 9.5, 9.10,
   9.23
International Petroleum Exchange, 5.28
International standards on auditing, 9.15
Internationalisation, 9.1–3
Inter-Professional Conduct, Code on
   (IPC), 5.33–40
Interviews, complaints investigations,
   4.49–53
Investigations, 3.34
   complaints procedures, 4.29–31
   acknowledgements, 4.32, 4.33–4
   analysis of documents, 4.54–6
   balancing evidence, 4.59–61
   conclusion, 4.62
   interviews, 4.49–53

Investigations—*contd*
obtaining expertise, 4.57–8
scope of, 4.45–8
time limits, 4.32, 4.35–6
Investment business in UK, regulation of,
5.41–96

Jurisdiction, market abuse, 7.68–9

Key indicators of risk, 2.18–20
Knowing receipt, money laundering and,
6.48–52

Legal department, 1.7
Legal status, 11.10
LIFFE, 5.27
Lloyd's, 5.21–5, 5.65–6, 5.89–91
Local compliance staff, 8.18, 8.21
Local regulators, 8.22
Location of offices, 11.10
London Clearing House, 5.30–1
London Code of Conduct, 5.33–40
London Metals Exchange, 5.28
**London Options Clearing House
(LOCH),** 5.19
London Stock Exchange, 5.18–20

Management, 11.77–8
access to senior management, 1.19
approved persons regime and, 8.50, 8.51
of change, 3.5
competence, 11.12
compliance responsibility, 8.10–45
line management of compliance risk, 2.62
responsibility for breaches, 1.35
risk management, 1.1, 1.2, 10.42–4
Managing investments, 5.80–1
Manual of procedures, 3.30, 3.33, 8.33
Market abuse, 7.1–3, 7.38–69
behaviour, 7.42–3
code of practice, 7.49–52
distortion of market, 7.53
FSA and, 7.47–8, 7.49–52, 7.66–7
information and, 7.44–6, 7.63–5
jurisdiction, 7.68–9
requiring and encouraging, 7.47–8
safe harbours, 7.55–62
Measurement, risk, 2.59–61
Meetings, 1.30
feedback meetings, 10.23–9
Memoranda of understanding, 9.32–44
Misleading statements, 7.71–7
Modelling techniques, 2.7
Money laundering, 3.34, 6.1–118, 9.17–18
awareness and training, 6.74–6, 6.113
civil law issues, 6.37–58
grounds for constructive trusteeship, 6.38,
6.42–7
holding property to the order of another,
6.53–6
knowing receipt, 6.48–52

Money laundering—*contd*
suspicious transaction reports and civil
liability, 6.57–8
client acceptance,
checking identification, 6.25–30, 6.67–9,
6.90–8
general guidelines, 6.89–100
situations requiring additional
diligence/attention, 6.101–5
client file updating, 6.106
control responsibilities, 6.111
criminal offences, 6.9–17
acquisition, possession or utilisation of
proceeds, 6.13
assisting another to retain the benefit, 6.10
concealing or transferring proceeds of drug
trafficking, 6.9
disclosure, 6.11–12
failure to disclose suspicion, 6.14–15
penalties, 6.17
relevant parties, 6.21–4
terrorism and, 6.7, 6.18–20
tipping-off, 6.16
definition, 6.1–2
FSA and, 6.59–84
monitoring, 6.77–8, 6.110
record keeping, 6.79–81, 6.114
reporting, 6.35–6, 6.57–8, 6.71–2, 6.112
reporting officer, 6.66, 6.77–8
staff training and, 6.74–6, 6.113
suspicion of, 6.31–6, 6.57–8, 6.70, 6.107–9
failure to disclose suspicion, 6.14–15
using national and international findings,
6.73
Wolfsberg principles, 6.85–118
reasons for, 6.85–8
Monitoring procedures, 2.38–41, 3.30
money laundering, 6.77–8, 6.110
regulatory observance, 9.23
Mortgages, 5.68, 5.94–5

Near miss logs, 2.23
Notification to regulators, 8.37–8
Numbered accounts, 6.101

Offers of redress, 4.38–41
enforcement, 4.41
Ombudsman schemes, 4.3, 4.13–14, 4.23,
4.36–7, 4.39–40
Open-ended investment companies, 5.56
Options, 5.58–9, 5.97
insider dealing, 7.12, 7.23–6
**Organisation for Economic Co-operation
and Development,** 9.5
Oversight structure,
compliance systems, 3.4
money laundering and, 6.100
Ownership of risk, 2.32

Payment systems, 9.16
Penalties,
insider dealing, 7.20–2, 7.26
money laundering, 6.17

Pension schemes, 5.57, 5.85
Personal Investment Authority (PIA),
  10.31–3
Policy drift, 1.22
Principals, dealing in investments as,
  5.74–5
Procedures manual, 3.30, 3.33, 8.33
Processes prevent controls, 2.44
Professional indemnity insurance,
  complaints procedures and, 4.69–70
Professional privilege, 11.82
Profits, seizure of, 7.79
Public disclosure, 11.75–6
Public officials, money laundering and,
  6.105
Public perceptions, 10.31–6
Public securities, 5.51
Publicity for complaints procedures,
  4.23–5
Put options, 5.59

Rating agencies, 1.16, 9.31
Recording,
  disciplinary procedures, 8.42
  interviews in complaints investigation, 4.53
  taping telephone calls, 1.33
Records,
  access to criminal records, 11.64–9
  money laundering procedures, 6.79–81,
    6.114
Redress, complaints procedures offers of
  redress, 4.38–41
References, staff, 11.59–60
Regulations *see* RULES
Regulators,
  Bank of England, 5.16–17
  Code on Inter-Professional Conduct (IPC),
    5.33–40
  communication with, 10.60–1
  consequences of regulatory failure, 9.29–31
  derivatives exchanges, 5.26–9
  EEA authorities, 5.32
  facilitating regulatory observance, 9.24–5
  feedback meetings, 10.23–9
  gaming contracts, 5.97–101
  internationalisation and, 9.1–3
  investment business in UK, 5.41–96
  Lloyd's, 5.21–5
  local, 8.22
  London Clearing House, 5.30–1
  London Stock Exchange, 5.18–20
  memoranda of understanding, 9.32–44
  monitoring regulatory observance, 9.23
  national co-ordination, 9.4
  need for risk-based compliance, 1.3–4
  new regulatory structure, 5.1–2
  notification to, 8.37–8
  objectives of, 10.55–9
  objectives and principles of securities
    regulation, 9.20–1
  regulatory ability, 1.23
  regulatory culture, 8.23

Regulators—*contd*
  relationship with, 10.1–29
  review by, 1.15
  risk assessment, 1.26
  size of regulated entity, 1.24
  visits by, 10.18–22
  wholesale market activities, 5.33–40
  see also AUTHORISATION; ENFORCEMENT;
    FINANCIAL SERVICES AUTHORITY (FSA)
Relationships,
  with compliance department, 1.5–17
  compliance systems policy, 3.20–1
Remedies, complaints procedures offers
  of redress, 4.38–41
Reporting,
  compliance systems policy, 3.24, 3.25
  management of rule breach reporting,
    10.11–17
  money laundering, 6.35–6, 6.57–8, 6.71–2,
    6.112
Reporting officer, money laundering,
  6.66, 6.77–8
Representatives, appointed, 8.55–8,
  11.48–51
Reputation, 10.62–3
Research department, 1.11
Review of business structure, 11.52–4
Rights in investments, 5.69
Risk, 1.18–36
  analysis and surveying, 2.1–70
  building systematic approach to, 2.4–9
  tools, 2.10–28
  training and competence, 2.65–8
  breach logs and near miss logs, 2.23
  change and, 2.8, 2.69–70
  compliance systems risk policy, *see*
    COMPLIANCE SYSTEMS
  control identification, 2.35–7
  differing views of, 1.31
  escalation triggers, 2.21–2
  high-risk money laundering situations,
    6.102, 6.104
  identification, 2.29–34
  internal audit reports, 2.24
  key indicators, 2.18–20
  line management of compliance risk, 2.62
  management of, 1.1, 1.2, 10.42–4
  maps and process flows, 2.15–17
  measurement, 2.59–61
  need for risk-based compliance, 1.3–4
  ownership, 2.32
  regulatory risk assessment ,1.26
  risk and control framework, 2.42–58
  action plans, 2.52–5
  back-stop detect controls, 2.46
  detect controls, 2.45
  external risk data, 2.56–8
  front-line prevent controls, 2.43
  processes prevent controls, 2.44
  relative costs, 2.47–8
  use of technology, 2.49–51
  risk and control monitoring, 2.38–41
  self-assessment of, 2.12–14
  special areas of compliance risk, 2.63–4

Risk management department, 1.8
Rules,
    management of rule breach reporting,
        10.11–17
    review, 3.28

Safe harbours, 7.55–62
Safeguarding assets, 5.82–3
Sales department, 1.10
Secure areas, 1.32
Securities and Futures Authority (SFA),
    8.10
Self-assessment of risk, 2.12–14
Settlement systems, 9.16
Shares, 5.45–8, 7.12
Solicitors, professional privilege, 11.82
Staff,
    access to criminal records, 11.63, 11.64–9
    compliance systems policy and staffing
        requirements, 3.23
    contracts of employment, 11.79
    credit checking, 11.61
    employment history, 11.58
    employment issues and enforcement,
        8.46–58
    fit and proper status, 11.55–63
    internal disciplinary procedures, 8.39–45
    knowledge of complaints procedures, 4.26
    new employees, 1.36, 8.30
    qualifications, 11.62
    references, 11.59–60
    restrictions on compliance staff, 1.21
    training, *see* TRAINING OF STAFF
    treatment when in breach of FSA
        requirements, 11.83–9
    turnover of, 1.25
    whistleblowing, 11.74–82
Stakeholder pension schemes, 5.57, 5.86
Standards,
    accounting standards, 9.14
    auditing, 9.15
    compliance with, 11.11

Suitability, 11.10
Supervision of banks, 9.19
Swap contracts, 5.63, 5.97

Technology, risk and control framework,
    2.49–51
Telephones, taping calls, 1.33
Territorial limits, 7.19
Terrorism, money laundering and, 6.7,
    6.18–20
Threshold conditions, 11.10–12
Time limits, complaints investigations,
    4.32, 4.34, 4.35–6
**Timescales, compliance systems risk
    policy,** 3.22
Top-down assessment of risk, 2.14
Tracing, 6.39–41
Trading department, 1.10
Training of staff, 1.28
    complaints procedures and, 4.26, 4.66–8
    compliance culture and, 8.29–34
    in compliance systems, 3.27, 3.35–6
    money laundering and, 6.74–6, 6.113
    risk analysis and surveying, 2.65–8

Unit trusts, 5.56
United States of America, 9.34

Vision, compliance systems, 3.2
Visits by regulators, 10.18–22
    feedback meetings, 10.23–9

Warrants, 5.53, 7.12
Whistleblowing, 11.74–82
**Wholesale market activities, regulation
    of,** 5.33–40
Wolfsberg principles, 6.85–118
    reasons for, 6.85–8
World Bank, 9.5, 9.23